Dropping Pebbles in Still Water

Breaking the Unbroken Whole of the Universe

Alexander S. Holub, Ph.D.

ISBN: 978-0-9844733-4-2

Published By:

Bridger House Publishers, Inc.

PO Box 599, Hayden ID, 83835

1-800-729-4131

www.nohoax.com

Printed in the United States of America

Layout / Typesetting:
Julie Melton, The Right Type, (www.therighttype.com) USA

10 9 8 7 6 5 4 3 2 1

Table of Contents

In 1971 Apollo 14 astronaut Edgar Mitchell had experienced a profoundly moving altered state of consciousness during his return trip from the moon; something he described as a "spontaneous epiphany experience." Ask yourself this, what is the hardest part to accept, that a man should have a profound and moving altered state of consciousness or that it should happen to him on the way back from the moon?

— Anonymous

The metaphor is probably the most fertile power possessed by man.

The Dehumanization of Art (1948)
José Ortega y Gasset (1883-1955)

Introduction

We are living in a time of change. Everything about our experience of life on the Earth is in a state of flux. There are "doom-and-gloom" prophets claiming and expecting the Earth to be destroyed within the next few years.[1] Others are claiming that prophecies of centuries past have predicted earth changes and the end of life as we know it by the year 2012. Still others have said that there will be amazing technological advances and that there will be contact with extraterrestrial visitors.[2] Many others have claimed to have been in contact with angels and have seen images of Christian religious personages.[3]

Something is happening. The noted psychotherapist, Carl Jung said that whenever humanity is experiencing a period of stress the psyche creates and projects into visual consciousness images which will promote hopefulness and faith in the future.[4] These

1 Unfortunately, there are politicians who buy into the "end-of-times" scenario and actually see themselves as "an instrument of God's work" and are doing what they can to make it come about.

2 If the tabloids are to be believed, both former presidents Bush (41) and Clinton and Barack Obama as well as Putin of Russia have already made friends with extraterrestrials.

3 Richard Bandler, the co-developer of Neuro-linguistic Programming paraphrased Carl Jung when he said, "When one person claims to talk to God and see angels and demons they lock him up. When a whole group claims the same thing, it's called a religion."

4 Interestingly, it is hopefulness and faith in the future that got Barack Obama elected the President of the United States.

images may be deific, angelic or even extraterrestrial. According to Jung they are all *archetypal symbols* and represent some of the deeper aspects of the Collective Unconsciousness of humanity.

We are going through a period of stress. We have experienced the end of a millennium. It is a time of stress because we have no idea what the rest of the century holds in store. To top it off the less reputable of the "prophets" are claiming that all of the "signs" or "omens" are here for the total Biblical destruction of this planet.[5] It is interesting to note that these same "omens" have predicted the total Biblical destruction of this planet just about every hundred years *since the end of the first century of this era.*[6]

Many scientists are concerned with what is happening to our planet. Human beings have always been extremely wasteful and destructive. Anthropologists have discovered that the earliest settlers to North America did not hunt like the later Native Americans. When they would hunt buffalo, for example, they would stampede the herd directing them over the rim of a precipice killing them by the thousands. Later they learned how to hunt in order to be more conservative. In Europe in the Middle Ages water pollution due to human activity was so horrid that if you drank the water you were assured of contracting, at the very least, dysentery.[7] In Central America the Mayans and Aztecs would use "slash-and-burn" farming destroying the forests. When the industrial revolution came around the air was so polluted with gasses such as methane, carbon dioxide and carbon monoxide as well as solids such as soot that breathing was definitely hazardous to your health. Today we have companies such as McDonald's stripping the rain forests for cattle grazing land for future hamburgers and Mitsubishi tearing the rain forest land apart for the resources that are on and underneath. We must also remember that

5 Religious fanatics are actually praying for the end of the world for they assume something better will transpire.

6 In the first half of the 4th century, the Church historian Eusibius said that all of the signs were there and that the end of the world was inevitable.

7 This is when the use of wine became an important part of the European diet.

strip mining is going on around the world for available minerals and valuables. These latter actions appear to be causing problems with the ozone layer, oxygen and temperature levels on the Earth. Consequently, people are concerned with what the future holds for them and future generations.

Just about everyone is familiar with what is happening on the Earth itself. Very few are aware of what is happening *to* the Earth as it progresses through the galaxy as there has been little if any publicity regarding this progression. Few people know that as our Solar System orbits the galaxy that it goes through periods of change as well. These periods of change affect what is happening on the Earth. To briefly describe: The Milky Way Galaxy is like a large bicycle wheel with innumerable spokes. (Figure I-1) Each of the spokes is a line of *magnetic flux*.[8] [i] When the Solar System makes its trek around the galaxy it goes in and out of these lines of magnetism. As it goes out of a line of magnetism there is a change in life on this planet. There are Earth changes as well as changes in whatever living things can be affected by these influences in this

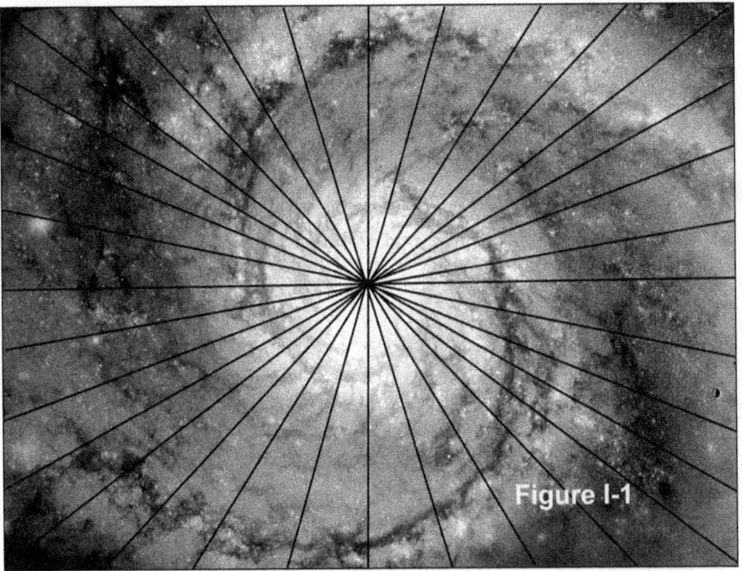
Figure I-1

8 This is how it was described by Dr. Robert C. Beck, D.Sc.

magnetic shift. At the present time our planet has gone out of one of these magnetic lines of flux and is moving toward another. Some scientists believe this is the reason that there is such confusion and so many planetary changes occurring at the present time.

We are at the point now with which the early Americans of more than ten thousand years or so ago were confronted. If we continue on the same path we are going to end up destroying ourselves. Human beings will be gone but nature will keep on going and will evolve new species which will relate to their environment in their own specific way. So, something has to change. That something is human thinking: our thinking about ourselves, our place on this planet, our place in the Solar System, and our place in the Universe. We need to change our focus and that change of focus must include a new perspective of our responsibilities to each other and to this planet.

It is an interesting point to note that whenever most people claim to see and converse with a vision or claim abduction by extraterrestrials many of them come back with pretty much the same idea. That idea was echoed in the previous paragraph: humanity must change its focus if it is to survive and become a member of this Universe. In the pursuit of power we humans have blurred part of the picture. If we begin to re-clarify some of the blurred areas we will end up blurring another part of the picture.[ii] In order to better understand our position we need to take a step back and look at the big picture and reframe our thinking to be more in harmony with the whole.

In order to reframe our thinking it is necessary to have a better understanding of what is going on when we do think. The current research delving into the workings of the brain are simply amazing. Researchers are finding the parts of the brain that are active when we think, act, and perceive. As yet, there is no idea what those parts of the brain are actually doing. The knowledge of the areas that are working is a fundamental breakthrough. From this knowledge we are able to have a better understanding of where specific information is being processed. How it is processed is the next step. Through different branches of scientific research we are finding more out about the workings of the human psyche than the past century and a half of psychological inquiry.

At the present time psychology is at an impasse. A dichotomy exists between those who could be called the "fundamentalist" psychologists and psychiatrists on the one hand and the "eclectics" on the other. The fundamentalists have their pet theories concerning the reasons for human behavior and the eclectics are looking into other branches of science for help in understanding the human animal. One of these sciences being explored is theoretical physics. This is one of the most unbiased of the sciences and many of the physicists are coming up with theories of their own regarding the human psyche and its workings.

When Einstein first postulated his theories of relativity, he began to usher in a whole new scientific inquiry. It became necessary to begin to think in terms of speeds in excess of one hundred eighty-six thousand miles per second. This changed the whole idea of the construction of the Universe.

Gone was the idea that the Universe was one huge machine in which "the gears of the gods grind slowly." Gone were the simple concepts of up and down, forward and backward, length and width and height: basic three-dimensionality. A new view of the Universe has been constructed. In this view the place of human beings is changed as well. Ideas of interconnection, complementarity, causality and acausality, implicate order, nonlocality, and many other concepts previously spoken of by mystics using other terms came into vogue. Since Isaac Newton, physics and the general sciences have been concerned with the "what." Now, especially with the advent of theoretical physics, we are looking for the "why."

Not only is the Universe taking on a new look, humanity's place in the Universe is changing as well. Human beings are about to take that giant leap — that *quantum* leap — into a whole new realm thus transforming humanity forever.

The concept of humanity, our place, our behavior and our very existence in this Universe is undergoing a radical change. It is almost as if humankind is slowly rising out of the primordial slime, the muck and mire of traditional scientific and religious thought, to become a star. With the use of the PET (positron emission tomography) scan and especially fMRI (functional Magnetic Resonance Imagery) the processes of the brain are being laid open so we can see *what* is going on *as we experience our life*. The whole mind/body relationship is beginning to be answered and soon we will have the answer to the very essence of consciousness itself.

Still, though, there are people, groups, philosophies, organizations, and governments who continue to hold the mind of humankind in abeyance. Often we hear and read about fear-oriented fundamentalist religions, brain-washing cults, quasi-religious "potential development" organizations, and "self-help" groups that keep their members afraid to make any real change in their lives and gurus, teachers, preachers, ministers, and politicians of one sort or another that demand your allegiance and more importantly, your money and your life. None of these groups and individuals truly cares to bring the individual up to his true potential, even though some may claim they do.[9]

As science is raising humanity up from its imposed bonds these philosophies will be forced to take a good, hard look at themselves and what is happening around them. For no matter how these organizations and people attempt to continually hold humans down, science is going to raise us up.

In the article, *Visions of a New Faith*[iii] Mary Long intimates that the priests of the coming eon are not going to come from the religions at all. They will be coming from the ranks of the scientists. Their meditation mandalas will be formulas on whiteboards and particle tracks on photographic plates. Their mantras will be thought experiments and the ruminations made while working on their formulas. The fact is that many of the theoretical physicists

9 Consistently, down through the centuries the "Truth" has always been taught *free* to those who will listen and can understand. Even in the Gospels there are admonitions against taking money or paying someone to teach the Gospels. The teacher should work for a living, not live off of the believers.

have a strong metaphysical inclination. Even Einstein at one time said that the deeper you delve into physics, the closer you come to metaphysics.[10]

We are moving ahead in this Universe. A new age is being ushered in. It is an age where human potential will become more fully realized. It is an age where thought will become matter. It is an age of thinking, doing and being: an age of more complete expression.

In all of this forward momentum, is humanity really taking a quantum leap ahead?

Strangely enough, the answer is "no."

"There is nothing new under the sun" as the old adage states. So what science is "discovering" is nothing new. What is new are the terms being used. The irony of it is that we must go backward in order to go forward.

The advances in the field of physics are forcing us to look backward in order to understand our own deeper selves, our reason to be, and the whys of our behavior. In fact, all of the empirical sciences find it necessary to go back to the basics and redefine themselves and, consequently, what they are all about.

Too many scientists have deemed it appropriate to disregard or reconstruct our past in order to maintain a status quo and concentrate on our present.[11] It is necessary that we identify with

10 The author had a voice teacher who told a story of a dinner she had attended. She was seated beside a Nobel Prize winning physicist. In the process of getting acquainted he asked her if she knew anything about physics. Due to the way she was raised she said that she only knew about metaphysics. The response from the physicist was, "My dear, there's no difference."

11 Historians and archeologists, for example, in order to be published will continually reinforce the ideas and beliefs that are the status quo even though proof exists for opposing points of view. Often you will read about archeologists in the Middle East finding part of a building or some artifact fitting an ancient description in the Bible and it immediately "proves" that this person or some event actually occurred and the Bible is wholly correct. Upon further research this consistently is found not to be so. With the "publish or perish" dictum present in academia many historians and archeologists will interpret the findings according to the status quo because that's the only way to be published, that's also what the administrators believe and that's how they hold on to their jobs.

our past in the most positive and objective ways in order to accept our future for this is the only way that we can understand how we got to where we are now and where we are going.

In order to better identify with our past we must accept our failures as well as our successes. We must break the bonds of bias, bigotry, intolerance, hatred and self-inflicted ignorance thus bringing ourselves out of our self-imposed exile with our deeper self. We have been taught for centuries *what* to think. Now we must learn all over again *how* to think, to do and to be.

We humans seem to be finally growing up. Many people are beginning to look in other directions for an understanding of ourselves. The rats in the laboratories,[12] the traditional philosophies and approaches to our being simply do not give us the answers. People are coming not to accept "pat" answers such as "You just *have to* believe," or "Because (some person or some book) said so." These kinds of responses didn't satisfy you as a child but they are expected to satisfy you as an adult. Simply, we are finding out that one book, one person, one philosophy, one branch of science does not have all of the answers.

There is a new objective for the new experience of humankind. The best way to describe this objective is that it is the total integration of each individual's inner and outer being. It is the union of all the parts of a person in order to have optimum functioning with optimum efficiency. It would be to assist in the transcendence of the individual from where he is without a dependency on past learning and conditioning to a greater understanding of and the ability to make better and more viable life's choices.

How this all will be achieved is by understanding that there is no such thing as a truly unbiased observer.[iv] As soon as we observe anything we immediately disturb it on the particle level. Anything disturbed on the most basic level eventually disturbs the higher levels as well. "But" some will say, "it doesn't matter if the particles

12 Richard Bandler, the co-developer of Neuro-linguistic Programming has said that the only people rat research benefits are exterminators.

are disturbed when it comes to something as complex as a human being." The fact remains that as soon as the particles of an object are disturbed the *whole* object is changed.[13] From this point intervention can be made. The only problem here is that the biases of the observer affect the particles of the observed in such a way as to manipulate the object from the *inside*, or *quantum* level, out. So consideration needs to be made with regards to the observer's thoughts.

For centuries we have been taught to believe that whatever happens to us is due to: 1) the will of some deity; 2) some evil entity out to lead we humans astray or to destroy us; 3) a group of gods playing some game such as chess with humans as the pawns; 4) karma from a past life; 5) the fault of where we were born or raised; 6) the fault of our parents; 7) predestination; 8) just the way life is and there is nothing you can do about it; 9) the nebulous "they"; 10) someone specific or some group who has control over our life and world's events,[14] 11) it is in the stars and we have no choice but to live it out.

Science is now showing these excuses to be major fallacies in human reasoning. The fact is no one is out to manipulate or control your life except you. No one has the responsibility for your total existence except you. You are where you are due to your choices and nothing else. What is more, you remain where you are

---

13 The Hawaiian Kahuna (priests) said that there was a permanent bond that exists between people when they meet and interact. This bond is called the "occa thread." It continues to exist until one person dies.

14 Many want to believe that a group such as the *Illuminati* actually exists. (The term *Illuminati* is a medieval term for the Freemasons.) Supposedly this group has been in control of world events down throughout the history of humankind. What these believers don't understand is that a group known as the *Cogniscenti* opposed the *Illuminati* and opposing the *Cogniscenti* were the *Intelligensia.* Needless to say these were such secret groups that no one has any actual information on their existence. Some, though, claim their existence due to speculative construction of obtuse data. One of the major problems with many human beings is their stubborn refusal to accept responsibility for their own choices. To paraphrase an old axiom: If you don't learn from the past you will be doomed to repeat it. The term Illuminati is a metaphor for the human ego.

due to your choice to do so. All of this occurs on the unconscious level and you are unaware that you are even making the choice.

In the mechanistic view of the Universe, humans are no more than pawns being controlled by whatever forces there may be. We have literally no control over our existence. We must passively sit back and accept all of the consequences which may be in store for us. We are nothing more than observers of all of the seen and unseen forces of the Universe. We can do nothing more than exist. We do not live.

While this mechanical Universe was being proposed, the philosophy of life reflected the same conceptualizations. We are at the mercy of some despotic deity in the sky which not only created the universe, as incredibly vast as it is, but also directly involved himself[15] in the lives of every single human being on this speck of dust on the outer rim of this average-size galaxy. It was, and in many cases still is, obey this despot or else. You are not allowed to think or reason or truly live. You *must* do as you are told.

Both the mechanical universe and forced obedience, hopefully, are being laid to rest. New questions are arising and answers are being formulated for them and for the age-old questions that we humans have pondered for centuries.

No longer is anyone truly forced to believe in something that makes little, if any, sense. No longer are the answers to most questions, "Because that's the way it is," or "You don't question it." For now answers are coming forth and science is at the forefront of the means of explaining many of the "mysterious" occurrences in life which were at one time relegated to the realm of "religious experience."[v] What is being found out is that the only mystery is that *there are no mysteries*. All that is, was, or ever will be has some rational explanation. In other words, *nothing* is supernatural. Everything is absolutely normal and natural for the Universe.

15 For some reason, this deity just happens to be a male.

Science sees human beings as co-creators of the Universe. We create our whole existence to fit our understanding of ourselves. We create our life to be exactly what we desire it to be. We are at the mercy of only one thing: *our own creating thoughts*. For it is in our thoughts that we and we alone will either reward or punish ourselves. It is in our thoughts that we will be ill or well. It is in our thoughts where we will succeed or fail. It is in our thoughts where we affect whatever we observe.

Our thoughts are powerful and the more we think a thought correctly the more chance we have of that thought becoming a manifested reality. But thinking is only part of the story. We must understand the workings of the physical manifestation of thought before knowing how to affect any sort of change.

Endnotes

i Phillips, Tony (12.23.2009) *Voyager Makes an Interstellar Discovery*, **Science@NASA**, science.nasa.gov/…/23dec_voyager.htm, extracted December 29, 2009

ii Michael Talbot (1981) *Mysticism and the New Physics*, Bantam Books, New York, NY

iii Mary Long (Nov. 1981) *Visions of a New Faith*, **Science Digest** Vol. 89, No. 10, 36-42

iv Gary Zukav (1979) *The Dancing Wu Li Masters*, Bantam Books, New York, NY

v Bigna Leggenhager, Tej Tadi, Thomas Metzinger and Olaf Blanke (24 August 2007) *Video Ergo Sum: Manipulating Bodily Self-Consciousness*, **Science**, Vol. 317, 1096-1099

Greg Miller (24 August 2007) *Out-of-Body Experiences Enter the Laboratory*, **Science**, Vol. 317, 1020-1021

Henrik Ehrsson (24 August 2007) *The Experimental Induction of Out-of-Body Experiences*, **Science** Vol 317, 1048

By convention there is color, by convention sweetness, by convention bitterness, but in reality there is atoms and space.

Democritis (c. 460-400 BCE)

Chapter 1
What is Reality?

You have undoubtedly heard of the brain being compared to a computer. This is not quite a correct comparison. There are some similarities between the brain and the computer but the brain is far more complex in construction and response than any computer. On the most basic level, the computer works through *serial processing only*[1] while the brain works *partially* in *serial* but *mainly* through *parallel processing*. This means that the brain is able to work on many different things at the same time. In the computer the closest that is possible at this time is what is termed *multi-tasking*.[2] But the parallel processing of the brain is far greater in complexity than the multi-tasking of the computer. Also, the computer needs to be programmed by an outside source while the brain can do its own internal programming. The programming language of the

1 Serial processing means that one command must be completed before the next can be engaged. It is no different than having a large job to do and breaking that job down into a number of smaller jobs that must be executed before the large job is completed. Each of the smaller jobs is dependent on the previous one for its ability to function. When the smaller jobs have all been executed then the large job functions properly.

2 Computer multi-tasking is the running of several programs at one time but accessing only one at a time. The parallel processing of the brain is accessing several programs simultaneously.

brain is your own thoughts and the language you use. Since your thoughts and language control your brain then what you perceive and achieve is a direct result of what you think and tell yourself.

Statistics have shown that if you were born into the middle class, for example, you will tend to stay in the middle class throughout your life. The reason is that your upbringing, learning experiences and socialization and even your genetics have programmed you for the middle class with its values, attitudes and life-style. Take the rap artists as an example. Many of them came from the lower middle and lower classes and they still maintain their class and gang disposition in spite of having large amounts of money available to them and access to better opportunities.

Many psychologists have stated that at least 90-percent of your personality was formed by the age of five. Both heredity and environment are intimately involved in this process. In fact, research seems to show that there is a 50-50 relationship between heredity and environment with the strength of the environmental influences coming from the society. Since much of your time, experiences and relationships in earlier life are with your family and your family essentially teaches you from the society's training doctrines then the thoughts that you were taught to think early in your youth will tend to adhere to you throughout much of your life. Some researchers are now saying that the main contributions of heredity to personality are *predispositions* to certain behavior patterns, values, ethics, attitudes and morality. These predispositions will move you into a direction but it is the environment that will create the specific behaviors that you will perform. That is, as soon as you encounter something occurring in the environment these predispositions can become overt behaviors. So, with the middle class ethic being deeply embedded in your experience (and apparently in your genes and nervous system) so soon in life it is easy to see that you will continue to stay in the same behavioral patterns progressing no further than what your family had programmed you to be.

It may seem that this pretty much predestines you to be what you are. In reality, you are actually an active participant in your own life. You were not predestined nor were you left at the whims of an unkind or unthinking Universe. You make the choices and direct your life as you progress. You can program your mind to do exactly as you would like your life and yourself to be. You construct your reality to be as you expect it to be, and your mind which does not want to make a liar out of you, will give you the experiences you feel you deserve. You create in your mind an environmental experience and it becomes an objective reality to show you that you were correct. Further, your environment and the experiences of that environment in turn recreate you in a continual self-perpetuating feedback loop. In essence, you are in a continuous feedback loop with every aspect of your environment throughout your lifetime which is constantly creating and recreating itself.

Do You Create the Environment or Does the Environment Create You?

In order to answer this question, it is necessary to have an understanding of several important concepts. First, everything in the Universe seen and unseen is some form of energy. Energy itself has the *potential* to become mass and mass has gravity as well as having a magnetic field[3] element. This magnetic field element is a space where magnetic lines of force are active.[i] Since one of the main functions of a magnetic field is attraction, it stands to reason that every body in the Universe attracts, or at least exerts some sort of force or *influence* on every other body in the Universe. This magnetic element then determines how the energy will manifest and, in turn, what it may directly influence.

Second, you are a *biogravitational, self-conscious organizing field*.[ii] Simply put, you tend to attract to you those things (people, events and conditions) which correspond *directly* to this field. It seems that you do not generate this field, but it *may* generate you.[iii]

3 In physics, a field is a region of space under the influence of an agent.

So, according to this idea, it is highly possible that your parents somehow "organized" the filed which you eventually became and then this field generated you. It was probably with the union of the egg with a *specific* sperm that this field began creating you. Some theorists have even hypothesized that the egg "chooses" the sperm that will fertilize it. It is known that there is a biochemical marker that the sperm has that allows it to penetrate the lining of the egg. As the fertilized egg developed from embryo to fetus this field became stronger eventually developing into you. After you were generated by the field you then reorganized it with your learning experiences and your perceptions in order to "prove" it was organized correctly in the first place.

After you had been organized fully into this field you then began to influence it with your own thinking. Your thoughts brought into your reality all that this field was organized to be, to have and to perceive. Every thought brings into your perceptions and into your conscious physical awareness what its basic intent is: For you must have the thought of or *conceive of the possible existence* of something either consciously or unconsciously before you can perceive it.

Humans have also been described as a *biocosmic resonator.*[iv] What this means is that you will echo or resonate some aspect of the Universe.[4] This resonance will be seen in your physical expressions: your thoughts, attitudes and behaviors. In essence, you vibrate to the subtle electromagnetic field which is surrounding you. You need to realize that all *things* around you are subtle *electromagnetic fields* vibrating in differing micro-pulsations. Many of these fields were created by nature but some were created by your own and others' experience. These pulsations affect your state of consciousness, your attitudes and your over-all internal clock and its rhythms. As a biocosmic resonator you pick up and express these micro-pulsations through the effect that they

4 Look at the idea of the biocosmic resonator being like a microcosm. As a microcosm you will be reflecting the larger Universe or Macrocosm.

have on your neurotransmitters, the rest of your brain chemistry and eventually your DNA. Consequently, your life deals with organizing those things which will reflect your consciousness and your consciousness in turn affects what you are organizing. Remember, though, that all things vibrate at their own frequency and you pick up on those pulsations with your nervous system. It is the multitude of these frequencies which your senses perceive as your external environment.

Third, what you perceive as reality is nothing more than the cognitive building blocks present in your mind. These building blocks are based on nature and nurture. This means that the conditions that your senses are born with affect *how* you will perceive *what* you perceive. It is what you learn after you are born which directly affects *what* you will perceive. Essentially, your reality is the thoughts associated with what you have previously experienced as being real. This means that what you are experiencing at the present time is based on your past experience (including your thoughts, daydreams, and other experiences) and the labels that you have learned and placed on your experience and your previous choices. The experience known as your reality depends *directly* upon the choices of what and how you choose to observe and your interpretations of those observations. Those choices depend on the content of your thoughts and your thoughts depend on your expectations and your desire for consistency in experience and in your perceptions.[v] It is important to understand that it is your brain which organizes your discontinuous experience (see below) into a unified whole. This organizational property of the brain is inherent and helps to make your experience predictable.[5]

The fact is there is no reality until that reality is perceived and all elements of that reality have been identified.[vi] This identification

5 The brain of every living thing organizes that organism's perception of its environment to optimize their survival in that environment. With the human the beliefs, attitudes, etc. in turn organize the perception of their environment. This is what makes one person see the glass as half full and another see it as half empty.

depends directly on your experiences and your choices. In essence, this can be considered a "participatory anthropic principle." This was first described by John Wheeler. The idea here is that the universe is "biocentric." What this means is that the universe is created by the perceiving organisms in that universe. Hence, we see a Universe that *we have created* and all sentient organisms in that Universe are participants in that creation.[vii]

It does not matter how accurately your interpretation of your environment may be, your perception of your reality is directly related to what you were taught *or believe* reality is *supposed* to be. What you generally refer to as *your* reality can be defined in terms of *your* experience; past, present and expected. Hence *your expectations* are the precursors to the experience and perception of your reality.

Whenever you observe an object as a solid, you are forced to choose what to observe. If it is seen as an abstract form there is no choice. The manifestation of what you see is through the choice of the available alternatives. (Figure 1-1) It is this feedback loop of creating and recreating that is continuous throughout your life.[viii] If you are confronted with an object that you have never seen before, you will make an association to it through your previous experience. Due to previous experience you will similarly label the newly experienced item. Through this labeling process you will be *expecting* the new object to act in the same manner as any previously experienced similar objects. If it does not then your expectations are challenged by a different

Figure 1 -1

reality and something needs to be changed. This change could include your expectations of the object, your view of your reality or the object itself.

What is Reality?

The term "reality" is derived from two words: *res* meaning a *thing* and *revi* which means to *think*. Reality can be defined as everything about which you can think.[ix] Probably one of the best ways to define reality is: ***All of the possible stimuli available to you at a certain moment in time and point in space***. This definition implies that you can have the experience of reality-upon-reality with the possibility of glimpsing insightfully into how you may be interpreting your reality.

When it is said that reality is: "All of the possible stimuli available ..." it means not only what you see on the surface as a physical object but also your *interpretation* of that stimuli based on your expectations, your labels and what you have learned. According to physical science, you perceive about *ten-thousand bits of stimulation per second* by your eyes alone! Since this information comes to you in bits it means that the basic structure of the physical universe is discontinuous or granular (i.e photons of light are in the form of *quanta* or packets).[6] [x] Trying to take in all of the information at once can easily overload your neural circuitry. Consequently, what your brain does is select what you will be responding to as well as what you will be experiencing.[7]

The process of choosing what you will respond to is rather complicated in itself. There are parts of your brain which automatically pre-select stimuli for you to experience at a basic survival and unconscious level. For instance, some stimuli may

6 If you look at a color photograph in a magazine with a magnifying glass you will get an idea of what discontinuous or granular means.

7 The brain processes about 400 billion bits of information at a time, but we are aware of only about 2000 bits.

be too faint, too dim or have too low a volume[8] and you will not react to them. Another stimulus may cause you some sort of emotional upheaval and it will be repressed. Then, there may be some stimuli which you will unconsciously interpret as being too overpowering and your system will shut-down in some way (e.g. faint). Consequently, the process of choosing how you will be responding is based on heredity and environment; that is, your natural survival mechanisms and your learned responses. The fact is, when your brain perceives sensory input the first thing it does is to check it for a physiological survival value. If it is important to respond the input will be sent to the appropriate areas of the brain for immediate action.

It is important to not only consider your present external stimulation as well as your automatic censoring devices but also the stimulation brought about through previous learning. This previous learning and automatic censoring ends up becoming the choices that you make. It is your previous training that teaches you basically *how* you will respond, *when* you will respond and to *what* you will respond. It also defines your reality and your experience of reality. This cannot be changed by anything you do in the present. It is only through being aware of this that you can set about to make the changes in your present that will directly affect your future.

Of course, you will not react exactly the same ways at age twenty-five as you did at age five in a certain situation. You will have learned different things and other kinds of responses and you will modify those earlier responses. Your basic responding will still be there. The point is that, in essence, your reality will remain consistent with earlier levels of your experience because much of your thinking and responding is still at an immature level.

8 Consider subliminal perception in this instance. Research has shown that the brain doesn't react to subliminal stimulation on anything other than the preconscious level. This means that subliminal stimulation actually doesn't motivate behavior.

What this means is that the reality you perceive will generally remain at a rather unsophisticated level and will only be *modified* by later experience. There are many researchers who say that at least 90-percent of your personality was formed by the age of five. Understanding this gives insight into the lower level of responding we have. Then, it seems, your perception and mental definition of your reality comes from a relatively immature level of experience.

Changing Reality

In order to change your reality you need to change your thinking by getting a different perspective on life. Everyone and everything is a reflection of yourself and your *interpretation* of reality. Essentially, all of the realities that you perceive are directly related to the unconscious thought patterns you entertain and the sensory experiences that you have associated with them. Your experience of reality, then, is learned and to the extent you can accept the possibility that a particular concept can become "real" it can become "real."[xi] That reality, though, can become factual *only for you.* Consequently, by changing what you accept about your reality as true can change your reality — or rather your decisions related to those "truths" associated with your *interpretations* of your reality. By changing your judgments the associated realities can either become more real or immediately no longer exist in the same manner. The existence or non-existence of a certain specific reality or concept is only for the particular individual who accepts it. Some other persons may still choose to accept the existence of a reality or concept completely different from yours and that reality or concept's existence will exist *for those persons only.*

Often this accepted reality is defined as a belief. When discussing belief many people equate belief and faith together as being essentially much the same thing. They are not the same. Faith is usually defined as the confidence that something will happen or that a certain thing does exist. A better definition of faith is the ***acceptance of expectation***. This means that you are simply *assuming* that what you may be *imagining* to occur or to exist actually will occur or does exist. This is nothing more than what psychologists have defined as superstitious behavior. Because of the assumptions and expectations involved in belief and faith, groups have placed "articles of faith" (bones of previous believers, meteorites, "unexplained" works of art, medieval forgeries, and so forth) in front of people in order to give them "proofs" for the existence of their beliefs. These articles of faith have usually nothing more than tradition backing them up and tradition is another aspect of what people would *like* to be, not what actually is.

Beliefs are *generalizations* that are taken to be inclusive as they are inferred from some usually, *singular aspect* of the environment. Consequently, since there is an assumption from experience you will operate *as if* the beliefs are universally factual. This makes beliefs *idealizations* of experience. An example of a generalization is the statement, "I can't do *anything* right." Often when you make this statement you are usually referring to one particular thing. Unfortunately, since it is such a general statement it ends up enveloping your whole life.

Beliefs are based on ***opinions*** or ***judgments***. They most often are *not* based on facts. If a belief is based on facts the facts are usually incomplete, misconstrued and/or misinterpreted. The truth of something is not in whether you are convinced of its possibility but in its existence ***in actuality***. In other words, beliefs are taken on *faith* (expectation) *alone* and cannot be substantiated by direct proof only anecdotal "evidence." Once a belief system is formed you tend to delete *everything* which is contradictory in order to support that belief system. Such as the statement in the previous paragraph ("I can't do *anything* right"). Once you have made that statement anything that you have successfully done is forgotten.[9]

---

9 There are many who are successful at failing. Consequently, they are successful at something.

Beliefs are sets of expectations about how things *should* be or how things *should happen*. In other words, when you hold on to a belief you see *only* what you want or *expect* to see or to happen thus preventing what *can* happen or *can* become from actually occurring. Faith is the acceptance of that expectation. Essentially, you accept that what you believe in can happen while no direct proofs exist regardless of the lack of its possibility. If things do not happen according to your belief you react in some way that will reinforce that belief. After all, you would surely hate to find out that something that you have made a part of your life, something with which you have identified yourself with so strongly, is not true. So, you will insure its reality by refusing to deal with facts. What you end up doing is arguing intensely for your unsubstantiated beliefs.

The main component of belief is *faith*. ***Faith, likewise, is not based on proof but on expectation. This expectation is founded on what you were told while simply <u>assuming</u> that what you were told is true — or even <u>truthful</u>.***[10] The expectancy comes from the assumption that what you have been told is factual and that the person or source relating the information is knowledgeable, trustworthy, aware and truthful. Remember, the proof of the belief in something is not in words alone but in the actual manifestation of that belief in physical existence. Belief in a concept does not necessarily or automatically mean that the concept exists. It must be made manifest on the physical level and become an object of the senses. Until that point it is nothing more than a thought pattern, most often, without intent.

Beliefs and objective reality are *not* the same things. Beliefs are essentially what you *would like* to see — not what is. Beliefs are nothing more than ***opinions* acted upon *as if* they are facts**. Alfred Korzybski, the founder of General Semantics essentially said that *people build beliefs when they don't know what's real*. So,

10 One of the universally accepted "articles of faith" is the value of the U.S. dollar. There is literally *nothing* backing the dollar. It is taken on *faith alone* that the dollar has value. This is what is referred to as "fiat currency."

beliefs are built upon unexplored *hypotheses* and the hypotheses are used as evidence for those beliefs. There is a difference between *assuming* something to be (a belief) and *knowing* that it exists (direct experience). Consequently, a separation between the two can create in you frustration, anger and even acting-out toward those who do not hold the same beliefs — or even toward those who hold the same beliefs, but in a different way.

There is a major distinction between belief and knowledge: A belief *assumes* that something exists or occurs and knowledge has factual *proof* that it does. You do not *believe* that the sun will "rise" in the morning. This is a statement of fact as long as the Earth continues to turn on its axis. You can *believe* that there is such a thing as an "ætherial tube,"[11] for example, because it is only an *assumption*. It cannot be proven. In another example, you can believe that the color blue inspires you. Knowledge of the color blue places it in the electromagnetic spectrum at a specific frequency and so forth. Consequently, knowledge is direct experience and is quite different from belief.

The argument always proceeds: "Just because *you* don't believe in it doesn't mean that it doesn't exist." The true test of a belief is if you can realistically make it an object of physical reality thus proving the efficacy of the belief and the actuality of its being. Often, predictability is mistaken for actualization. It is in predictability where belief lies. It does not matter if the prediction is incorrect or that it does not come about, all that is necessary is to believe that it *might* happen. Then, simply by making the prediction the belief is strengthened. Another way that beliefs are strengthened is through the assumption that something in the environment actually proves the existence for the foundation of the belief. It's like saying, "Since apples exist then oranges exist" or "If X then Y." What those promoting this assumption are forgetting is that the brain perceives the environment according to the experience of the perceiver. It

11 This is another "new age" buzz-word made up by someone who considered himself an enlightened teacher.

is the perceiver that *interprets* those perceptions a particular way.

Argumentation and philosophical dissertations have been proposed and promoted concerning beliefs of all sorts but have proven nothing. The problem is that the tools being used (words) are meta-symbols: symbols of symbols. The beliefs are symbols and the tools of argument, words are also symbols. Consequently, the use of symbols to explain symbols is ludicrous. It just does not prove anything except that one arguer is more effective than the other with the use of his or her particular set of symbols. Besides, as soon as the statement is made it is *assumed* to be factual. Hence, the argument for or against the existence of God *assumes* automatically that a thing called God exists. If you are arguing against, then as the old adage in war goes: "The attacker must totally destroy; the defender need only overcome." Hence, the defender needs only to make the use of anecdotal and emotional "evidence" using a smattering of manipulated facts in order to prove that their beliefs are correct.

Conversely, just because someone professes a belief in something does not mean that it exists. The existence or non-existence of something is not found through belief and argumentation but through direct testing, proofs and physical experience. Even then it is still not to be taken without question for, "*The truths of one era become the myths of another*." Hence, there is a *relativity* for both belief and truth or knowledge. Beliefs are relative to the individual. Knowledge is relative to the time, the space and the experience.

It is interesting to note that many ancient philosophers felt that all you perceive is illusion or "maya." They felt that the senses could easily be deceived, so they did not rely on them unquestionably. Verifiability is the only way that something can be experienced. Hence, believing that what you experience with the senses as well as the experience of the senses themselves as experiencing *absolute* reality is indefensible.

Knowledge does not require belief. It is pragmatic. Knowledge refers to something which can actually be experienced with the senses. It is based on your verifiable experience of the physical reality. It is not based on what you would *like* to exist but on what *actually* does exist. It is something that cannot be disputed. If something's existence or processes can be argued then its existence or its processes are taken on faith, not on fact, and beliefs must be formed to verify that faith. In essence, ***whatever is arguable is hypothetical NOT factual***.

This same process can be seen in the difference between actual scientific study and those that disguise themselves as a science looking for respectability.[12] A science is any study and *experimental system* based upon that study which seeks to understand some aspect of nature or natural processes. It is founded upon *direct observation* of nature or natural processes and it *builds hypotheses and theories* initially established upon these observations. After the hypotheses and theories are set up then *experiments* are performed in order to find if the hypotheses and theories will hold up. From this point, the theories will be brought together into a coherent system that can be proposed in an attempt to illustrate that aspect of nature or the natural processes being observed.

One of the marks of a true science is that it is *amenable to change*. That is a science can propose a theory that, at the time of its proposal will be correct. Later, after more experimentation and measurement, new information may be found that may prove it to be incorrect or incomplete and that particular science will change its theories to accommodate the new data. In this context it means that knowledge and science do change. As Einstein put it so well, "***Science is conditional truth***."

On the other hand, once you acquire a belief you may hold on to that belief in spite of factual information and proofs to the

12 This includes the pseudo-sciences such as phrenology, many of the "alternative sciences," and "Creation Science" now known as "Intelligent Design." One commonality that all of these ideas have is their stubborn refusal to accommodate any sort of change as well as the fact that there is literally *no* scientific experimentation done on their hypotheses or claims.

contrary. Hence, beliefs are structured in such a way that opposing viewpoints and proofs are ignored and even disregarded. This makes them and their proponents unresponsive to information and to change.

Beliefs are associated with particular states of consciousness. They are characterized by an intense focus of attention[13] which would then limit your experience and responsibility. In essence, you would be "hypnotized" or "entranced" by the belief. While in that belief state you could be manipulated, controlled and otherwise directed by anyone who was adept at producing and controlling the particular state.

Beliefs are trance states. As trance states, beliefs tend to be relied upon strongly when induced thus actively deleting any opposing and contrary information. The value of holding on to a belief is based mainly on the *consequences* of having or not having the belief. Quite often fear is the great inducer and preserver of a belief. Fear will lead you to accept a belief without question. You will be assuming that there are positive gains (consequences) received from having the belief and punishments from not having it.

Beliefs perform the function of being a filtration system for experience. That is, they limit your ability to perceive, analyze and thus, respond appropriately to your environment. They set up predispositions or assumptions which are difficult to get around, consequently, they tend to determine what you will pay attention to and how you model, experience and interpret your world. In essence, your beliefs limit the sort of information that you get and the responses and distinctions you make as well as the behaviors that you will engage in as you are reacting to your world.

Your value system is tied to your beliefs and your judgments of "right" and "wrong" are based on this value system. It is these

---

13 Carl Jung called this intense focus of attention a *complex*. Once a person had a complex, that person's behavior and experience revolved about the complex. A complex is essentially a concept with a series of behaviors, emotions, thoughts, values, etc. supporting it, hence, it comes to function as a whole personality.

values that you bring into your interaction with your environment and with others. As soon as you decide what is right or wrong, good or bad you have made a judgment about it. You must remember, these judgments are based on what *you* have decided is appropriate or not in any given situation. It does not matter what your decision may be it is tied to your beliefs about its benefit, value and usefulness to you.

Beliefs are not based on what you know about a particular thing. They are based only on your *opinion* of it and opinions and beliefs do not need to be supported by facts. People will die and kill to preserve their beliefs even though there are often no facts or reality to back those beliefs.

Beliefs tend to be built-up when you do not know the facts. They are only an incomplete abstraction of the experience and not the experience itself. Your support or opposition to a belief is based upon how well that belief seems to hold up in your experience.

Beliefs are acquired the same way as any habit: through the conditioning process of imitation and modeling, reward and punishment, superstitious behavior, and so on. They are generalizations. Generalizations help to make some sense out of the world and to give the world some sort of stability. So, beliefs help to make the world a bit more predictable. It is this predictability that is often mistaken for the actualization of that belief. This predictability is based upon what you *expect* or *want to have* or feel *should* happen,[14] not on what is. Beliefs are the products of immense biases causing you to make incorrect interpretations and decisions concerning your environment.

Beliefs cause the omission, the misrepresentation and the misinterpretation of both incoming and outgoing information. Beliefs invariably have emotions attached to them thus causing you to make identifications with them. In effect, when you accept a belief you *are* the belief. It is not an idea that you have chosen to accept. It is part of who you are. Identification of the self with

14 That is, it is based on faith.

the belief likewise does not automatically make it factual. It is this identification of the self with the belief that can cause you to strike-out in some way. Giving up the belief, in essence, means giving up part of yourself. Once you identify with the belief it makes you somebody and gives you a reason to be.[15] Without it you are nothing. So, holding on to the belief is an absolute necessity.

Beliefs are unconscious in operation. You do not realize that you have acquired the belief and you also do not realize that you are acting upon it. Hence, whenever you have acquired a belief it will tend to govern your behavior unconsciously the same as an emotional or trance state. It is this motivational aspect of beliefs that gives you the problem. Since you will be acting in a certain way, perceiving in a certain way and thinking in a certain way you will not be open to other possibilities which are available to you. So, you will not explore any of the potential that is accessible to you because you have erroneously interpreted and perceived your existence. Your whole existence will be based on a highly biased and limited experience both internally and externally.

Beliefs are self-fulfilling prophecies containing the product of a limited experience and a biased point of view. In it you have little or no way of experiencing anything which is outside of the opinions holding the beliefs in place.

Beliefs do not create reality. Your choices and your intent to experience something combined with the creative thought processes may bring about creation. No matter how strongly you profess a belief in something, until it becomes a product of the senses it does not exist in reality. It is nothing more than a subjective phantasm with no direct relation to reality. Beliefs can actually prevent you from experiencing something in reality. The reason this happens is because beliefs have emotions tied to them and these emotions bring with them their own unique trance states. Consequently, when you are attempting to experience the object of your belief the emotion of the belief blocks the actual experience.

15 This is one of the motivators for suicide bombers.

Many people have claimed to have experienced the object of a belief. A surge of emotions or the brain creating a mental image and projecting it into objective reality is not actually an experience of the belief. If the object of the belief is not a physical reality you can never have knowledge of it. As it is said in one of the Upanishads: "Once you find it, you can't name it: Once you name it, you can't find it."

Objective and Subjective Experience

There is a difference between your objective and subjective experiences. Your objective experience is one which is verifiable by concrete methods; your subjective experience is not. Your subjective experience tends to be dependent upon your beliefs, prejudices, attitudes, wants, needs and desires which are part of your *learned traits* and are *inferred* from experienced internal states. Your objective experiences are based upon the experience of the senses themselves. You tend to assume more from your subjective experiences because they are *biased* by your personal *interpretation* of what is going on inside of you and their accompanying emotions, not by what exists in reality as well as the many identifications placed in your subjective field. Consequently, subjective experience is unverifiable and judgmental and its interpretation is *highly* influenced by your personal biases and your internal states. Subjective experience is also susceptible to a lot of unfortunate mislabeling. This is due to the fact you were taught which emotions were appropriate, in what situations they are appropriate and in what quantities and qualities they are appropriate. Because of this quite often you have no idea what your true emotional experiences are. This is where the mislabeling comes in. Since there is so much emotion and personal identification attached to your beliefs, especially the beliefs that you stubbornly hold on to, and since the chances are quite high that you have no idea what emotions you are truly experiencing the beliefs attached to those emotions are mislabeled and subject to error.

It is important to remember that the existence or non-existence of any reality is simply a matter of choice. You choose whatever you have decided to make real in your life. You choose whatever you have decided to experience in your life. You choose whatever you have decided your life to be. No one or nothing outside of you "makes" you choose, controls you or in any way manipulates you so that you will do, say, or think a certain thing. You are free to choose. You construct your reality every instant of your conscious life through the choices you make. Reality, then, becomes what you choose to perceive it to be.[xii]

The western world has been given many convenient cop-outs for irresponsible behavior. They are all signs of irrational and careless thinking. Freud gave your parent's way of dealing with you as you were growing up; sociologists, social psychologists, and psychiatrists gave you your deprived environment; behaviorists and social learning theorists gave you rewards associated with conditioning and modeling of behavior; Christianity and Islam gave you God's will and God permitting the Devil to do whatever it wants. Nowhere in these areas does it say that you made a choice to do what you are doing. Nowhere is personal responsibility even as much as implied. It is so much easier to lay the blame on something or someone that is not around and/or doesn't even exist to defend itself, assuming its existence, or that cannot possibly make any sort of defense.

Looking at Reality

The world itself exists only as potential until it is observed. What you observe as your reality is a perception of only a small portion of what you understand reality to be. All particles, indeed, all things exist potentially as different combinations of other particles and things. Each combination of particles has a certain probability of occurring. Each part of the physical reality is fashioned from all other parts of that reality and its expression is based on the interdependence of all things as they interact with each other.[16] [xiii]

What appear to be "real" objects are actually transitory illusions which result from your limited state of consciousness. The illusion is that parts of a complete essence are actual objects (observables).[17] Self-actualization (Individuation to Jung) is the experience that objects including "I" are only ephemeral essences stripped of separate existences: momentary links between the illusions of the past and future expanding in the illusion of time.[xiv]

Three kinds of reality have been proposed:

1. The *measurable reality* which is the physical knowable reality of the senses.

2. The *psychic or mental reality* where thoughts, dreams and pictures that symbolize or resemble the external reality exist. You may recognize it as similar to the Collective Unconscious as described by Carl Jung.

3. The *intermediary reality* containing attributes of both realities at the same time.

All realities are superimposed upon or in superposition to one another. What you perceive is the reality that you have chosen to perceive.[xv]

In the intermediary reality, cause and effect manifest. It is not physical objects that follow these laws but a different form of matter. Their only dependence for their functioning is space and time for they change in very orderly, causal ways when they are not observed and disturbed. There is actually no possible way to observe without actively interfering and disturbing what is being observed.[xvi]

---

16 This interdependence is based on all of the co-creators in the "mass reality" being experienced by all perceivers in that reality. See what follows.

17 An *observable* is defined as a feature in nature that is considered fixed or determined.

Each reality is composed of an infinite number of Universes co-existing, interpenetrating and connecting. Whichever Universe you choose to observe is a total mental construction. Even if the reality is some sort of physical object it is still a part of a generated or constructed field.

For reality to exist there must be the thought, or rather, the *intent* for the action of existence by an infinite number of Universes[xvii] or experiencers. In essence, all beings who are part of a certain Universe and who themselves are other smaller universes (microcosm) create the different realities of the Grand Universe (Macrocosm). It is through their intent to create or bring something into some objective reality where a perceivable reality comes into existence.

In the creation of reality you may also consider the possibility that creative or morphogenetic[18] fields[xviii] exist. According to this concept, morphogenetic fields embody the idea that all living existences are based on previous existences and the similar fields that those previous existences have generated. There are fields for organs of the body, for different physical forms, and even for behaviors. The concept of morphogenetic fields may be to what the idea of "self-organization," that was discussed earlier, is actually referring. This may be, likewise, the explanation for simultaneous inventions, concepts and construction around the world, as well as of archetypal symbolism being so similar from culture to culture even though there was no direct contact. It could be the explanation for Jung's idea of the Collective Unconscious.

At the very basis of an existence in a reality is the initial intent. Next comes the thought and finally the construction of that reality. Without the initial intent neither the thought nor the construction of that reality could possibly exist. Interestingly enough, a reality *may* exist if a single individual intended it to exist. Usually the existence of a reality takes the cooperation of all those existing in

18 The concept of *morphogenesis* refers to the idea that the structure or forms of characteristic fields (e.g. molecules, crystals, cells, tissues, organs and organisms) are influenced, shaped and maintained by fields derived from previous similar systems. The more the field is replicated, the stronger it becomes.

that reality before it can become manifest. It is not necessary that a *duplication of intents* or the *cooperation of* the infinite number of *Universes* occur. Each Universe, though, must have the intent for existence in order for its existence to occur. The singular intent which can bring about a reality simply needs the Universe to be flowing in the direction of its manifestation. With the Universe behind you going in a specific direction creating of a reality along the lines of that same direction becomes quite easy.

As soon as the initial intent for a reality is made it is necessary that consciousness be altered in order to adjust to the new reality. For as soon as the new reality starts to manifest other separate but equally possible realities are created to aid you in organizing all that is necessary so you can perceive the new reality. Since you are an organic living system you are self-organizing, and all self-organizing fields generate matter. So, you can generate matter through intent, thought or desire and construction (i.e. visual imagery).

Self-organization involves bringing together all of the physical objects, including persons, conditions, situations, and so on, associated with a certain basic intent. For without the intent nothing can be organized. The concept of self-organization implies that you will first organize yourself from the inside out. In order to organize yourself from the inside out it is necessary to alter your consciousness and place it in the proper state for total acceptance of the intended action. It should be understood that every existence is an action and not an object.

How often do you really pay attention to the thoughts that you are thinking? The fact of the matter is that you spend very little time considering what you think. Your main concern is what someone else will think of you: Would you be loved if you performed or acted a particular way? A lot of your time is spent in judging your position in relation to another's point of view without any direct information as to how the other person really thinks. All you are doing is "mind-reading" and that is really not that easy to do. Mind-reading is *assuming* to know what the other person is thinking by virtue of *your own* experience. Hence, you will decide how the other person feels and will *react* opting to do the "right thing," as you see it. For it is always better to please another than yourself. You will think that to consider your own feelings, emotions, mental, physical and psychological well-being is somehow wrong because it is supposedly egocentric. It seems that another's total well-being is more important and that somehow this type of activity is "spiritually" rewarding. You are not very important and this is your "lot" in life.

How can something be spiritually rewarding that totally or even partially denies *your* individuality? To deny one aspect of yourself leads to the denial of the whole self. This denial brings in many types of emotional, mental, psychological and physical disorders. It distorts your perception of yourself and your reality and leads to a narrow view of your total existence.

The denying of your selfhood brings about an inner chaos and leads to emotional disorders. Without a clear understanding of who you are all that is evident is confusion, misinterpretation of your experience and fear.

The Truth About Reality

Once you have made a decision as to the existence or non-existence of a reality it then becomes a represented aspect of *a* truth *for you*. It does not matter how accurate the *mental construction* of a reality is, it only represents *an* aspect of *a* truth, and not *The Truth* itself. Just as your physical perception will be selective so also will be the points or aspects of truth represented by that reality. You cannot possibly experience the total reality or *The Total Truth* of *a* reality so you will select some aspect of that reality and of *a* truth in reference to that reality and often will assume that what you have chosen to experience is *The Total Truth*.

The fact is that there are other realities which to you are true simply because you believe they exist. Because you believe in their existence does not necessarily mean that they are *The Truth*.

It just means that due to your experiences, or rather, *what you have chosen to experience*, these realities are aspects of various truths for you.

As you were growing up you experienced the many different realities of many different people. Each person with whom you had an encounter had his own realities which he had believed to be true. As a child your mind was filled with awe and wonder with the desire to learn and experience far away from your initial experience of reality prior to birth. You knew no better and accepted bits and pieces of others' realities to be your own and to be true. So you took on from those other persons, through the processes of imitation, role modeling, conditioning through reward and punishment and various and vicarious learning processes, their viewed realities and their associated truths.

With the assumption of these realities you then began to organize yourself and *your* reality to conform to those learned concepts, actions and so on. You then became a direct extension of others' realities, and being self-organizing, creating a uniform Universe that corresponds to what you have assumed to be true. You drew to you all of the people, conditions, activities, physical objects and total experience of those assumed realities which were made available to you. You were not permitted to view reality through your own eyes or experience reality on your own. You began to accept everyone else's view of what they had chosen as their reality.

In direct association with *a* reality is its associated truth. Whatever reality exists for you is some sort of inclination toward *a* truth. Since your previous experiences had clouded your perception of reality then the truth which is associated with the reality is clouded. Remember, any reality can only point to *a* truth and not be representative of *The Total Truth*.

Not only does previous experience directly affect you in this respect but what you choose to believe as being real also clouds your experience of what reality is. Only after you have transcended all realities, especially believed realities, can you find *The Truth*.

For *The Truth* is a direct experience from your total being. It exists without the limitations and uncertainties of your human nature or any contrived ideas, concepts, philosophies or beliefs from your personal experience. You will then begin to understand that all experienced realities are basically a means to an end. They can be seen as sign-posts telling you what seems to be the problem with your experience. Through the transcendence of the personal experience of many realities you can gain greater insight into your interpretation of your own inner reality in association with the realities of others.

"There are many roads to the top of the mountain," stated Gautama Buddha more than twenty-five hundred years ago. They are all, at some point in objective time, valid due to the realities experienced and the truth to which they are connected. No one path should be adhered to for longer than is useful. Whenever anyone says that they have "the way" or the "perfect path" or something similar, you can be sure that they do not have anything in which your involvement is worthwhile. They will do whatever they can to manipulate your experience of your reality so that you will become dependent upon them as a surrogate parent or demigod. They will stifle your individuality and uniqueness for the sake of conformity. Then, your self-esteem will be manipulated and made to oscillate up and down at their whims in order to keep you in line. Your self-concept will be made into what the individual or group wants it to be. You will no longer be living, breathing, thinking and choosing for yourself but as a member of a group out to force your imposed reality on to the realities of others.

What these groups refuse to see is that due to your own uniqueness as a member of the Universe, in your life experiences and in the chosen way you conceive of yourself *you have your own path*. Psychological problems can be attributed to a lack of awareness of this path. A lot of frustration and hostility develop due to being out of synchronicity with your path. By accepting another's view of reality as your own you get turned aside from your path and your reality and end up living another's experience.

Maya

All conceived realities must, at some point in time, be set aside. All believed in realities need to be discarded. All that you experience, or rather choose to experience must be logically questioned and, as soon as it becomes categorized, released so that you will not become obsessed, possessed or consumed by it.[19] All that you experience is what the ancients termed *maya* or illusion. For it is a transitory and imagined reality.

What the term *maya* really means is that what you perceive as physical reality is an illusion. You are interpreting reality through your physical perceptual senses and your senses do not always function at their optimum. Further, you need to remember that in the whole electromagnetic spectrum,[20] the entire visible light spectrum is from 400 millimicrons to about 700 millimicrons, simply *less* than *one-one millionth of a meter* of the whole electromagnetic spectrum. (Figure 1-2) Then, add to that the fact that whatever you see is only *reflected* light and that you will choose what you will be responding to with your senses being most inefficient systems of perception, although your senses do function well for what they evolved to do. The fact is you experience so little of the Universe that you cannot make any realistic judgments about any aspect of it. For when you make a judgment you are reflecting some portion of your previous experience which tells you what you have decided to accept as your reality. Essentially, your judgment expresses some aspect of yourself, not of what the Universe actually is.

All conceived realities are temporary. All that which you physically perceive to exist will not last. That is why your physical reality is considered *transitory* or *maya*. All that is in the physical Universe at some point dies. It must for new growth to be stimulated. Stars and planets are continually being born; others

---

19 Obsession leads to possession. Once someone is possessed by a thought, idea or possibility they become consumed by it and it becomes part of their identification.

20 The electromagnetic spectrum runs from 10^{-14} meters for Gamma Rays to 10^{10} meters beyond AC circuits.

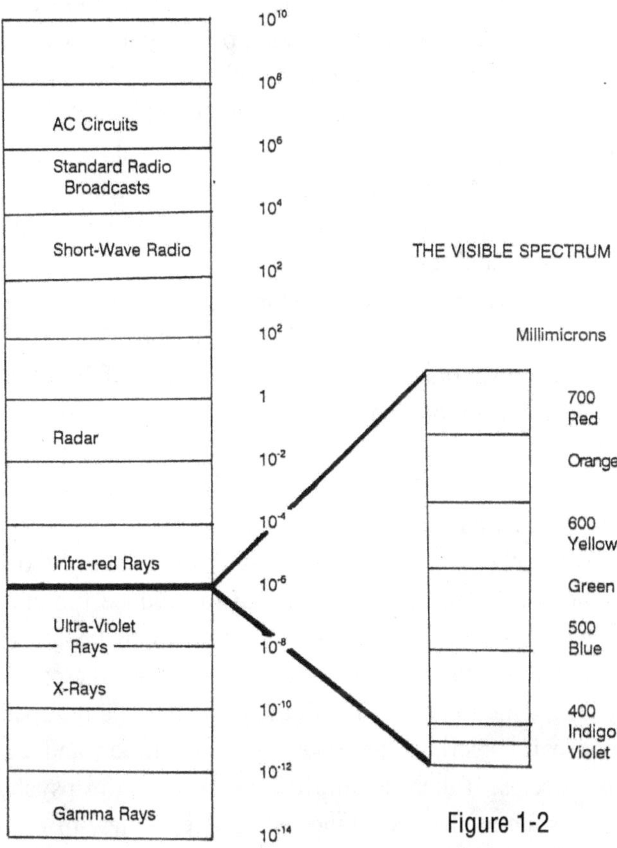

Figure 1-2

The visible spectrum is only 1/1,000,000 of a meter of the whole Electromagnetic Spectrum.

are dying. With each new death comes a birth or rather a rebirth. Another way to describe this process is the changing of energy from one form to another. For energy can neither be created nor destroyed, but it can be changed into another form. The Universe cannot exist with something totally missing or with actual empty space or a true vacuum. There will, of course be those who will argue that black holes are empty space. That is not quite true. Whether they are mini-black holes (as has been theorized) or black holes that take up light years of space, they are *not* empty space. They obviously take up space or they would not exist. They are more like a whirlpool in the ocean, possibly a doorway to some other reality whether it be on the other side of a galaxy or this Universe, into another physical Universe, into another dimension or into the negative side of this Universe, they do exist. No one or nothing known has gotten close enough to a black hole to find out what it is doing where it is so just about anything within reason can be postulated for its existence.

All life involves growth. The fact is the Universe is inundated with all of the elements which can produce life. The present scientific endeavors know of only one kind of life and that is terrestrial and carbon-based. There may be other forms of life which no one is able to understand and which are not carbon-based. Silicon-based life-forms have been theorized and no one has any idea what they would look like or how they would act or even what other forms of carbon-based life would be like.[21]

The whole Universe is equipped to produce life and all life must grow and evolve. That growth is not strictly physical growth. This includes emotional, mental and psychological growth as well. Anything which interferes with the growth that any aspect of the Universe is experiencing produces degeneration and extinction of the species. If there is interference to mental or psychological growth, such as the acceptance of another's view of reality, this will inhibit you from the experience of your true reality and your inner being. In order to have this experience you need to leave the world of constructed realities. You need to see that all that the five senses experience are constructs of your individual thoughts. By your experience of a certain thought you can bring a certain reality into your physical existence. The truth is that a reality does not exist until you have constructed it and only then will it exist *for you*.

---

21 Consider all of the extinct carbon-based life-forms that lived on the Earth. There may be insectoid or even reptilian life-forms that could have involved into sentience on other planets.

Throughout human existence billions-upon-billions of ideas, concepts, realities and truths have been postulated, existed for a time and died. What is the truth, the reality of one age is found to be the fallacious reasoning of another. Those truths that you now hold to be part of your realities will soon go the way of the gods of civilizations long since dead. All things, including religions and social philosophies and institutions devised by humans will soon pass away. The only real constant in the Universe is *change*. All things are in different forms of change and are often imperceptibly changing.

Psychological and physical problems develop due to your denial of your deeper inner self and the acceptance of change. This denial forces you away from the direct experience of your deeper reality and in this denial you will hold on to your constructed beliefs and unknowingly accept them as true reality. So, in order to balance your outer being with your inner being you will distort your experience to fit your belief system. You then will repress a lot of your internal emotional experience and eventually give yourself experiences which form the basis of the realities you intended into existence.

Since the only real constant in the Universe is change, each reality which you experience is constantly changing. Due to your experiences each reality is constantly forming and attracting all other appropriate realities to it. The point to remember is that these attracted realities do not all have to exist in this same space-time dimension. There are realities beyond that which the mundane senses can experience. There are experiences of which you have absolutely no knowledge or understanding. But due to your experiences in this physical reality, the reality in which you have chosen to experience, you attract other realities that exist *concurrently* in association with this reality. This means if you happen to have a strong enough intention based on some mystical system or philosophy you can bring into your life the manifestations pertaining to that philosophy. Often, you will assume from your emotional responding and assumed changes in those emotions that based on your intent the mystical system has become manifest. The truth of any mystical system is its actual manifestation in physical reality, not because some book or some person or people have said it exists. Remember, the manifestation of it does not mean that it is *The Reality* or *The Truth*. It just means that the reality in which you are involved is, for you at a certain point of time, the object of *your* experience. That is one main reason that you should never hold on to a certain constructed reality or stay with one certain path for any long period of time. Once you have experienced some aspect of a truth or a reality, holding on to it restricts your evolution. You must let go in order to gain new experiences and insight into your deeper reality. For as you gain this insight into yourself you begin to gain insight into your own and the whole Universe. You are nothing but a miniature reflection of the Grand Universe and are in total unity with the Grand Universe. Essentially, the Universe will manifest to you according to your capacity to understand it. The Universe's manifestation will be a reflection of what you have understood it to be, what you intended into existence and you will experience that which you have intended.

One mistaken conception to which many people adhere is the idea that the reality which is perceived is a single reality. The fact is that you exist on all Universes and realities at the same time. What you perceive is the interpenetration and interconnection of an infinite number of realities co-existing. Your thoughts of each of the perceived realities then become what your experience has taught you to categorize as a single perceived reality. By simply remembering the fact that you experience about ten-thousand bits of information per second you can see that even on the physical level you do not perceive a single object. All that you actually perceive are the *representations* of the objects you are perceiving; or quantum wave functions.[22] [xix] It is your early training and

22 A *Quantum Wave Function* is a description of an observation, not the observation itself, determined by mathematical models which are continually changing thus leaning to the imprecision in its description. It is an endless pattern of spherical waves flowing in a logical manner rippling and pulsing outward from a center much like pebbles dropped in still water.

conditioning that comes into play here and you will select out of that experience.

Summary

The basic structure of the physical world is determined by how you choose to look at it. How you understand your reality to be is a creation of your thoughts. Whatever you choose to truly intend to be will become manifest in your physical reality. Further, whatever you, through your basic intent, bring into your outer experience, will be. You are constantly in a process of becoming as is the whole Universe. Your realities and your perception of your realities are constantly changing. Consequently, nothing remains the same for more than a fraction of a second. As soon as it is perceived, it is changed. But in order to make the world more stable, you perceive the physical world or some object as simply being there and possibly moving from point to point.

All realities, all events, all phenomena in the whole Universe are integral parts of an inseparable, harmonious whole. Consequently, there is no division between you and any other aspect of the Universe. Whatever you perceive you create in order to perceive it. Every moment of every day you are manifesting the Universe out of the innumerable possibilities available. As soon as you choose and identify with some aspect of the Universe you, the observer, and the observed become one and both realities are immediately altered.

There is really nothing until you choose to see it. That is, nothing exists "out there" until you look for it and find it.[xx] All that you are doing is discovering part of yourself everywhere you look. That is why there's the paradox of the object and its opposite everywhere you look. Because of this you are constructing the experience that you have of reality from what you have within yourself and your internal concepts constantly.[xxi] That is also why there is no such thing as an unbiased observer. Further, that is also why the Principle of Indeterminism[23] holds validity, even in the field of human behavior.

You are, in actuality, an essence, not an existence.[xxii] Like the virtual particle, you exist only in principle. The Universe embraces all possibilities because consciousness can conceive of all possibilities. Nothing can exist without an observer to bring it into existence. You are the creator and have the right amount of freedom to create anything that you want.[xxiii]

The Universe acts more like an event than an object. To paraphrase Buckminster Fuller, "The Universe is a verb, not a noun," for the whole Universe is nothing more than all of the beings and objects within it relating and interrelating. It is reality-upon-reality continually attracting, connecting, interpenetrating, dying, being born and reborn, and manifesting itself in whatever ways that the beings in the Universe perceive it to be. The Universe is not like a machine but a unified whole. It is more like one great thought the deeper you delve into it. The more you remove your dependency upon temporary realities the more you will see the interconnectedness of the whole Universe.[xxiv] Then truly the concept of you being a small representation (microcosm) of the Grand Universe (Macrocosm) will become realistic. It is then possible to experience more on a grander scale: more of yourself, others, nature and the whole Universe. Not only that, but you will begin to express yourself in the most positive, constructive ways — the ways in which you were intended to express yourself. You are here to express the aspect of the Universe which you are, not to be a self-centered expression but a total representation of the whole Universe on a small scale. You are here to experience the many realities which you are for they lead to many truths, the transcendence of which leads to the experience of *The Truth*.

Your experience of the Universe is a personal one. How you relate to the Universe is also personal. As long as you accept the

---

23 *The Principle of Indeterminism* states that it is impossible to actually predict the outcome of an experiment no matter how much information we know about it consequently a prediction is uncertain.

realities which you constructed as being The Truth you cannot fully experience nor can you relate to yourself, others or the Universe. What you are doing is voluntarily cutting yourself off from part of the Universe and how it relates to you. It is adjusting your perception of your Universal Reality to fit a physical concept or some man-made conception.

The Newtonian view of space-time is a dynamic picture of events developing with the passage of time. Time is one-dimensional and moves forward. Past, present and future occur in that order.

Einstein's Special Theory of Relativity sees time as a static, non-moving picture. Space-time is a continuum where events do not develop but just are. Everything exists in total on the fabric of space-time. Past, present and future are all here now. The illusion that events "develop" in time is due to your particular type of awareness that allows you to see only strips of the total space-time picture at one time.[xxv]

Direct experience is the only way to remove yourself from constructed realities. You can then fully experience a reality and return with a concept of that complete experience for you can never really return with the experience itself. Hence, you will view reality as an experience and not a static event.

You need to remember that a computer will only do what it is told and that its output is only as good as the individual who programmed it. The same goes for each individual. Look at the programming that you have. Look at what you accept as being reality. Look at what and how you perceive. Then look at your choices. It is here where you will find all that you need to know concerning your personal view of the Universe: For as these are inseparable parts of the unified whole individual, you are an inseparable part of the Unified Whole Universe.

Endnotes

i Bob Toben (1975) **Space-Time and Beyond**, E.P. Dutton, New York, NY

ii *IBID*

Michael Talbot (1981) **Mysticism and the New Physics**, Bantam Books, New York, NY

iii *Op cit*

iv Norrie Huddle, **Interview with Robert Beck, D.Sc**. Taped Jan. 1983

v Fred A. Wolf (1981) **Taking the Quantum Leap**, Harper and Row, Publishers, San Francisco, CA

vi Robert Lanza and bob Berman (May 2009) *The Biocentric Universe*, **Discover**, 53-55

vii *IBID*

viii *Op cit*

ix Gary Zukav (1979), **The Dancing Wu Li Masters**, Bantam Books, New York, NY

x *IBID*

xi Michael Talbot (1981) **Mysticism and the New Physics**, Bantam Books, New York , NY

xii Fred A. Wolf (Dec. 1981) *Taking the Quantum Leap*, **Science Digest**, Vol. 89, No. 11, 88-92

xiii Fred A. Wolf (1981) **Taking the Quantum Leap**, Harper and Row, Publishers, San Francisco, CA

xiv *IBID*

xv Lawrence LeShan (1966) **The Medium, the Mystic, and the Physicist**, Ballantine Books, New York, NY

xvi Fred A Wolf (1981) **Taking the Quantum Leap**, Harper and Row, Publishers, San Francisco, CA

xvii Jeff Love (1976) **The Quantum Gods**, Samuel Weiser, Inc, New York, NY

xviii Rupert Sheldrake (Oct. 1981) *Rupert Sheldrake's Hidden Force*, **Science Digest**, Vol. 89, No. 9

__________ (1989) **The Presence of the Past: Morphic Resonance and the Habits of Nature**, Vintage Books, New York, NY

xix Gary Zukav (1979) **The Dancing Wu Li Masters**, Bantam Books, New York, NY

xx *IBID*

xi Michael Talbot (1981) **Mysticism and the New Physics**, Bantam Books, New York, NY

xxii Fred A. Wolf (1981) **Taking the Quantum Leap**, Harper and Row, Publishers, San Francisco, CA

xxiii *IBID*

xxiv Jeff Love (1976) **The Quantum Gods**, Samuel Weiser, Inc., New York, NY

xxv Gary Zukav (1979) **The Dancing Wu Li Masters**, Bantam Books, New York, NY

It is not the consciousness of men that determines their existence, but on the contrary it is their social existence that determines their consciousness.

Karl Marx (1818-1883)

Chapter 2

What is Consciousness?

Consciousness is the *creative element* of the Universe. It is at the basis of everything and exists without being associated with any living system.[i] Without consciousness nothing can become manifest.[ii] Consequently, no matter what your conceived realities appear to be, prior to their perception, you must be conscious of them in order to perceive them.

No doubt you have used the term *consciousness* many times without really concerning yourself with its meaning. It is one of those "buzzwords" that many people assume everyone knows the meaning of so no explanation seems necessary. Simply defined, consciousness is ***a state of awareness***. Consciousness is actually much more than that. Some researchers consider it an organized arrangement of mental (psychic) or internal elements. What consciousness is not is thoughts and thinking. Thoughts and thinking are only the *after-effects* (the epiphenomena) of consciousness. This means that your thoughts are doing nothing more than *reflecting* your consciousness. Consequently, by paying attention to what you are thinking you will be able to get an understanding of what your state of consciousness is at the time you are thinking the thoughts.

It is important to note that consciousness is *something that the brain does*. It is a *subjective experience* that arises from the normal functioning of the brain and, consequently, is impossible to experiment on directly. One of the main reasons that consciousness is so difficult to experiment on is because there is no useful and acceptable definition for consciousness. For associated with consciousness are its main processes: perception, learning, thinking, memory, and emotion.[iii]

The psychologist, William James saw consciousness as a stream of thought. The allusion to a stream recognizes the fact that it is constantly changing on a continuum. The fact that it is changing constantly implies that it has many diverse elements. Your experience of consciousness shows that it has an organizing unity in these elements. If it did not have this unity it would be a series of separate and discrete elements and you would be constantly experiencing a jumble of perceptions from the environment. With the research that is being done today, defining consciousness as a continuum appears to be closest to defining what the brain's experience of consciousness is.[iv]

Consciousness, as seen by Carl Jung, is both a blessing and a curse. As a blessing it is in "higher" consciousness[1] where you have the clarity and certainty which is needed to see problems through. It is a curse because for every problem you look at you are forced into greater consciousness (states of awareness) and further away from the innocence of childhood unconsciousness.[v] In theoretical physics consciousness is seen as the element which is outside of the physical Universe and which collapses the quantum wave function. The quantum wave function collapse produces an observed result from its range of possible states.[vi] In other words, whenever a wave function collapses you will perceive a physical object.[2] As long as the wave function continues progressing there is only possibility, not physical reality. Consciousness is the process

1 Seeing consciousness as being "higher" or "lower" is ridiculous. Without a workable definition we have no idea of what consciousness is in the first place.

2 The collapse of the quantum wave function is the basis for perception according to theoretical physics.

wherein potential reality becomes physical reality. Hence, the wave function isn't the total representation of the physical world. There is a "hidden variable" that specifies 3-dimensionality. At any time it is this "hidden variable" that determines our experience.[vii] It is the awareness of any particular branch of parallel universes of which you happen to be aware. It is the process by which you stop time in its progression in order to create what you perceive as your physical reality.

Consciousness is important because of the fact that you are shifting through different states of awareness and you go through and experience these different states all day long. Since your awareness of your environment is constantly shifting your consciousness is likewise constantly shifting. Take a look around you right now. What are you aware of? Describe the environment in which you are sitting. To describe each item in your environment you must constantly shift your consciousness in order to become aware of, for example, the lamp, then the table, then the window, etc. This goes for the descriptions of each item: its shape, color, location, placement and so on. Your consciousness must reorient itself constantly to the environment by refocusing its attention. Do not get the idea that consciousness and focused attention are the same. They are not. Focused attention is the main process producing consciousness; not its main component. There are a number of theories of what consciousness is and what causes it. Researchers at this time do not know all of the components involved in consciousness.

Since your consciousness is constantly shifting and altering every moment in time and at every point in space many researchers feel that it is very possible that there are as many different states of consciousness as there are for each and every reality and everything in that reality you perceive. So with each perception there is a state of consciousness needed to perceive it. Some theories have gone as far as to suggest that most likely everything existing has its own state of consciousness to be what it is or it would not be. This is easy to understand when it comes to something animate such as a dog or a cat. What of a tree or a rock or blade of grass or a mountain or a cloud? Do these also have consciousness? All objects, living or inanimate, may have differing forms of consciousness. There is no way of finding this out at this time. A theory exists that all of the objects you can perceive are perceiving you in return. With the combining of consciousnesses of all things participating the present reality is created. The implication is that realities sort of create each other by being self-excited systems and they are brought into being by the participation of all those beings who take part in their construction.[viii]

Your personal consciousness distinguishes you from all other things. You have your own unique consciousness to be who and what you are and it is this unique consciousness which distinguishes one consciousness from another or one object from another. In philosophy this is referred to as either the separation of the *"I"* from the *"non-I"* or the *"I"* and *"thou."* In essence what is being described is the fact that one way to know who you are is by looking at and describing what you are not.[3] Remember all objects that you perceive are part of your created reality and that they are progressing toward becoming what they ultimately will become. Hence, you can never really know what an object *is* only what it *does*. Consequently, there are no nouns, only verbs. So the term "object-event"[ix] is used by some theorists to describe the things "out there" which you perceive. Being an object-event implies that its own uniqueness is constantly changing. The only way that an object-event could be totally experienced is whenever you have intended, thought and willed it strongly enough that all of the realities involved in its manifestation would come into harmony. Only then would it come into existence. This means that your intention, thought and your

3 If you want to do an interesting experiment, take a sheet of paper and write down all of your "I ams." You can begin with something like, "I am (John Jones)." Then, "I am a (man/woman)." Then to "I am (American/French/ Austrian)" "I am a (student/barber/teacher)." Go on from there. You'll find some interesting things out about yourself from this exercise. (See exercise 1Pp. 27-29 in **From Victim to Victor: Defeating a Victim's Consciousness** by Alexander S. Holub, Ph.D.)

will are the three main factors in stopping an object-event in its progression making it an object of the senses.

Consciousness is both *awareness* and *the creation of experience*: the *being* and *knowing* of experience (knowing is mind and being is matter).[x] Consciousness seems to constantly be streaming in from the outside in the form of sense-perceptions. Sense-perceptions tell you that something is "out there" but not *what* is out there. This is told to you by the process of *apperception* (that is, conscious perception)[4] and this may be either directed, as attention, or undirected as fantasy or daydreaming.[xi] The process of apperception means that you are conscious and that you are perceiving. This form of consciousness is based on where your attention is directed. If it is internal you will be aware of what is happening inside of your body. If it is external you will be aware of external events and objects. Apperception, then, involves choice and this choice is intentional and not unconscious.[xii] With every experience you have the intention to perceive that experience and this intention precedes the actual perception.

Brain researchers have found that something happens in the brain moments before you make a choice to do something. As an example, moments before you make the movement of even your finger there is an activity in the brain indicating that an unconscious choice is being made. Once this activity occurs then the action occurs. There appears to be a similar thing that happens prior to your choice of your experience of reality as well. Researchers have found that there is a recognition "spike" on EEG (electroencephalograph) tracings immediately after you see and identify an object. It may be that the consciousness of the possibility of that experience is what brings about the actual perception of it.[5]

---

4 It is important to remember that it is the brain which *interprets* the neural stimulation created by the sense organs. This interpretation is influenced greatly by past experience.

5 There are researchers at this present time who are hoping to use this information to aid paraplegics and quadriplegics.

Consciousness affects you on all levels of your existence. It has been known for some time that there is some prenatal awareness and some interesting theories have come about regarding this awareness. It is known that whatever the mother experiences emotionally the fetus feels as well. It is also known that the fetus is aware of sound vibrations and things said prior to birth from at least the beginning of the third trimester in utero. These things can be remembered and transferred into one's lifestyle. Some recent evidence for this was found by some medical researchers as well as non-traditional therapists and hypnotherapists doing age regressions.[xiii] Consequently, not only does life outside the womb affect you and your consciousness but it seems that shortly before birth there is consciousness awareness and this also has an effect. Closely aligned to your perception of your reality is your consciousness and there is a constant feedback loop between you and your environment. That is, what you perceive reacts in a particular way to your awareness of it and you in turn react through your conscious awareness in that reality in a particular way. As soon as an action is performed and it is observed, it alters both yours and the observer's reality instantly. The observation disturbs the unbroken wholeness of the Universe and through the act of observation each observer separates himself from the rest of creation because both the observer and the observed have been affected by the observation. Observation brings in knowledge. Unfortunately, the price of this knowledge is that of becoming increasingly more isolated[xiv] by becoming more estranged from reality instead of a part of it. This is why Jung described consciousness as a curse. The more experiences that you have the further you progress from that wholeness you had experienced in infancy. The more observations you make the more you separate yourself from that initial unity.

The Limitations of Consciousness

Your mind has the ability to become conscious of many realities and to experience them in different ways. You can react to many different consciousnesses and become intimately aware of them. Assuming that all living things have consciousness, an oak tree, for example, is aware that it is an oak tree and does not have the potential to be anything else as long as it is an oak tree. For the sake of discussion, let us say that an oak tree is totally conscious of itself being an oak tree and that its awareness of the future is that all it will ever be or produce or experience is only what is related to and concerned with its present consciousness of being an oak tree.[6] [xv] All that it can do is react to the other consciousnesses around it as an oak tree. In a violent wind it cannot bend like a palm tree. Its acorns cannot produce roses. So its consciousness is locked into being an oak tree. All of its experiences are based on the consciousness it possesses.

Every consciousness has its own special uniqueness which gives it an individual perception of what it considers reality. You can experience more realities and more consciousnesses than any other living thing on this planet. You can experience what appears to be the consciousness and reality of the oak tree but the reverse seems to be most improbable. You can become intimately aware of more things due to your ability to place your consciousness into them and return with the apparent sensations of the experience. You can, by virtue of your thought processes, transcend time, space and dimension to gain greater insight into your own and the Total Universe. Whether or not these experiences are real

6 There are some rather unusual theories concerning plant consciousness and communications. One person has gone so far as to use a plant as an antenna to attempt to communicate with extraterrestrial intelligences and "inter-dimensional" beings. Others have claimed that plants are conscious of other consciousnesses in their area. At this time it is rather questionable that the results are viable for experimenter bias can unconsciously influence the results received. Further, plants don't have a nervous system as animals do so their ability to react as animals do is rather questionable.

is up for conjecture. You have no way of knowing if what you are feeling when you focus your attention and awareness into an oak tree is the actual experience of the oak tree. Suffice it to say that your mind is only limited by the limitations that it has placed on it. These limitations alter your consciousness so that the perceptions experienced are not fully experienced. Like the oak tree's consciousness, your consciousness has its initial limitations placed on it by virtue of being human.

Further limitations on your consciousness come from the fact that you were most likely born into and raised by people who themselves had a limited consciousness. The initial experience of selfhood which may be encountered at birth soon was set aside for statements which told you who and what you were and dealt with lack and limitation. Remember also that there are prenatal influences which must be taken into account as well. Consequently, the birth experience could very easily turn out to be rather traumatic thus adding another limitation. This is why the initial experience of selfhood may not always occur at birth.

Carl Jung saw that there is no consciousness at birth. The child must go through the process of *becoming* conscious. Jung described this process of becoming conscious with three stages of consciousness. The first stage of consciousness is the simple connection made between two or more mental elements. This is your basic associational stage. In this stage you learn to connect, for example, a face or an object with a word or a name. In this way you learn to identify objects outside of yourself automatically separating yourself from your own inner experience. You can also learn to connect an internal feeling with an external experience and learn that a certain experience can produce a specific emotion. The ego begins to develop throughout this stage and it develops by identifying those things "outside" as the *non-I.* At this stage those things are simply understood as "out there," instead of "not me." The second stage is that of the developed ego complex being self-centered. In this stage your ego begins to separate itself from the environment taking on its own unique existence.

As this happens your ego becomes the focus of its own world-view where identifications are made with things and feelings (e.g. "That ball is *mine*," "*I'm mad* at you"). Here you identify yourself with the objects that are "outside" or the feeling being expressed. This action further separates you from your initial experience of yourself. The final stage is the dualistic state[xvi] where the *I* and *non-I* are recognized and identification becomes a matter of what you are not. You become more conscious of what is outside of you than of what is inside of you. Here you realize that those things outside are "not me" and that there is something which is either felt to be or known to be "me" or "I" which has nothing to do with the things outside. It's the experience of the environment that affects consciousness and vice-versa. Here there is an understanding of states of awareness which are different. This idea gives rise to the whys and whens of your consciousness's limitations.

Assuming that you were born with a self-concept that is intact and your awareness of your self is fitting, your encounters with others tended to limit more of your self-consciousness. In most cases the limitations by others was not deliberate. They just do not know any better. What you encountered were the problems, setbacks, failures, insecurities, and so on of those with whom you had the closest contact. These things were placed on you thus limiting more and more of your consciousness, perceptions, responses, experiences, and reality. In essence, you began experiencing yourself, your life and life in general through other peoples' eyes.

More limitations were placed on your consciousness from the society. The structure of the laws of most societies sets limitations by stating what is not to be done. No one can think of a way to run a society by stating what can be done. Add to this the childrearing practices of most societies follows this same tradition: "Don't do that!" "Stop that!" "You shouldn't do that."

More social limitations to your conscious awareness are the present religious concepts. Very few, if any, religions of the world allow you to think for yourself, to experience in order to gain knowledge for and of yourself and your world and, in essence, to grow. As a member of a certain sect or denomination you *have to* fall in line and be *exactly* like everyone else thus subverting your individuality. Being exactly like everyone else is only part of the problem. You also have to think exactly like the leader of the group and that means that you have to think like everyone else. There are no variations allowed. If you think and reason and question you risk some sort of expulsion and rejection by the group in general and its members specifically. In order to insure that everyone thinks alike some "religions" have gone to the extreme of using direct coercion and modified brainwashing procedures. Directly or indirectly, virtually every religion uses some sort of coercion whether it be directed at this life and your experience in the group or the existence of some postulated life after death.

To be conscious of something means that at a certain point in time you have conceived of its existence. The main function of your consciousness is to recognize and assimilate your external world through your senses and to translate into visible reality your private world within. Consequently, the only things you experience immediately are the components of consciousness,[xvii] those parts of consciousness that you are aware of at the moment you are experiencing them. This means that you have brought something into your sphere of reality and have experienced it, or rather as much of it as your limitations would allow. It must be understood that consciousness actually conceives while thinking adapts that conception.[xviii]

Consciousness makes you aware of the *I* and *non-I*. Without being aware of what you are not you could not have much awareness of what you are. Through this awareness of your own self (the *I*) and another (the *non-I*), existence is brought into your reality. Due to the fact that you do have limitations set on you, first of all by being born and later by what you have been taught, the *I* / *non-I* awareness — the subject-object distinction — becomes rather limited. Since this distinction can become blurred you end up identifying yourself with those objects outside of yourself to which you have become emotionally attached. Once an object[7] is imbued with emotion you are unable to separate it from yourself and it becomes an extension of yourself and, quite literally, it becomes you. It will be given the identity of "*I am …*"

Slowing Potential

Everything is in constant change or in potential. Consequently, as soon as you conceive of the existence of another object you slow down and stop its potential and at this point it becomes an object of perception. This process of separating the *I* from the *non-I* is the basis of perception and perception, as has been shown, is seen as a collapsing of a quantum wave function. Also as soon as an object-event *(non-I)* is perceived it has been separated from you *(I)* and you recognize it *(non-I)*. You then become aware of its existence.[xix] Remember that consciousness is an *internal* process and this process involves more than simple awareness. Without the consciousness of an object's possibility for existence you could not perceive it. Hence, you are separating the object from the "inside" and placing it on the "outside" in order to perceive it.

The *I* that does the perceiving is the common link that connects light as particles and light as waves. For light has both properties[8] and, you'll recall, all that you perceive is reflected light. It is your choice *to* perceive which gives you *what* you perceive. The different way that light behaves, either as particles or waves are properties of interactions[9] of the perceiver and the perceived. What the perceiver *expects* to perceive is based on his previous experience. This previous experience creates expectations. These expectations are major influences on what you perceive. Take a

---

7 This would include philosophical viewpoints as well.

8 This is termed *complementarity*. Complementarity means that light has the properties of both a wave and a particle but cannot be both at the same time.

9 The term *interaction* refers to when one thing influences another. The idea of observing and disturbing is an interaction.

look at your life and you will see that all of your perceptions are an unbroken unity of things and events that you "know" to exist. It is impossible for you to perceive what you do not know. Things that you believe in continue to stay unmanifested because they are not realities in the first place. Only those things that you "know" to exist will be manifested for you to experience. Consider this, only those things which have the highest *possibility* for manifestation will be perceived and experienced.

The world that you perceive consists not of things but of *interactions* or influences: Everything is influencing and interacting with everything else and in these interactions possibilities are brought into expression. What you experience is not external reality, but your *interaction* with the external reality and the influence that reality has on you and vice-versa. It is only through contact with things and people that the *I* is in contact with the world and vice-versa.[xx]

The properties that objects contain belong to *interactions*, not independently existing things. All of the things in the Universe that appear to exist independently are actually parts of one all-encompassing animate *pattern*. No part of the pattern is ever really separated from it or are any of those parts separated from each other.[xxi] This means that there is constant contact between all parts of the Universe. Since this contact exists every part of the Universe influences every other part of the Universe. It is this influence which increases the possibility of the perception or experience of one object over another. The contact (influence) that one part of the Universe has with (on) all other parts of the Universe has been termed *information*. It is this information that is passed from particle-to-particle through a *Superluminal Information Transfer*.[10] Consequently, there is no such thing as

10 *Superluminal Information Transfer* refers to the concept that information travels faster than light. Bell's Theorum states that once particles have been in contact they will never lose that contact no matter how far apart they are. Consequently, if one particle is affected in some way the other particle will show a similar effect.

separate parts in the Universe. Everything is interconnected.[xxii] This is the reason that Einstein said he could move his finger and disturb the farthest star and this is the reason that your whole experience of reality appears as an unbroken whole.

To become conscious of something outside of yourself means that you have slowed the momentum of the thing down to human perceptual speed. The perceived object-event in return does the same (recall that some researchers say that everything has a consciousness). When the consciousness of two object-events collapse a quantum wave function what occurs is that both consciousnesses become aware of each other. From these two awarenesses comes the awareness of other consciousnesses and from them other consciousnesses ad infinitum and reality-upon-reality is created. Hence, you can see that all conscious beings are combining their conscious awarenesses in order to create your reality as you perceive it.

When a consciousness perceives it immediately splits the Universe into reality branches. Each branch of reality is inaccessible to the other branches of reality[xxiii] because of perceptual choice. Consequently, you exist with and around many different realities. You have some awareness of thousands of realities all of the time but you are selectively responding to only one reality at a time. What you see occurring is that your level of awareness is shifting automatically and your consciousness changes the patterns of the construction of the object-event to create what you perceive.

Consciousness is the foundation of everything and directed intent is its essential and central characteristic. Consciousness can be seen as the state of having an intent duplicated by another.[xxiv] When an intent is communicated between two or more individuals consciousness occurs. So, consciousness becomes sort of an *information transfer* between individuals. This duplication of intent needs to occur before there is perception of reality. Most researchers are looking for the what, where and how of consciousness. The key to understanding consciousness may be the *interaction* between the observer and the observed.

Consciousness *may not* be an individual experience at all. What could be necessary for consciousness in the first place may be a subjective and objective *feedback loop.* The most important aspect of any feedback loop is the *interaction* between those involved.[11] A simple example of a duplicated intent is this: a child was told that it was awkward and uncoordinated. As soon as the mind of the parent (or caregiver) becomes duplicated by the mind of the child, it would become a reality. The child would then have the consciousness of awkwardness and a lack of coordination. The feedback loop would be the communication from parent to child and the duplication of that communication by the child. Once the parent reacts to the child confirming that the child has duplicated the parent's communication the child reacts in such a way to confirm that it is doing exactly as the parent had intended it to do. Later this feedback loop becomes self-perpetuating and self-reinforcing. If the child does not duplicate the intent it would not become a reality. If a specific reality does not exist there is no consciousness for that reality and therefore it would not exist although the idea of its possibility can still exist. It may exist for another but not for that specific individual.

Whenever consciousness begins, the realities associated with that level of awareness slow down to become perceived. This occurs with both the perceiver and the perceived. Some type of detection apparatus by the observer is required to collapse the wave function of what is observed into a physical reality, otherwise what is observed does not physically exist except as endless potential or possibility. Whenever the wave function collapses (i.e. perception occurs) the endless possibilities that produced reality branches[xxv] immediately reduces. It is your choice which focuses your perceptions onto one particular branch of the experience of that reality. Without the process of perception, the Universe continues on unimpeded. We can see this in the Zen koan; "If a tree fell in

11 The family therapist, Virginia Satir (1916-1988) said; "The meaning of the communications is the response that you get."

the forest and there was no one around to hear it, would it make a sound?" Without a perceiver the Universe simply becomes what it will become at its own pace.

As soon as an intent is duplicated by another, consciousness occurs. Thus, as an observer entertains the possibility of the observed's existence and intends the experience, as soon as the observed's intent for the existence of the observer occurs a dual consciousness is developed and both perceive each other. It does not matter what the perceiver and the perceived may be: a blade of grass, a stone or another human being. Both must have the intent and the consciousness for the other's existence prior to each becoming a reality to the other — or rather two realities being experienced on the same level.

Consciousness alters the world by altering you. Consequently, consciousness may be independent of the intent — but not the intender. It affects your appraisal of the future by altering your perceptions. Since the quantum wave function contains *all* possible futures (or your total potential), it is your will and intention (*not* your belief) that changes those probable futures into a real present. This happens as a result of the impressions you gain through your interactions[xxvi] with others and the environment.

Consciousness creates through the initial intent of itself to express itself in some way.[12] To intend something or to want something enough to will it into existence begins the process which will change the object of the intent and of the intender. The director of this pattern of change is your *thought processes*. In essence, each thought that you think has the potential for becoming an actual physical experience. Physicists say that particles exist potentially as different combinations of other particles (thoughts *may* contain particles of some sort, other than particles with biochemical properties, that is). Each combination has a certain probability of occurring. Just as the whole Universe exists in

12 This implies that consciousness has some form of self-consciousness. That is, it is aware of its potential and has some influence on whatever outcome it may be intending. This, in part anyway, appears to be true.

potential, each part of the physical reality is constructed of all other parts and its appearance is based on the interconnectedness of all things.[xxvii]

Thoughts are a different reality on a more subtle level. What makes a thought a reality is the fact that it is your intent to think it. Without the intent to think a certain thought you would not think it or experience it on any other reality level. You will experience some other thought because that other thought is the one that you had intended.

All experiences are available to you at any time. It is your choice to experience one thing over another that narrows your experience.[13] No matter what you do, think or say it is a result of a choice. What prompts this choice is your past experiences setting your expectations, your perception of the situation and the possible outcomes available and projecting them into the present experience and into possible futures. The fact is that many of the choices that you make are habitual and are *reactions* instead of deliberated actions. This means that most often there is no thought involved, just reaction continually being performed.

Through the choices that you make you can get a view of your consciousness level. You can see how you perceive your reality through the choices that you make within it. You can see the kind of universe you have chosen to create for yourself. By looking at the choices of another you can see the same things for them. In this way you can begin to tune into your own realities, your own created universe and your own consciousness.

The Center of Innocence

You need to remember, as it has been said, that about 90-percent of your personality was formed by the age of five. Consequently, a lot of your present consciousness level has not grown beyond that time period. In essence, then, as an adult you are still basically

---

13 This choice of narrowing of experience is called *attention.*

operating from a child's consciousness but far away from the innocence of your initial experience of the world. This is not as bad as it seems — if you were in touch with that consciousness. Most often what you will try to do is to compensate (really, it's an overcompensation) for that child's consciousness by "acting like an adult." It is here where problems begin.

In the western Euro-American culture acting like an adult has never been defined. So there are individual and cultural perceptions of what an adult is *supposed* to act like. Some believe that acting like an adult means to be very sexually active. What they lose is the child-like spontaneity that makes sex exciting. Others think that acting alike an adult means to make grand material gains. What they lose is the child-like enjoyment of self-discovery because the things accumulated become their identification. Still others feel that acting like an adult means to manipulate others for power and to get what they want. What they lose is the child-like experience of deeper inner communication and empathy with themselves and another. There are also those who think that acting like an adult means to cause another undue worry and emotional pain. What they lose is the child-like joy and awe gained from simply "being" with another.[xxviii]

It seems that as humanity has become less "primitive," where the limits and actions are clearly defined, it also had become less childlike and out of touch with that innocence within. There is much that an adult can learn from a child. The child within is no exception.[14]

Notice the absolute fascination with which an infant views his world. He lies in his crib wide-eyed, barely blinking for he does not want to miss anything. He cannot take in enough stimulation and experience. He is in awe of all that is happening.

Notice again a child with a butterfly. There is an incredible attunement that the child experiences with it. As it flies away

14 The child within is the sense of awe, joy and wonder experienced with life, not some pseudo-psychological concept.

the child goes with it until it is out of sight. He is not where he was standing or sitting. The child and the butterfly are one consciousness until one consciousness breaks that union.

Notice also the way that a child is completely enchanted with a flower. The flower is a total experience, not just something colorful to look at or pretty to smell. The colors, the fragrance, the consistency of the stem, the leaves and the petals are a complete experience.

How many adults have lost themselves in a contrived world of materialism and became frustrated and angry with everything and everyone, especially themselves. It is hurry, hurry, hurry! Make quick gains! Do not care how it is done for it is appearances that count most. Since the early 1980s both a husband and wife had to go out of the home and work in order to keep up with their most basic needs. This has had quite an effect on the family. Since there is a strain on them there is a strain on the rest of the family. This change in awareness and consciousness level has brought the average wage earner into a different reality. This reality was that of personal gain and appearances instead of dealing with the reality of the times.[15] The reason many want to put up appearances and go into debt is because of what their ego wants. It is necessary to look as good now as prior to the economic problems which started in the early1980s (and continued into the 2000s). With this there has been a complete change in the family structure and their goals.

The child who just wanted nothing more than to live in a "Garden of Eden" was thrown out due to the intervention of the parents and their ideas of what life is *supposed* to be. The ideas of right and wrong replaced the experience of completeness and attunement with life. You were taught to be ashamed of yourself and to cover yourself with an unnatural skin of some other animal: that is, to assume a façade so you do not show who you are. So, your child-like wonder and joy is suppressed and you are given

15 The generation in the 1980s was called the "me generation."

lack and limitation. No longer can you just "be" but you have to be *somebody* and/or *something*, in most cases, that you are not.

The innocence within is also an important creative center. That child-like quality is always present in extremely creative persons.[16] The desire to experience all that you can, to be in tune with all that is and the awe which is encountered with the completion of the total creation is a quality that few possess today.

This child-center, the center of innocence, is very creative and desires nothing more than to express itself. It is this area that gets little exercise and a lot of repression. The more constricting the habits that are laid upon it the less creative it is. The more rules and regulations are placed on it the less expression occurs. The more titles and names are placed on it the less individual it becomes. The more the ego is placated instead of the expression of the child-center the more of the self lies stifled and constricted. What then happens is that by adulthood the center of innocence becomes bound and gagged and finds no expression in any form.

The consciousness of this center affects the whole being. This center is an area of individual expression and if not allowed to express itself your whole being becomes unbalanced and any conscious intents that are directed tend to become frustrated. With intents frustrated and blocked, you will either revert to hostile actions and/or immature and irresponsible behaviors and intents. There will not be any growth, only stagnation. When you have resigned yourself to a certain level of stagnation then complacency sets in and you become satisfied in that position or your place in life.

If the child-center is allowed expression you will become more creative acting in a more creative manner. Decision-making is not black-and-white but is based on the same type of preconsciousness that a child exhibits when confronted by a new experience: "How

---

16 It is unfortunate that many creative persons think it is necessary to act like spoiled brats throwing temper tantrums and getting heavily involved in drugs, alcohol and other disruptive behaviors instead of the pleasure of knowing others enjoy what you are doing.

much can I learn from this?" The child shows the way to all of us by becoming in harmony with the event and flowing with it. Its expression is an inward experience and an outward fascination in everything. It is not until it is told what to think, to do or to be that this fascination becomes limited.

Confronting Choice

The place where you are right now is the outer expression of your consciousness and your view of reality. You can only express that which you believe yourself to be or what you are conscious of within. Whatever you have the awareness of is what will be expressed as the reality of your existence. You cannot conceive of or believe yourself to be anything other than what you are right now. If you could conceive of something different you would not be at this point nor would you be who you are.

One of the main areas of instability within those with personality and psychotic disorders is that they consciously try to see themselves as someone else doing something else while deeply hidden in the recesses of their unconscious they cannot accept that premise. Consequently, they do what they can to somehow adjust the communication between their conscious and unconscious mind in order to bring internal balance and harmony to themselves. But this does not work. It causes them more problems than they feel they can deal with effectively. Their consciousness is set at a certain specific level and anything beyond that level causes a shut-down response.

On a smaller scale this psychological adjustment response occurs with the "normal" members of a society as well. As you have been trained, as your consciousness is set, then you will react in certain ways to certain things or events. If you encounter something which confronts your personally accepted norm you will most likely refuse to see and accept it. This is a simple example of the psychological adjustment response in the vast majority of individuals.

There is an adage that says: "People will only see what they want to see and hear what they want to hear." This adage refers to individual awareness levels. Wherever your consciousness is placed these are the specific needs that you will seek to satisfy. Consequently, you will see and/or hear only those things related to the satisfaction of those needs associated with that particular level of consciousness.

As your consciousness changes, so also do your needs. You cannot seek to satisfy needs related to a different level of consciousness for these present needs are part of your present created reality. You must satisfy your present needs first.

This same idea concerns the choices that you make. At a certain state of mind you can only make the choices related to that state. You will not be able to go beyond them without having to deal with your internal psychological responding. This is one of the problems with socialization processing. Many people become confronted with a situation and the only solution they conclude they have is an "either/or" response. Basically, this means that they see nothing but a forced choice. They have, in actuality, disregarded other possible choices thus leaving only the two which are perceived. The fact is that you always have more solutions than you feel are available but due to other factors (e.g. preconditioning, procrastinating, tunnel-vision) you accept only a forced choice which means that you are accepting little or no responsibility for the choice.

Everything reacts to consciousness in its own particular way. Your awareness sets the limits to your level of perceptual reality and your reality is in turn limited by your awareness. This is one of the main reasons it was said at the beginning of this chapter that it may be possible to influence the reaction of a plant.[xxix] Both are levels of consciousness and each can influence the other to a degree. The physiological reactions of humans are well-documented. Physiological reactions of plants are still up for conjecture.

Throughout your whole existence there is one undeniable fact:

You are at the basis of the manifestation of your total experience. Your consciousness creates what you perceive as your reality. Whatever you experience in your life was your intent to bring into existence on some level. You are totally responsible for who, what and where you are. What you need to understand is that you have a level of consciousness deep within your unconscious mind which is separate from your physically conscious reasoning. This influences your unconscious responding and it is this consciousness which is the picture that you see of yourself and your world. It is usually different than the picture you would like to see. It is made up of your beliefs about yourself and your existence both of which have been given to you since before you were old enough to understand anything. You have complete choice about your life. You are totally responsible for your existence now because being a rational, thinking individual you can choose what works and what does not. You can continue to accept the same conditions, situations, attitudes and so on or you can make the choice to change all of that. It is simply the choice for growth or stagnation: to accept the same old consciousness or to grow into a new one.

Choosing Change

Many people choose to remain at the same level because it is quite comfortable. They have resigned themselves to their own personal law that what they have now is the best that there is — for them. So, they choose to stay. Basically, what you need to confront is fear — plain and simple fear. Fear can motivate you to move quite quickly or it can do just the opposite. It can make you follow another and even do things that you would not ordinarily do. The biggest problems are the subtle fears that you encounter daily. These subtle fears are nothing more than anxieties which pertain to future outcomes and the "*What if*s …" that keep you doing the same things. They are the "butterflies" in the stomach, the woulds, shoulds, have tos, need tos and musts of personal demands. These fears surround all of your dealings for in them you have no idea what will happen next. With them you are afraid of the loss of security, the loss of love, of success and so forth. All of these are taught to you and you learn them through direct instruction as well as imitation and modeling of important other people. Many fears are cultural and are imbedded in cultural norms. Fear can help you manipulate another. As long as the consciousness for fear exists there will be problems and you will always find that you will be getting in your own way in relating to life and to others. You will find that there will always be someone who will be willing to manipulate you through your fears and you will find that there is always someone who will be willing to be led by his fears.

In order to make changes in your life you must make changes in your consciousness. There are brief times when you do alter your consciousness and the things with which you are familiar seem somehow different. But these are only for brief moments. In order to alter your consciousness permanently you must make definite changes in your perceptual outlook on life. You must view reality in a totally different way. Once you can get to view your reality in a totally different way you will see new choices available and life will change. Once you can get a new view of your reality you can then see your whole life differently. In order to alter your consciousness you must make a fundamental shift in the awareness[xxx] of this reality. That is, your awareness must be all the way down to the most basic level. You have to reach down into your belief system and question all that you were taught to believe. You need to do this with an open mind and with the realization that you are growing in mind, body and conditions throughout your life. You will find that a lot of what you believe about yourself and your life is incapable of supporting you and your present and future needs. You cannot wear the same clothes you did when you were three or four so why continue to tenaciously hold on to that level of consciousness?

When your consciousness is altered you view the world as if it were structured differently.[xxxi] You see what you are used to from another perspective or see it changed. Your whole existence takes on a new meaning. You start to see the change that was there from the beginning. You will begin to understand that whatever it is but only for the moment of time that you recognize it as being what it is. For as soon as you recognize it immediately it is changed.

You always experience slight alterations of consciousness constantly. As soon as you notice something different about a familiar object it is due to a shift in awareness. Whenever you experience new knowledge about yourself or part of your existence which causes a change in behavior, attitude, viewpoint, and so on, you have undergone another shift. Whenever you go to sleep and dream you are in a totally different consciousness and space. The space that you would want to be in is one where you recognize the Universal constant of change in all that is and can experience the change that is there, no matter how slowly the change seems to proceed.

Summary

As soon as two consciousnesses intend an object a slowing of the constant change of that object begins until the object comes to a perceptual level. Even though it may be at a perceptual level it still continues on its forward motion toward becoming but at a slower rate. If you view an object-event the same from day-to-day without the experience of its change it is because you have placed the block in your mind through your level of consciousness. You are not aware of its changes because your consciousness has not grown. This lack of growth will affect the rest of your existence.

All of your life is a direct extension of your level of consciousness. This means that you have accepted all that you are now and all of the necessary planes have been affected. You are who you are, where you are and having the experiences you are having due to your level of consciousness and the acceptance of all that has involved at that level. That is why some people always seem to have everything go their way and others not. The new situation can only be an objective reality after the consciousness has affected all of the planes necessary for its occurrence. When this happens it sets up a series of events (e.g. being at the right place at the right time) that will bring about the particular object-event. What generally causes things to function improperly is that you are either attempting something that you do not have the consciousness for or you are not following the flow of the Universe. You then have to get yourself into harmony on all levels and you can create a more positively charged life.

One of humanity's greatest assets is the ability to adjust to change. In order to make this adjustment you must alter your consciousness, your awareness, your view of reality and your thinking. If one of these four necessities is in any way unable to be changed then the adjustment is difficult or impossible until the level of consciousness has been changed: For adjustment begins in the mind — the same place where the experience of your whole Universe begins. Whenever you are in the proper state of consciousness for the acceptance of a certain object-event all of the planes of all of the Universes necessary for the objectification of that certain object-event are affected and you will experience it.

Every day is a new reality. You should not see an object on two different days as being the same. As time moves forward so also do all of the object-events in your personal Universe. The only real constant in the whole Universe is change and everything changes constantly.

The ancients of the Western world have described man (as well as all existence) in terms of four elements: Earth, Air, Fire and Water. These elements refer to our physical, mental, spiritual and emotional natures respectively. Modern psychology describes individual selfhood and the selfs and the description could be equated with the four elements in this manner: the physical self, the ideal self, the real self and the self-as-a-concept. (Figure 2-1) Above and beyond the four

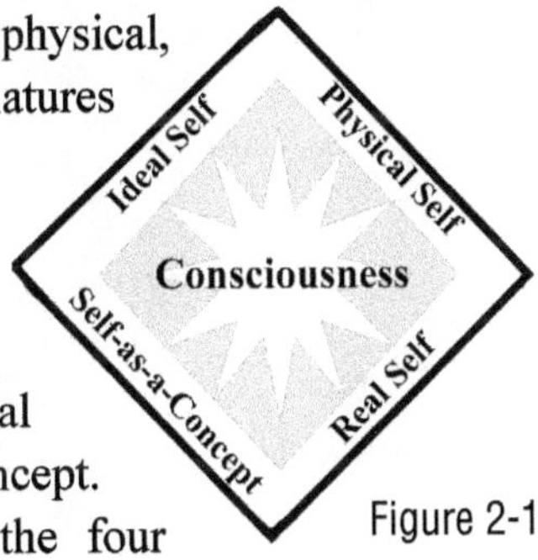

Ideal Self
Physical Self
Consciousness
Self-as-a-Concept
Real Self

Figure 2-1

elements and our four natures or the four selfs is the fifth element which constructs and holds all four together: *consciousness* which the ancients described as the *æther*. Without consciousness the elements could not exist in and of themselves. Consciousness must be there to begin the process of intending in order to bring something into objective reality. For as you are conscious of those things which are the *non-I* you could not differentiate what the *I* is. The consciousness of who and/or what you are makes you aware of all that you are not. All of your existence works through your consciousness under the direction given it through your thinking. Your level of consciousness and the acceptance of that level by you is what creates your whole Universe. Along with your thinking processes (included here is your belief system and the intents of other consciousnesses), your consciousness puts together the compound of elements called reality but your choices do the creating.[xxxii] For without the physical thought of who or what you are you could not perceive or choose your physical existence. Consciousness creates; Thought adapts that creation.

Endnotes

i Michael Talbot (1981) **Mysticism and the New Physics**, Bantam Books, New York, NY

ii Fred A. Wolf (1981) **Taking the Quantum Leap**, Harper and Row, Publishers, San Francisco, CA

iii Roger Penrose (1994) **Shadows of the Mind**, Oxford University Press, New York, NY

Richard M. Restak, M.D. (1994) **The Modular Brain**, Lisa Drew Books, New York, NY

iv Susan A. Greenfield (1995) **Journey to the Centers of the Mind**, W.H. Freeman & Co., New York, NY

Benjamin B. Wolman (Ed.) (1973) **Dictionary of Behavioral Science**, Van Nostrand Reinhold Co., New York, NY

v Joseph Campbell (Ed.) and R.F.C. Hull (1971) **The Portable Jung**, Penguin Books, New York, NY

vi Fred A. Wolf (1981) **Taking the Quantum Leap**, Harper and Row, Publishers, San Francisco, CA, P. 216

vii Peter J. Lewis (2003) **Life in Configuration Space** at http://philsci-archive.pitt.edu/archive/oooo/272/o1/ Configuration -Space-2.doc, extracted 4-2009

David Z. Albert and Rivka Galchen (March 2009) *A Quantum Threat to Special Relativity*, **Scientific American**, Vol. 300, No. 3

viii Joseph Campbell (Ed.) and R.F.C. Hull (1971) **The Portable Jung**, Penguin Books, New York, NY

ix *IBID*

Jeff Love (1976) **The Quantum Gods**, Samuel Weiser, Inc., New York, NY

x Fred A. Wolf (1981) **Taking the Quantum Leap**, Harper and Row, Publishers, San Francisco, CA

xi Joseph Campbell (Ed.) and R.F.C. Hull (1971) **The Portable Jung**, Penguin Books, New York, NY

xii Patrick Haggard (8 May 2009) *The Sources of Human Volition*, **Science**, Vol. 324, No. 5928, P. 731-733

Michel Desmurget, et al (8 May 2009) *Movement Intention After Parietal Cortex Stimulation in Humans*, **Science**, Vol. 324, No. 5928, P. 811-813

xiii L. Feher (Winter 1997) *Natal Therapy and Theory*, **Journal of Psychohistory**, Vol. 4, No. 3, P. 309-317

Morris Netherton, Ph.D. and Nancy Shiffrin (19780 **Past Lives Therapy**, Wm. Morrow and Co, Inc. New York, NY

Thomas Verney, M.D. and John Kelly (1981) **The Secret Life of the Unborn Child**, Dell Publishing, New York, NY

Alexander S. Holub and Evelyn Budd-Michaels (1999) **Psychokinesiology: Doorway to the Unconscious Mind**, Bridger House Publications, Carson City, NV

xiv Gary Zukav (1979) **The Dancing Wu Li Masters**, Bantam Books, New York, NY

xv Victoria Gill (14 July 2010) *Plants 'can think and remember,'* **BBC News Science & Environment**, http://www.bbc.co.uk/news/10598926... extracted 14 July 2010

xvi Joseph Campbell (Ed.) and R.F.C. Hull (1971) **The Portable Jung**, Penguin Books, New York, NY

xvii *IBID*

xviii Jeff Love (1976) **The Quantum Gods** Samuel Weiser, Inc., New York, NY

xix *IBID*

xx C. Kracklaner (Spring 1972) *Exploring the Life-World*, **Journal of Phenomenological Psychology**, Vol. 2, No. 2, P. 217-236

xxi Gary Zukav (1981) **The Dancing Wu Li Masters**, Bantam Books, New York, NY

xxii *IBID*

Fred A. Wolf (1981) **Taking the Quantum Leap**, Harper and Row, Publishers, San Francisco, CA

xxiii *IBID*

xxiv Jeff Love (1976) **The Quantum Gods**, Samuel Weiser, Inc., New York, NY

xxv *Op cit*

xxvi *IBID*

xxvii *IBID*

xxviii Alexander S. Holub, Ph.D. (2007) **From Victim to Victor! Defeating a Victim's Consciousness**, Bridger House Publications, Inc. Carson City, NV

xxix Victoria Gill (14 July 2010) *Plants 'can think and remember,'* **BBC News: Science & Environment,** http://www.bbc.co.uk/news/10598926, extracted July 14, 2010

xxx Lawrence LeShan (1966) **The Medium, The Mystic, and the Physicist**, Ballantine Books, New York, NY

xxxi *IBID*

xxxii Lawrence LeShan and H. Marganan (Mar. 1983) *Discovering Alternative Realities*, **Science Digest**, Vol. 91, No. 3, P. 71

You see things; and you say, "Why?" But I dream things that never were; and I say, "Why not?"

George Bernard Shaw (1856-1950)

Chapter 3

What You See is What You Get?[1]

One of the dreams of mankind is to be able to stop time in its tracks. Just about everyone at some point in their life has wished that time would stand still so that an experience they are having would go on indefinitely: A beautiful sunset, a moment of true realization, an evening with a loved one are all times we would like to stay immersed in for years. Sometimes it seems so unfortunate that our memories are so transient and imprecise and that we are not able to reexperience these beautiful moments exactly as they were at any time we desire.[2]

Science has also gotten its hand into this area of attempting to slow down and possibly reversing time. Einstein has theorized that the closer a person gets to the speed of light the slower time becomes until at the speed of light time would stand still. Others hypothesize that once beyond the speed of light it is possible to go either forward or backward in time. There are also other theories about creating a "warp bubble"[3] around a vehicle which will slow

1 Apologies to the late comedian Flip Wilson (1933-1998).

2 Maybe it's best we don't experience them exactly as they occurred because we would surely find that they weren't as we remembered them.

3 Interestingly, the mathematics has already been done to prove that this is possible. All that remains is the technology to build the means for creating and navigating within the bubble and hence in time. (See: http://members,tripod.com/da_theoretical1/wdtheory.html)

the advancing of time and within which the vehicle could either move forward or backward or stand still and go from one point in space to another almost instantly.[4]

The actual stopping of time in order to "savor the moment" may be a pipe-dream and the actual slowing or stopping of time may be decades or centuries off into the future — or it may be a literal impossibility. The fact of the matter is that we do actually slow time down although it does not appear that is what is happening.

Energy into Matter

Let us begin by looking at the Universe as a living system with the main goal of self-perception. All parts of this system exist *synergistically* creating an harmonious whole. Throughout the Universe there is not one part that is better than another or operates without the "cooperation" of the other parts. One of the main reasons for this is that the main component of the Universe is *energy*. All that exists is energy and this energy exists on all planes and levels. Energy exists in all forms comprising everything that we are aware of and perceive physically as well as that of which we are not aware. At the highest level is *Pure Energy*. *Pure Energy* exists totally without form and substance in and of itself or as form and substance. *Pure Energy* itself is incomprehensible and imperceptible. We cannot in any way begin to understand *Pure Energy* or what may be beyond it. What is beyond can only be described as a *Void* or *Nothing*. This *Void* has been characterized in many ways by many different philosophies: It is the *No-Thingness* of the Existential Philosophers, the *Ain-Soph* of the Kabbalists, the *Tao* of the Taoists, the *Paran-atma* in Hindu Philosophy and the *Chaos* of the ancient Greeks. The thing to remember about the *Void* is that it is *not* empty space. It can be equated with *Pure Consciousness*. *Pure Consciousness* is at an extremely high level

---

4 According to current quantum theory it would mean the vehicle and all of its occupants would be transformed not into energy but into *information*. Remember, accordingly space and time are intimately tied together.

of vibration and is not able to begin the goal of self-perception. All *Pure Consciousness* is capable of doing is organizing. It is not until *Pure Consciousness* organizes itself with the intent of perceiving of itself that self-perception starts. This is when it begins to become something. That something is *Pure Energy*. It is through the slowing of *Pure Consciousness* to *Pure Energy* that the different levels of what are usually understood to be physical reality come to be seen.

Energy can be described as the beginning of or the initial organized intent of *Pure Consciousness* to perceive itself. Even at that high level of Being, *Pure Consciousness* is unable to perceive of anything other than its pure state. Consequently, in order for *Pure Consciousness* to perceive of itself it must alter itself. This means that it must slow itself down even more until it takes on a form slow enough that a distinction begins to exist between the *I* and *non-I*: For in order to make the *I/non-I* distinction there has to be a differentiation among inherent parts. You will recall that probably your first means of identification is that of looking out and seeing things outside of yourself and identifying with those things. Later you learned that those things are not who you are and may have realized that it is your consciousness which created them. Consequently, you can gain a basic sort of understanding of who you are by looking at the things that you have created. The same goes for the Universe. The main idea here is that at some point perceiving, volitional beings who are able to distinguish between what they are and what they are not will enlighten the Universe as to its existence and of who and what it is. These beings, though, are not the ultimate goal of the Universe for even these beings are subject to change.[5] So, in order to be able to understand itself the Universe must separate itself from its complete unity and become different things. This separation occurs when energy slows down in order to become matter. By experiencing different things the Universe gets an understanding of who or what it is. On

5 Everything must evolve and in that evolution the change that is produced allows the Universe to perceive of itself in a little different manner.

the physical level, you slow energy down when you perceive the objects that you have created in your personal universe.

The first order of slowing for the Universe comes when *Pure Consciousness* becomes *Energy*. (Figure 3-1) This is the area of postulated concepts such as Einstein's tachyon or L. P. Hughston's

The Path of Energy Into Matter

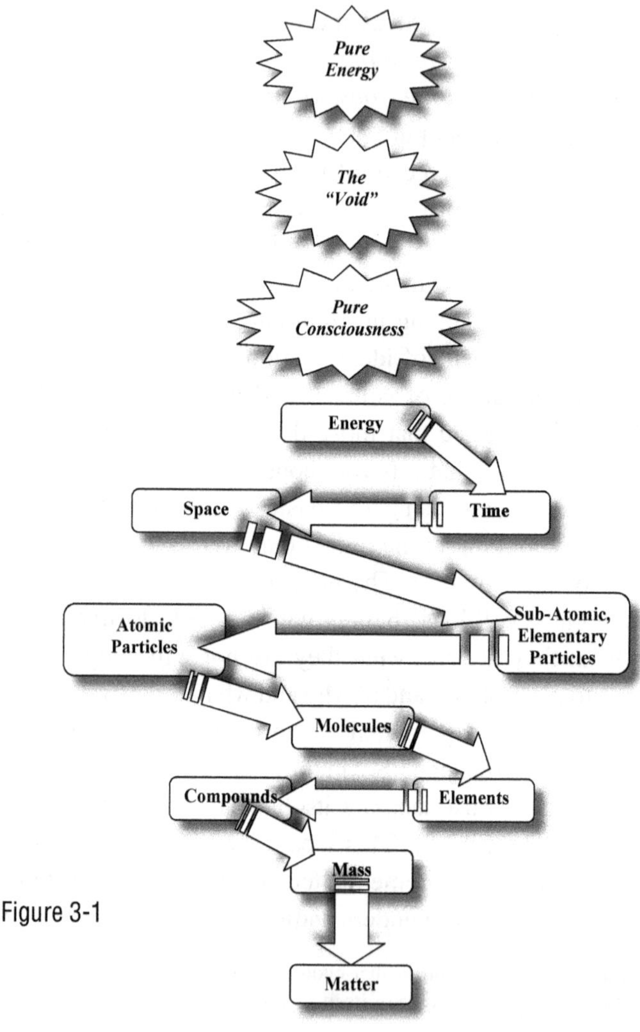

Figure 3-1

and Roger Penrose's twistor.[6] [i] The energy at this point is merely potential and is in the process of becoming. (Remember, *Pure Consciousness* and *Pure Energy* just *are*.) The potential available is incalculable and it has the capability of becoming all forms. For now though, the energy is just beginning to slow down and beginning to assemble. It may be seen as a whirlpool slowly turning and being directed toward a point. This is the indication of organization or what is referred to as *implicate order*.[ii]

As the slowing continues and *Energy* is drawn more and more together it begins to differentiate itself and starts to gain boundaries and limitations. The first limitation is *Time*. Time in this instance is a synchronization of the upper levels of existence with the lower levels of change. Hence, the Universe begins to understand its existence in terms of time. Although this concept of time is beyond the human understanding of time; time begins to exist for *Energy*.

Inseparable from *Time* is *Space*. On the Universal plane *Time* and *Space* are intimately tied to each other, but they are separate entities. They are like the Yin and Yang in Chinese philosophy. As soon as *Time* comes into existence then in order to have that existence in *Time* there must be *Space* to contain that existence. So *Time* and *Space* begin to slow down in order to contain the initial *Energy*. This is the point of *real Space* and *Time*[7] which is still beyond the human conception and understanding of space

6 Roger Penrose began developing the idea of a twistor in the late 1960s. L.P. Hughson first wrote about it in the early 1970s. The twistor is an eight-dimensional virtual particle shaped somewhat like two funnels placed end-to-end in this manner: ⧗. It is now referred to as the "twistor-string theory" due to the work of Edward Witten's relating twistor geometry with string theory in 2005.

7 One characteristic of real space and time is that it doesn't change. Real or absolute time is time which whenever and wherever it is measured is *exactly* the same everywhere. Real or absolute space has the same measurement property. The mystics characterized real space and time as "the circle whose dot is everywhere" and wrote it as: ⊙. Mathematical time is a continuum from past into the present and into the future. Mathematical space has length, width and height: that is 3-dimensionality.

and time. It is not until an *"I"* is able to perceive a *"non-I"* that mathematical space and time are defined. At this point there is no separation of the perception of the *I* and *non-I*. Everything is still *Energy*.

On the more physical level, after *Time* and *Space* begin to bring the *Energy* into a more solidified form then *The World of Sub-atomic, Elementary Particles* comes into existence. This is the level of the ground state of the atom, of photons, quarks, mesons and so on. These particles cannot be seen at the present time even through the most powerful electron microscopes. The only real evidence there is of them are the tracks that they leave on photographic plates in particle accelerators. This is the first hard evidence of substance beginning to take objective form. This is also when *Energy* begins to separate itself from virtuality and moves into actuality.

From sub-atomic particles the next step is *Atomic Particles*. We are able to view some of these atoms through high-powered electron microscopes. Here we can see the electron, proton and neutron of the atom operating in an harmonious unity and know what atoms comprise what will eventually form. Here are the very basic units or building blocks of all matter whether it is carbon-based or not. At this point you can begin to understand what parts the forming matter may consist of by looking at the separate atoms of the substance.

From the atomic level you start to gain a greater understanding of the form which is coming into perception through its molecular structures. On the *Molecular Level* you can begin to separate different groups of molecules into basic concepts or perceptions. Molecules are capable of combining and existing in close proximity with other molecules and functioning separately. Molecules are the first indication of a specific substance.

After the molecular level you come to the *Elemental Level*. Elements are the constituent substances of which matter is composed. Water, for example is composed of two elements of hydrogen and one element of oxygen (H_2O). At this point the impending perception has a definite direction. Here is found the fundamental properties of the perception and the slowing of energy down to a more physical state. This conceptual level is not the Earth, Air, Fire and Water elements of Western Mystical thought but it is the basic ingredients of which the perception is composed.

Slowing from the elemental level produces the level of *Compounds*. Here the perception becomes more and more complicated when the elements begin to combine to form specific substances. On the *Elemental Level* are the basic ingredients of which compounds are formed. It is when two or more elements are combined that a compound is formed. Elements can be combined in many ways but they can only be combined in one way in order to form a specific compound.

Now you are getting to a level of extremely slowed energy. From the *Compound Level* you proceed into the level of *Mass*. It usually is only an unrecognizable lump of some sort at this point. Here is a quantity of something which as yet has not taken a complete form. It appears to be matter but at this moment in space/time is not anything specific, for there is no recognition of it as an object. It is usually a distinct formless form. That is, it does have some sort of form but it is indistinguishable.

When you first recognize and perceive of an object it had been slowed down in its progress. As soon as it is slowed down it is considered to be *Matter*. At this point the object definitely occupies space and as it does so also becomes limited in its existence in time and is considered an observable. It has now become an object of the senses and a total and complete perception. The *I* and *non-I* gain definition in time and, consequently, in space thus becoming a physical reality. As a physical reality the Universe now is capable of self-perception. That is, the Universe sees itself through us.

Take a look at this process. You will see that it describes the mechanism of *Involution*. Prior to evolution everything needs to come together into a form through which it can evolve. Once it gets into the most basic form then the process of *Evolution* can proceed from the simplest into the most complex physical form. On the Earth the most basic elements for life had to come together before they could combine in ways that promoted the whole process of life. Whether these elements were already here in some form when the solar system formed or came to the Earth from asteroids and comets from space, is still not known. What is important is that they did combine and life as we know it *evolved.* This is the way that Nature works. From the "big bang" to the presumed "final flicker" of the last star in the Universe, *everything evolves*. There is no single aspect of the Universe that does not exist outside of the natural processes of the Universe. It is necessary to understand that even the most complex portions of the Universe are still evolving. Your perceptions only tell you what things are, not into what they are evolving.

Once something has evolved into the highest level or form that it will go, it must *Devolve*. This devolution brings the evolved form back to its basic elements. From the basic elements it will continue on into *Energy* again. Then it *may* go on and go through the processes of *Involution*, *Evolution* and *Devolution* all over again. (Figure 3-2) This is the way of the Universe.

Figure 3-2

All that exists is an event which progresses throughout space/time on its way toward what it will ultimately become. Perception, the collapsing of the quantum wave function[8] is the process of stopping an event from continuing on its path. Once you have stopped an event and are able to perceive it you have made the distinction between what you are and what you are not. You can then bring into your existence a total Universe outside of yourself.

---

8 Perception is generally defined as the *interpretation* by the brain of sensory input.

The Paradox of Perception

There is a paradox in your ability to perceive. What you perceive as the physical Universe are realities and their opposites. You are not aware of both for you do not see both sides at the same time. The paradoxes of the physical universe are resolved by the choices that you make.[iii] When you respond to any situation or stimulus you are making a choice. It is totally impossible to react to all of the bits and pieces of information you receive each second, so you select the most important information and respond to that.[9] You have automatic filters and a censor in your brain stem (e.g. the Reticular Formation) which pre-selects the most important information or sensations before sending it on to the higher associational areas in the cortex. In the lower brain centers the most important of this information, especially that aimed toward basic survival, is given essential and primary association and selection and will be sent on to the cortex. In the cortex conscious action will be taken. You must realize that any selection or choice that you make is prompted not so much by the perception you are experiencing but by the conscious or unconscious *interpretation* you place on that perception.

To the ancients, the senses were not to be trusted. It is very easy for the senses to be fooled. This can readily be seen through stage magic and illusion. The ancient mystics understood this to a much greater degree than many do now. It is a fact that you do not perceive the total reality of an object-event or experience. All that you see are its *effects* stopped in that moment of time and space as the quantum wave function collapses. There is an even greater effect placed on the interpretation you have of that object-event or experience. For what you see ain't what you get but rather what you *think* or *expect* to see is what you get.

9 The brain receives about 4 *billion* bits of information at a time but is aware of only about 2000 of them. This is all that we choose to experience out of the environment.

The term devised by the ancients for the interpretation of reality is *Maya*. Maya literally means illusion. The mistake made by many when discussing the concept of Maya is they take Maya to mean that all that the senses perceive is illusion. Even Einstein in his Special Theory of Relativity stated that everything is *not* relative. It is only *appearances* which are relative.[iv] So, what a thing is and what you have defined it to be are *not* the same. Here in lies the illusion: On the surface is not the illusion. For all around are shapes, forms, structures and all kinds of objects. It is your *interpretation* of these things *as realities* that constitutes the illusion. Your previous experiences create expectations as to what you have the greatest possibility of perceiving so whenever your brain senses something it associates it with what had been experienced and interprets it as a certain object. Physicists have said that what we perceive are external *representations* of internal *concepts*. What are on the outside are not things at all. They are *ideas* which are evolving and changing. To the enlightened, a concept of matter as energy slowed down to visual speed makes sense. This energy/matter is interconnected with all other forms of matter throughout the Universe by way of *Superluminal Information Transfer*. This interconnection allows for communications between particles, and hence, the observer/object disturbance.

The fact remains that you can never be certain that what you perceive is actually what is. *The Uncertainty Principle*[10] in physics states that no matter how accurately you try to measure the position or speed of a particle (or any object in motion for that matter), there will always be uncertainty in the measurement: For to observe is to disturb.[v] The fact is, you can never know what an object is; only what it does. This means that since it is constantly evolving it is not what you are perceiving it to be at that particular moment in time and point in space that you perceived it. One reason is because, as infinitesimal a period of time as it is, the

10 *The Uncertainty Principle* (Principle of Indeterminism) states that you can never be sure of both the momentum and position of a particle at the same time. You can know one *or* the other.

reflection of the light from the object to your eyes shows you what the object *was*, not what it is.

Your definition of a thing is based on experience, learning and expectation. These help to not only make your experience of the Universe more predictable but it also detracts from your experience of the Universe. A natural process of the brain is the deletion of information in order to store it. This deletion is part of the *encoding* process that gives the experience a way of being brought back to the surface in order to be remembered. The greater the number of associations in the encoding the easier the experience is to remember.

What Influences Your Perceptions?

To the ancient mystics matter just existed. It neither was nor was not reality. You are unable to see it for what it truly is for your senses are rather poor tools for perception even though they are rather efficient for what they had eventually evolved to do. Your sense of sight picks up only about one-one millionth of a meter of the whole electromagnetic spectrum. (See Figure 1-2) Your sense of vision only picks up reflected light from the matter surrounding you. It must be remembered that it is only the surface of the object that you actually see. If you were truly able to see the object that you perceive you would see a complete Universe of dancing electrons, protons, neutrons and other subatomic particles glowing and sparkling. Consequently, what you see on the surface is not what the reality of the object is. You need to go within the inner workings of the object to view its reality.

With the visual sense being limited to reflected light you are unable to see into either the higher or lower end of the electromagnetic spectrum and consequently cannot comprehend the vastness of the total Universe. The fact is that astronomers and astrophysicists are constantly amazed the more they peer out into the visible Universe with their different instruments. The instruments that they are now using are picking up in the ultraviolet and infrared portions of the spectrum and consequently they are able to get insights into the Universe which light gathering telescopes cannot possibly give. The ultraviolet and infrared Universe is very different than the visible universe. If you could see into the unseen portion of your personal universe, how much more vast would this invisible universe of yours be?

All that you perceive as matter is nothing more than energy or particles and waves slowed down to a point of visibility. As energy slows down it begins to coalesce and form into visible substances. These substances then begin to appear more and more solid to the senses the more they slow. Further, the more the energy slows down and becomes heavier the more it curves space and with this curvature creates gravity. With the creation of differing levels of gravity certain forms of energy will become attracted together to form specific molecules, elements, compounds, masses and finally, matter. It is this matter which excites and activates your senses.

Remember that light acts as both a particle and a wave. The double-slit experiment[vi] first done in the early 1800s[11] has shown this. (Figure 3-3) The double-slit experiment goes like this: There is a beam of particles all traveling with the same speed which strikes a screen containing a narrow slit. The particles leaving the slit are all *defracted* so that their directions make various angles with respect to the initial beam. Observing these particles shows them to be striking in a much wider area than the area of the slit. Individual particles are neither replicated nor anticipated, only a pattern of distribution of hits is represented.[vii] When the two slits are open, the particles leave empty spaces on the screen adjoined by darkened regions in an *interference* pattern.

The iris of the eye is similar to the single-slit. The light which is reflected from objects hits the retina in a defracted, discontinuous pattern and your brain interprets the defracted pattern of light. (Figure 3-4) This sets up your perceptions of your physical reality.

---

11 Described by Thomas Young in 1803.

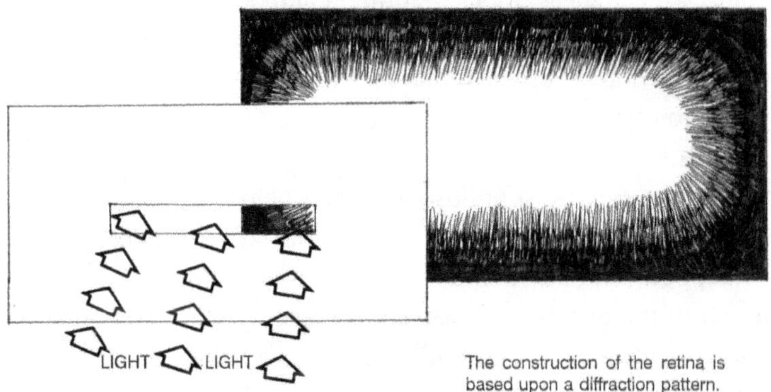

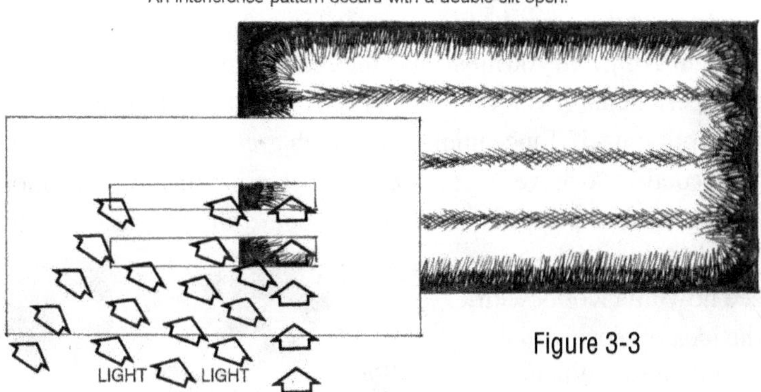

Figure 3-3

Figure 3-4

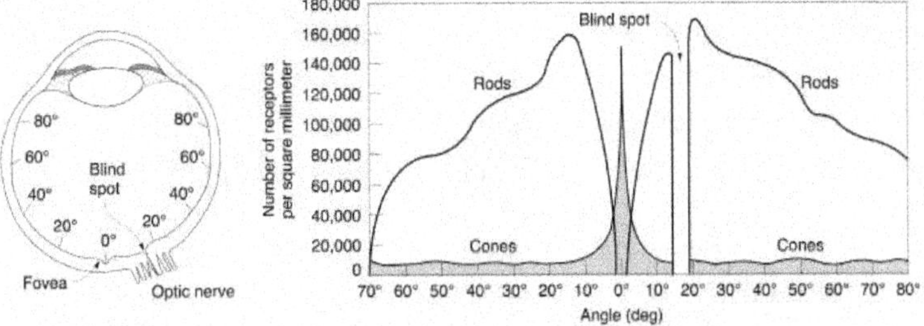

The pattern of rods and cones in the retina of the eye shows that a defraction pattern had evolved in the human visual system. The cones which detect color, bright light and detail are mainly in the center of the retina. The rods which detect low levels of light are on the outer areas of the retina. This gives the human eye a pattern for vision which is specific to the evolved species and to diurnal animals.[12]

To the empiricist philosophers and behaviorist psychologists the mind is a blank page (Tabula Rasa) at birth and all of the perceptions and sensations experienced write their messages on it. All of the experiences you encounter in your environment are indelibly etched in your mind and on your brain. As soon as you are able to perceive of a physical stimulus of any sort (it makes no difference if you understand it) it becomes part of your repertoire. You can and do easily file it away for future interpretation. By remembering that you must have the concept of the perception prior to experiencing it you can gain an understanding of the process of perception itself. Since humans are such great generalizers all that is needed is to have a *general* concept prior to the perception. This general concept is enough to become an expression on the physical level. You can see how this works with the idea of closure in the visual sense. Whenever you see an incomplete object your brain puts it together into a form which you will recognize. (Figure 3-5) The ultimate image is based on what you have experienced previously.

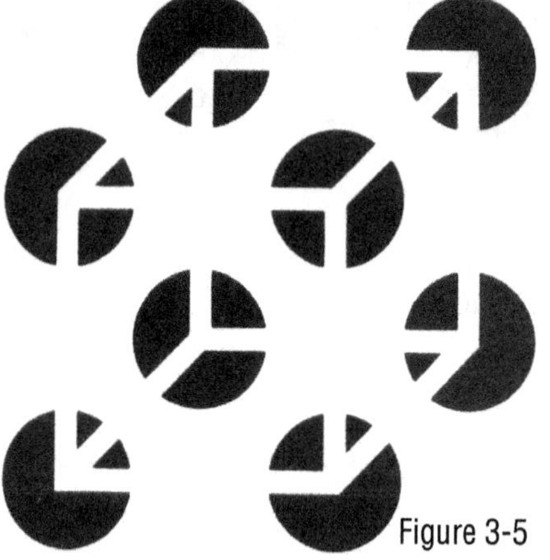

Figure 3-5

12 Human beings are *not* nocturnal animals. Anyone who claims to be a "night person" is wrong. Humans have not evolved to that point regardless of the fact that they may have adjusted their internal clock or has insomnia.

There are four main influences on how you will perceive what you perceive. The first of these is your *biological make-up*. This is based on genetics and you get this from your parents. If you are color blind this will obviously affect what you perceive visually. If you have difficulty hearing due to an abnormality, this will affect your perception of sound. Biologically, the cause of the perceptual problem does not have to be genetic. An accident or illness could bring about misperceptions as well. You cannot forget that your biological needs and drives will also cause you to perceive things related to the satisfaction of those needs. Food, thirst, the need for sleep, the need to relieve pain (physical and emotional), the need for sex and so on all motivate you in some way and you will perceive according to the satisfaction of the particular need. For example, if you have been driving for many hours and becoming hungry the road signs that you will notice most often will be those pertaining to food; restaurants and pictures of food.

The second factor influencing your perception is the *environment*. Under this factor is the weather. You will react and perceive things much more slowly and differently when the weather is inclement; too cold or too hot. Also, if it is dark or light as well as dawn or dusk perceptions will be altered. You can include the topology of the area itself as well (e.g. a flat plane, a wooded area, jungle, desert, city, etc.) as part of the environmental factor. Basically, you could say that everything in your created Universe will influence the what and how of your perception.

The third and extremely important factor that influences perception is *intrapsychic*. This means *what is going on within your mind:* the *thoughts* that you are thinking, the *feelings* that you are having, the *values* you possess, your *beliefs* and *expectations* all help to determine what will be perceived. Along with the intrapsychic factors you need to consider all previous experience and what you have learned from the first moments on this planet as other major factors influencing you to see things not exactly as they are.

Finally, the last factor that affects your perceptions is your *socio-cultural* influences. The society/culture in which you live directs how and what you will perceive. In today's modern world we're looking at the subcultures within the larger culture. Each of the subcultures has their own system of values, morals, expectations and belief patterns as well as their own acceptable and unacceptable behaviors. This not only goes for differing cultures but for those in different social classes within the culture as well. Hence, the environment is seen in specific ways by those from different areas of a society.

Much of the problem in correctly perceiving reality comes from the interpretation that is placed on the sensations being experienced. As a child you were told that whenever you had the experience of a certain object-event that it was a specific thing. This thing, or your interpretation of the thing, never really changed although it may have been modified. It still remains basically the same. As long as you view it as the same it means that you do not allow it to grow and change and become what it was truly meant to be. Moreover, it means that you have not changed. You essentially, are stopping time at this point in order to perceive something which you, in actuality, are experiencing in the past. When you perceive anything and slow down its progress, you are perceiving it as it *was* even though it may have been only milliseconds ago.

Whenever you encode an experience for later memory recall you are doing the same thing. This encoding takes the events and deletes much of their sensory experience and places all of it in the brain. Then, whenever the appropriate sensory input is triggered the experience is recalled. The difference is that much of the original data no longer is available to conscious experience and you have a lesser perception. The reason that a trauma appears so powerful is because it uses more sensory input in order to encode it. In a traumatic episode, such as a bad automobile accident, you have visual, auditory, feeling states (emotional and bodily states), gustatory (a "bad taste" in the mouth), and olfactory (usually subtle body and/or automobile smells) senses all coming together at once creating a mental image. This mental image has a series of cues of which a minimum number can decode the experience and bring it up to conscious expression.

Your consciousness creates your reality. It is through this created reality that you perceive. You cannot accurately perceive something that is outside of your reality and consequently not within your consciousness. With this being true, what you will perceive will only be what you presently understand to be real. What you understand to be real is a direct result of all of the learning experiences you have had and the choices you have made in relation to those experiences. As you were growing up you were told what your experiences were, how you were supposed to experience them and when to experience them. This refers not just to physical objects like trees, rocks, animals and so on but to emotional experiences and concepts like love, hate, relationships, apathy, fear, attitudes, in essence all emotion-based responses and objects and events associated with your emotions. The fact is much of your training was not direct. It was indirect through watching what others were doing and imitating their behavior. As soon as there was any kind of reward for these experiences you continued doing them.

The Brain's Part

All of your behavior patterns are controlled by a certain set of nerve cells (neurons) firing in a particular sequence. (Figure 3-6) Whenever you learn any habit patterns (e.g. writing), as you are learning it you are training specific groups of neurons (a cell assembly) to fire in order so that you can perform that action on cue at a later time. It is this cell assembly firing that brings about the behavior. If this action is modified there is a change in the neurons themselves as well as bringing other neurons into play. In this way there is no conscious thinking brought into your habit patterns. The habit then becomes imbedded into the nervous system making it somewhat difficult to break — although habits can be broken.

NEUROTRANSMITTER RELEASE

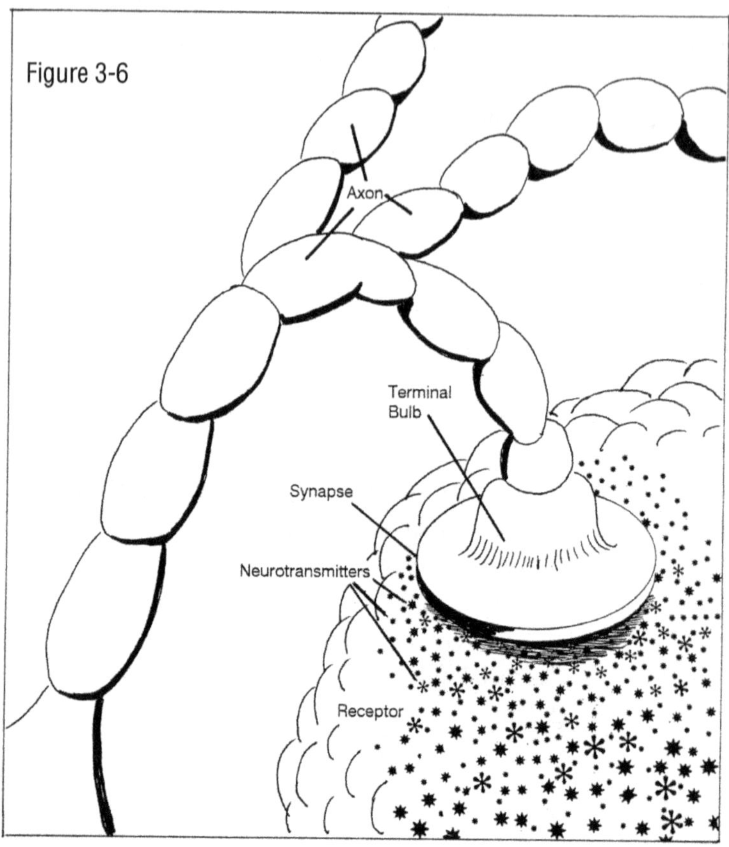

All that has been discussed thus far has been the physical aspects of habit formation. It is important to remember that many of your behavioral responses are learned through reward and punishment. The primary rule of behavioristic psychology is: "***Whatever you reinforce, you are going to get more of***."[13] Those behaviors that get rewarded will continue to be performed and become imbedded in the nervous system. Those behaviors which

13 This is E.L. Thorndike's Law of Effect which states: Rewards increase a rewarded response.

get punished will tend to drop off to the wayside — unless the punishment is viewed as a reward by the receiver. In essence, the bottom line of learning is the training of a cell assembly to fire at a particular time and sequential order. In this way a behavior, a thought or a memory can occur *on cue* with or without conscious consideration of any sort.

Whenever you think a consistent thought a cell assembly fires in order to produce or reexperience that thought. Your memory works in the same manner. The same way that you learn a physical habit is also the way you train your memory. The more cell assemblies that are fired for a specific thought, memory or perceptual object the easier is the recall. The easier it is to recall the deeper it is imbedded in your nervous system. The deeper it is imbedded in your nervous system the more a part of your consciousness and reality it is. On a personal level, the greater number of times you are told a certain thing about yourself, the more it gets conditioned into your nervous system until it becomes a habit then you will express it with your behaviors, attitudes, values, mores and beliefs. Whenever you see any action on the physical level you can be sure that it is a thought made matter and, hence, part of your reality and your level of consciousness.

One current view of consciousness[14] is that it appears to come from some sort of quantum mechanical (particle) reaction which takes place at the synapse,[viii] the space between the neurons. Another similar view is that consciousness is a quantum reaction in the microtubules inside of the neuron.[ix] Consequently, every neuron you have would contain a complete representation of your total consciousness because every neuron is actually involved in every experience you have. This involvement can be directly or peripherally. Thus each neuron has the consciousness or awareness

14 Actually, as you've seen the difficult thing about consciousness is attempting to define it. Whoever is writing about it defines it according to their perspective. Hence, a psychologist will define it differently than a neurologist, who will define it differently than a philosopher, who will define it differently than a theoretical physicist and so on.

of its job in the particular behavior as well as its relationship to the other neurons and their jobs in any behavior at any time. By introducing a certain thought or idea consistently every neuron can be programmed with the consciousness appropriate for its physical manifestation.

Like the neuron, the human body is an electrochemical system. Each thought or experience of any sort involves the production of differing amounts of specific biochemicals. Whenever a habit is learned, electrical and chemical reactions of sets of neurons combine to insure the successful completion of the appropriate behavior. Certain biochemicals (neurotransmitters) are released along the appropriate neural pathways and the behavior pattern is created. (Figure 3-7) Then whenever that behavior pattern is needed all that is necessary are suitable cues and the behavior will be engaged. With any new learning situations or whenever the initial behavioral pattern is modified many of the same neurotransmitters are released — but in differing amounts as well as with other biochemicals causing other neurons to fire. Some of the neurons will be firing in a little different manner. When this happens a new pathway is created as soon as the learning experience is imbedded strongly enough in the brain. On the surface — on the physical level — there appears to be another reaction to a certain stimulus or a new response entirely being created.

This same process is involved in what you think. Essentially, all of the thoughts you think, what and how you think are all programmed. You cannot conceive of a thought that is outside of your reality, your experience and your consciousness. Further, all of the thoughts you think are electrochemical reactions to some stimulus either internally or externally. So, if you think any thought, it is a cell assembly firing in a precise order and time giving you the experience of the thought. This holds for every thought you think whether in passing or consistently. But it is the consistent or habitual thoughts which will tend to become objectified. So, if you want to have some sort of experience you have to think it

THE NEURAL PATHWAY

Figure 3-7

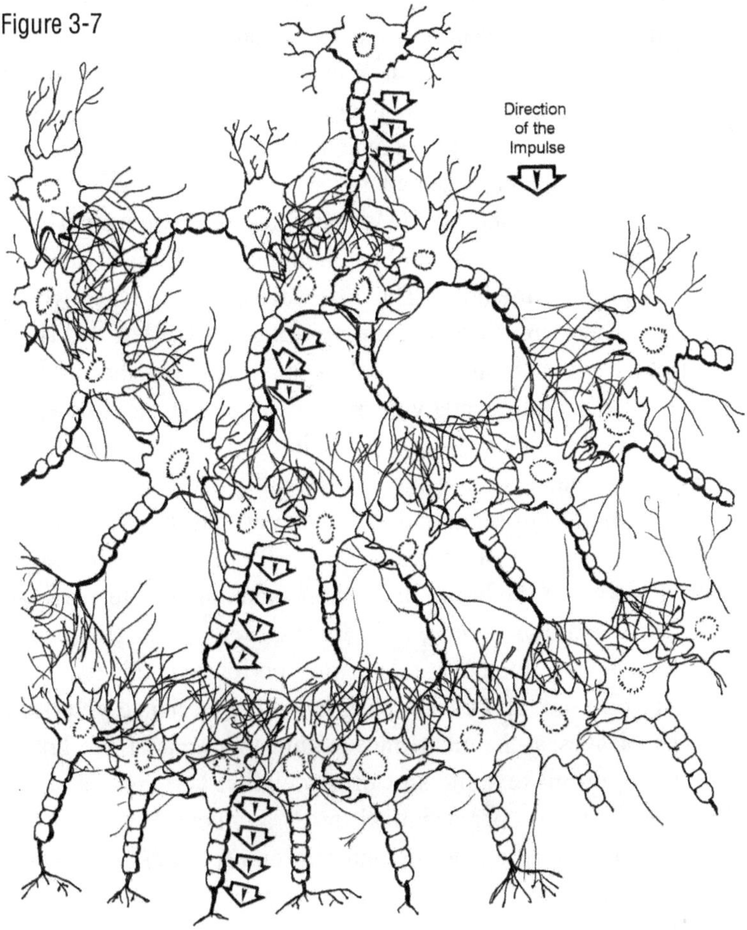

as being a reality in your life.[15] Thoughts program your "mental computer" so the more you think a certain thought the more powerful the programming. Further, the more input you have for a

15 An important point here is that the thought that you want to experience *must* be realistic. That is, you cannot think of yourself being or doing something that is unnatural. You can't fly no matter how strongly you think of yourself jumping in the air (or off a roof), flapping your arms and taking off. Gravity has the final word on that.

certain objective the greater chance you have of seeing the specific outcome. If you want to see something occur objectively you have to create the consciousness for it by introducing the possibility for its reality into your mind. When the correct cell assembly has been properly conditioned then the thought is on its way into your consciousness to become a physical manifestation. It is interesting to note that researchers using PET (Positron Emission Tomography) scans and MRI (Magnetic Resonance Imagery) have found that the thought of an object and the actual object activate the *same* areas of the brain. The difference comes in when words are used. There are differences in activation of the left and right hemispheres of the brain. Essentially brain researchers have found what has been said for many years: The brain does not know the difference between a physical and an imagined experience.[16] The brain, though can distinguish between reality and fantasy.[x]

Every bit of information that you receive has to be processed. This processing is most likely done in the 90-percent of seemingly unused portion of the brain. In this area (sometimes referred to as the *silent* or *association areas*) all of the associations, instantaneous calculations and memory relays are performed. Since every thought you think and every sensation and experience you have ever had leaves a chemical trace within this area of the brain, whenever you make some sort of association you are searching this area for the proper chemical traces and neural pathways in order to send a message to the outer portion (cortex) of the brain for your response.

The silent areas are also the places where the perceptual sensations are associated. So if there is a problem with your view of reality this is where it is first seen: Assuming, of course, that

---

16 Herein lies the rub. You can spend time visualizing something happening and it can be stored away in your brain as nothing more than a thought and never reaching your external reality. What is causing the problem of bringing it to physical reality are emotional blocks, accepted personal labels, the initial intent and whether it is realistic.

all of your senses are operating at their optimum. Even so, the chances are your perceptions will still be somewhat clouded.

You do not experience a perception as it actually is because of all that you have learned and the natural limits of your senses. Whenever you receive a sensation it will immediately be scanned by the lower brain centers then sent to the association areas. Here is where your past living events color and influence your present experience. Every possible association is immediately made with the sensation you are scanning. All that is remotely related is associated and all of this material affects what is sent on for interpretation and reaction.

You are continually constructing, deconstructing and reconstructing your reality every instant of your conscious life through the choices that you make — and you are constantly making choices. Reality then becomes what you *choose* it to be.[xi] These choices are greatly influenced by what you have previously learned and the experience encountered during and after that learning. The interpretation of an experience is based on the *assumed* results that you feel you will receive. These assumed results are based on the results that you received during the original learning as well as on the results you had already received in similar situations (remember the process of generalization). So your choice is not so much based on the future as on the past. Since your reality and consciousness level are at a certain point you will continually experience those object-events associated with that level of consciousness. At this level, for all intents and purposes, you are *fixated* in the past with responses based not on what you would like to experience but on what you *had* experienced some time before. The information that you had gained in the past is never really lost. What you are doing in this process is altering the potential reality making it actual:[xii] In other words, stopping the Evolution of the Universe.

Once you have assumed a certain level of response you tend to become complacent in it. You do not choose to change because it is comfortable and you can habitually respond without assuming any responsibility for the outcomes of the responses. This complacency also makes the world much easier to deal with and more predictable. Any changes that are "forced" on you confront that predictability and cause you frustration and anger. You do not like to change because you do not know how to respond to or in that change. So you opt for complacency out of fear of the unknown.

As a human being you tend to consistently view yourself and your universe pretty much the same from day-to-day. You do not even consider the idea that you are completely surrounded by constant and inevitable change. Nothing in the physical Universe that you had created and are now perceiving stays the same. It cannot. It moves on from creation, through physical existence, into oblivion or rather into another creation. But being on this physical level you tend not to see the changes all things must go through all of the time.

Summary

Nothing conceived of and executed by humankind survives for long. For none of it is based on the concept of consistent change. The assumption is made that whatever it is will stay exactly the same no matter what discoveries are made. So, in order to make things remain the same there will be distortions of reality made to insure a consistency. All of this can cause confusion, frustration and hostile acting out. Even though you are human you can transcend the physical realm of empirical knowledge and go onto the plain of growth and change. The first step is to begin to understand the concept that all you experience is constantly changing. Next you must realize that you are the creator of your universe and all of the realities in it. Beyond that you have to be aware that only through the changing of your consciousness can you change your reality. Basically, all that you are doing here is allowing yourself to grow and experience outside of the realm of constructed realities.

You can consider three major obstacles to your growth. First is what can only be termed *karma*. The term karma is a metaphor for the process of synchronicity *and* cause and effect. Karma, like synchronicity, comes from the deeper mind. Essentially it is negative returns that most people consider when speaking of karma. But when you want to understand how growth is restricted you must include both negative and positive returns.

The negative returns restrict you and get in your way because they are always stumbling blocks. They are the fixations that you have. These are areas where you reject change and growth. In essence, negative karma comes to you when you try to move against the progression of the Universe and out of the natural harmony between all interconnected aspects of the Universe. For the Universe always takes care of itself and will always be in perfect balance and harmony. Consequently, if you attempt to put the Universe into a position of disharmony by acting in a self-serving manner, deliberately causing others physical or emotional harm, if left to its own devices the Universe will compensate automatically.

Individual growth can also be restricted through positive karma when you become complacent in your position and will not opt for the consistent change that is available and the growth that change brings. Whenever you become satisfied with what you have, no matter how positive it may be, you set stumbling blocks for future development. In this way positive energy can have a negative outcome.

The second obstacle to your growth is the aspect of *maya* or illusion. Look at your view of reality and your state of consciousness in order to get a better understanding of this concept of illusion. An illusion literally is a distortion from your neural circuitry of an object-event or sensation which causes a misinterpretation. In other words, it is a false perception and consequently produces a *miss-taken interpretation*. Some illusions are due to imperfections in your senses. Remember, your senses are highly limited naturally. Much of your perception, though, is due to expectation. Into here is where the concept of maya enters.

You will recall that maya, although it literally means illusion, does not mean that all that you see is an illusion but that you mistake all of the things around you, which are concepts of the unconscious mind, for reality. Expectation comes into play from the fact that whenever you perceive an object-event you misinterpret it as a specific reality. Your previous training and learning create the consciousness for that particular thing and nothing else. You are interpreting the concepts you perceive as reality but remember you are only considering their surface appearances. You do not see beyond the moment for your expectations of all that you perceive are biased by your previous experiences.

Along with expectation restricting your growth and interfering with your interpretation of your reality you must also consider motivation. You will be motivated to interpret an object-event in a specific way due to your needs, wants and desires. Look, back again at your state of consciousness. It is these wants, needs and desires needing satisfaction which will drive you to misinterpret an object-event while attempting to see psychological, physiological and emotional harmony.

The third obstacle to your growth is your *egocentric attitudes and desires*. Whenever you seek the satisfaction of your own personal desires irrespective of anyone else's rights, needs, desires and wants you hold back your own growth. We all need each other but the degree of *assumed* need differs in all of us. You cannot place yourself above anyone else for any reason at all. We are all equal. By placing yourself above another you place yourself in a position where you cannot relate to any other human being on a person-to-person level. By not allowing any type of relationship to develop you lose out on the growth potential available from it. You cannot think of yourself as being better than another even though you may be able to do something better than that person or a number of people or have some title different from someone else or have more money or belong to some organization or religion. The chances are that the organization or religion to which you belong is a device of human construction and has little actual meaning outside of that which the founder(s), current leaders and you have given it.

Whenever considering egocentric attitudes you probably envision someone who thinks that he is the most important human being alive and that the world revolves around him alone. Often you would fail to consider that it is also egocentric to think of yourself as *inferior* to another. By placing yourself in an inferior position you are attempting to have the world revolve around you through sympathy and pity. It is *passive egocentricism* as opposed to the *active egocentricism* of the narcissist or egoist.

You are no better or no less than another and until you can accept this you cannot accept yourself or the universe that you have created. You will continually restrict your own growth and get in your own way and constantly live in a world of illusion and misinterpretation. As you are restricting yourself and your growth you will do the same to others or the outer world which is a reflection of your inner world.

Look back over the three obstacles to growth. You will notice a single concept emerging. This concept is: By imposing yourself on another, failing to recognize your own limits and the rights of another through your own self-gratifying actions and attitudes, you will misinterpret your own created universe and your position in the Grand Universe and reap the reward of negative returns. As all positive, life-affirming philosophies teach, it is only through selfless, altruistic service[17] that you will gain the greatest and most positive benefits.

What you perceive is constantly being modified but on the conscious level it appears to be remaining the same. Your senses perceive everything statically and without change or motion (discontinuously). What appears to be motion is a construction of your brain. As each image falls on the retina of the eye it does so like it appears on a strip of movie film: frame by frame. It is the brain

17 Altruistic service doesn't mean to be a "doormat." An altruist doesn't look for reward for any assistance he/she may render. It is done simply because it is the right thing to do.

which puts the separate static images together into a continuous flow. This is another important innate and natural process known as *continuity of movement.* This innate tendency helps to slow down the constant change in the Universe otherwise the Universe would be almost impossible to comprehend. You need a certain degree of stimulus change in order to stimulate the senses. When this change is either too great or too little your brain will work automatically to create a harmony. In the case of too little stimulus change such as during sleep, the brain will function to give you sensations of sight, sound and even feelings to compensate for the lack of external physical stimulation. This compensation is called a dream. In the case of too much stimulation, the brain will simply shut down the whole system or some part of it. This latter situation also occurs whenever you feel that the amount of stress, for example, being encountered is too great and equilibrium cannot be maintained. Then, after the system shuts down you will begin to create your own stimulation because there is no external stimulation.

You tend to make the mistake of assuming that your universe never changes because your perceptions appear, on the surface, to be unchanging. This is the illusion created by the fallibility of your senses and the point of space-time at which you as an energy form exist. Consequently, your view of your reality and your level of consciousness remain pretty much stable. You do experience modifications of your consciousness all of the time and you run headlong into these modifications mostly when you are forced into it. One of the major change experiences is when you age and find out that you cannot do the same things you could in your younger days. You have to then adjust your consciousness to fit your body and take on a new lifestyle. Then there are those who desperately attempt to hold onto the consciousness that is totally out of harmony with their actual life instead of allowing themselves the privilege of growing and learning and passing on their experiences graciously.

Your perception is consciousness-based and reality-directed.

This means that whatever you perceive on the *physical level* is based on your state of *consciousness* and directed by what you *view* your reality to be. These three are an interconnected, intertwined trinity: You cannot have a *perception* that does not exist in your *reality* and if it does not exist in your reality you do not have the *consciousness* for it. Once it exists in your consciousness it does not mean that it exists for you. Nor does it not mean that at some time later it will not exist or in some previous time that it had existed: As soon as you become aware on a deeper level of an existence and it of you then it is on its way to becoming part of your physical reality. You can also set a reality into being by making yourself aware of something and causing its attraction and awareness of you. Thus you are creating the consciousness in yourself for the reality which eventually brings about the perception of your reality.

Endnotes

i L.P. Hughson (1979) **Twistors and Particles**, Springer-Verlag, New York, NY
http://universe-review.ca/R15-19-twistor.htm;
www.maths.ox.ac.uk/~1mason/Tws/Nietzke
George Musser (June 2010) **A Simple Twist of Fate**, *Scientific American*, Vol. 302, No. 6, P. 14-16

ii Fred A. Wolf (1981) **Taking the Quantum Leap**, Harper and Row, Publishers, San Francisco, CA

iii Fred A. Wolf (Dec. 1981) *Taking the Quantum Leap*, **Science Digest**, Vol. 89, No. 11, P. 88-92

iv Gary Zukav (1979) **The Dancing Wu Li Masters**, Bantam Books, New York, NY

v Fritjof Capra (1975) **The Tao of Physics**, Shambhala Books, Boulder, CO
Michael Talbot (1981) **Mysticism and the New Physics**, Bantam Books, New York, NY
Fred A. Wolf (Dec. 1981) *Taking the Quantum Leap*, **Science Digest** Vol. 89, No. 11 P. 88-92
___________ (1981) **Taking The Quantum Leap**, Harper and Row, Publishers, San Francisco, CA
Gary Zukav (1979) **The Dancing Wu Li Masters**, Bantam Books, New York, NY
Ivan Dryer (Nov. 1979) *Science, Mysticism and the Future*, **U.S. Psychotronics Conference**, Taped Talk

vi Michael Talbot (1981) **Mysticism and the New Physics**, Bantam Books, New York, NY
Fred A. Wolf (1981) **Taking the Quantum Leap**, Harper and Row, Publishers, San Francisco, CA
Gary Zukav (1979) **The Dancing Wu Li Masters**, Bantam Books, New York, NY

vii Fred A. Wolf (1981) **Taking the Quantum Leap**, Harper and Row, Publishers, San Francisco, CA

viii Michael Talbot (1981) **Mysticism and the New Physics**, Bantam Books, New York, NY

ix Roger Penrose (1994) **Shadows of the Mind**, Oxford University Press, New York, NY

x Anna Abraham and D. Yves von Caramon (Mar. 2009) *Reality=Relevance? Insights form Spontaneous Modulations of the Brain's Default Network when Telling Apart Reality from Fiction*, **PLoS ONE**, Vol. 4, No. 3, e4741

xi Fred A. Wolf (Dec. 1981) *Taking the Quantum Leap*, **Science Digest**, Vol. 89, No. 11, P. 88-92

xii Fred A. Wolf (1981) **Taking the Quantum Leap**, Harper and Row, Publishers, San Francisco, CA

The vivid force of his mind prevailed, and he fared forth far beyond the flaming ramparts of the heavens and traversed the boundless universe in thought and mind.

Lucretius [Titus Lucretious Carus] (99-55 BCE)

Chapter 4
What's the Mind Got to do With It?

We are all unique individuals. The possibility of you being you and me being me, although finite, are phenomenal. Consider that the human genome contains about *3 billion* base pairs (nucleotides). Ninety-percent of the variation in the genome is found in a subset of *10 million* pairs of nucleotides. At the DNA level, only about *3 million* pairs of nucleotides distinguishes you from anyone else on this planet. So, as a purely physical being and the result of the union of an egg and sperm the possibility of you being a certain individual ends up being about *375.5 trillion* to one. Then, if we multiply that by the endless possibilities occurring in nature itself, as a totally distinct being on this planet, each one of us is incalculably unique.

You are an individual, unique but still the same as every other person on the Earth. You were conceived the same way. You were born the same way. You perform the same physiological functions throughout your life. Finally, at some point you must give up this body and may become transformed into another body of a different vibration, the same as everyone else.[1] While you are here you need to make the most of your life and experiences — but not at the expense of others. You need to create an existence which is comfortable and happy. You need to have a life where you love and are loved in return. You would also like to be free from excessive worry and stress. Even in this seemingly complacent picture there must also be growth: psychological, emotional and mental growth.

If everyone realized these ten premises, we would all be able to have happy lives and accomplish our desires:

1. ***There is no one better than or less than anyone else.*** Money, titles and possessing objects does not make anyone a *better* human being. The vast majority of people with money, titles and objects identify themselves by the *things* that they possess, not by having concern and care for others. So often it comes down to the objects possessing them, not the other way around. Many leaders of world governments also seem to forget that the greatest asset and natural resource that the country has is the citizens in that country. If you treat others as if they do not matter it says something about you, not about them;

2. ***All you really need emotionally is to love yourself constructively, positively and confidently,*** **not neurotically, narcissistically or egocentrically,** ***and to love others honestly accepting them as human beings and accepting their choices.*** You may not like the choices another

1 Whenever an electric circuit "dies" it produces its strongest surge of current. An example is a light bulb. At the point of burn-out the bulb goes dim then produces a very bright flash. It then "dies." The dark "tunnel" many having the near-death experience report seeing is most likely the system shut-down. The bright light at the end of the tunnel is the flash of current surging at the end. Recall that wherever there is an electric current there is a magnetic field. The field shut-down and immediate resurgence can produce a shift of some sort; a magnetic surge. Some researchers have claimed there are *21-grams* of weight *loss* at the point of death beyond the natural expulsion produced by the muscles. A relaxing body should actually *gain* weight. The 21-grams had been proven to be incorrect.

makes but their choices are theirs to own. If those choices interfere with your life, again, it tells you something about them;

3. ***No one really needs big cars, mansions or expensive things. You do need to be comfortable and have your physical needs met plus time and money for the enjoyment of life.*** The basic comforts of life everyone wants and needs. Sigmund Freud was right when he said that in order to be happy in life all you need is love and work. You need to love and be loved and to have creative outlets in order to enjoy life;

4. ***The more that is given freely the more is received.*** Expecting something in return is not giving freely. That expectation of something can be as simple as a "Thanks" from another. Thus "Thanks" can build your self-esteem. Even these simple responses being expected mean that it was not freely given;

5. ***No one is "out to get you" or to get something from you through manipulation or any other means.*** You will set yourself up. By setting yourself up you will let others have control of your life. By doing so you do not take responsibility for the choices that you make;

6. ***Everyone can be happy.*** Happiness is not something that only certain people are able to achieve. It is something that is available to everyone. By being able to know the difference between what your ego wants and what you really need happiness can be achieved;

7. ***The world is not made up of the rich and wealthy, the average wage-earner, and the poor and it does not operate on that premise.*** It is the human ego which makes these characteristics and distinctions. It is also the human ego that makes physical objects, titles and power and control more important than people;

8. ***Your thinking is the initiator of your creation.*** Understand that your thoughts are the programs to your brain and that the thoughts that you dwell on most as well as their attached emotions have the greatest chance of becoming manifest;

9. ***By changing your thinking you can change your experience of life.*** Changing your worldview gives you a totally new experience by which to live. As your worldview changes so does your experience of your world; and

10. ***You are part of a unified whole and you can and do affect the rest of the Universe.*** You are not at the mercy of an unkind Universe. You are the creator and controller of your total experience. It is up to you to take charge and make the changes you desire. It is necessary to realize that those changes must be realistic and achievable.

As idyllic as much of this seems, it is not impossible and unattainable. You need to remember that thought controls your brain and that your brain does exactly as it is told.

Looking at the Brain

You can begin this by looking at your brain. By now you have some basic understanding of the brain and the process of thinking. In order to appreciate how the brain works it is important to know that the brain is made up of somewhere between 100 billion and 1 trillion neurons.[2] Each neuron is made up of an input side, the cell body where the processing of the input and basic cellular functioning goes on and an output side. (Figure 4-1) The way that the neurons are placed gives more than 30 trillion possible circuits for the dissemination of information. Every neuron has from

2 The brain's cells also include glial cells. There are more than nine-times more glial cells in the brain than neurons. Researchers are just beginning to find out about the functioning of these cells. They do more than just communicate with each other and with the neurons.

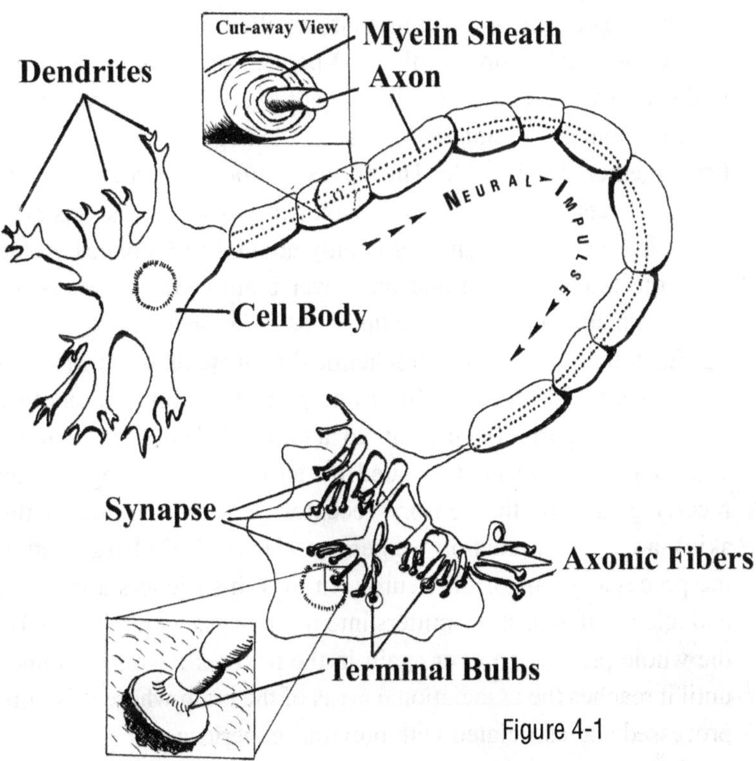

Figure 4-1

1000 to 5000 synapses (depending on learning) and each of these synapses connects to other neurons. What is interesting here is that with all of these connections there is very little redundancy. So, the nerve cell is an information distribution system that empowers the human thinking process itself with an ability that even the largest supercomputer is unable to achieve.

Both the brain and the neuron have input, processing and output. Your senses (eyes, ears, nose, tongue, skin, muscles and joints) send information to the brain through the neurons and the sensory pathways. Inside the brain, below the cortex (the outer portion of the brain) much of the processing is done. After the processing, this information is sent on to the cortex for decisions and output. The interesting point here is that over 90-percent of what you think, do, say and feel is influenced by *less* than *10-percent* of the brain. The part of the brain that has all of this influence is the cortex and it takes up less than 10-percent of the volume of the brain. To give you an idea of the size of the cortex, the brain itself weighs about 3½ pounds and is just a little larger than both of your fists together side-by-side. The cortex comprises, in area, the size of four sheets of 8½" x 11" notebook paper. The thickness is only about 1/8 inch. In weight this is only about 4 to 6 ounces. Aside from the limbic system and the lower brain centers, the rest of your brain apparently is made up of "association areas."

Each neuron is an electrochemical factory. Its basic function is to transmit information from one part of the body to another or from one part of the brain to another. Whenever the input side of the neuron is stimulated by an electrical change at the receiving area of the sensory receptor (e.g. the surface of the skin), a chemical reaction triggers an electrical discharge within the processing part of the neuron. In turn this triggers a reaction and release of neurotransmitters into the synapse which then starts the whole process all over again in the next cell.[3] This continues until it reaches the associational areas of the brain where it is fully processed and associated with previous experiences.

Do not get the idea that the brain does not follow some sort of pattern when processing information. There are general steps

---

3 In conversation with the late Dr. Robert C. Beck, D.Sc. a few years before he passed, he mentioned that the current concept of the neurotransmitter may be replaced by the concept of the *Soliton Electrical Wave Phenomenon*. A soliton is a self-contained energy source hence, it receives no outside energy. The neurons of the body are solitons. Aside from their synaptic connection, they appear to be in connection with each other via some type of information transfer similar to *Superluminal Information Transfer*. As the name states, there is an electrical wave phenomenon involved in the soliton. The reference is to very minute electrical pulsations. The neural impulse is driven by minute sodium, potassium and calcium ion changes through the myelin sheath of the axon. The chemical response occurs at the synaptic buttons and in the synapse itself.

which the brain goes through in order to learn anything. Once the brain has encountered an experience that requires any kind of learning, if the approach that it used in the experience was successful, it sends instructions to the memory to use the same approach when a similar situation is encountered. If it fails, it searches through all of its reasoning or computations to pinpoint the error. Adjustments are made in the faulty part of the program in order to bring about a workable solution.

You will notice that the brain *generalizes* its experience and the learning associated with that experience. Many times this ability to generalize gets in your way and causes more problems than it solves. Human beings have a great tendency to generalize the outcome of a singular experience to other similar experiences. From the generalizations it is assumed that all of the similar experiences will achieve the same results. This can cause frustration, anxiety and other emotionally charged reactions. Once your brain rationalizes or in some other way harmonizes your outer experience with your internal experience then a state of balance is achieved and the program is assumed adjusted. If this is not done then a state of stress is produced.

Once the brain has generalized, it has learned. This means that the information has gone into the association areas of the brain and has become accessible for the future. The implication is that the memory of the event has been retained and will be available for future access.

One of the requirements for the beginnings of intelligence is a good sized memory. There must be enough capacity for a large number of simultaneous associations to be made. Without the ability to make associations the organism will not be able to function with any efficiency outside of the environment in which it exists. Without a large size memory the organism tends to *react* mainly from a reflexive and instinctive mode and not according to a pattern of learning and adjustment in the environment.

Another requirement for the beginnings of intelligence is wiring that permits circuits to be changed through experience. This means that there must be facilities which allow the neurons to adjust to both the learning situation and the experiences encountered. It has been known for many years that rich environments produce heavier brains. This occurs because with richer environments there is greater potential for more learning experiences. In behavioral observations of both laboratory animals and humans actual changes in brain structure have been seen upon autopsy. With a more varied environment, organisms tend to be more curious and explore more to discover what is around the next corner or what does what. Curiosity and novelty seeking behaviors are natural in all mammals including human beings and are the basis for many learning activities: The richer the experiences the greater the increase in intelligence potential in an organism.

The brain does not need anything as exact as a specific order of stimuli in order to interpret the information coming in to it. It works on less precise methods of signaling. The brain has the advantage of being able to recognize patterns. The computer does not have that ability unless it is programmed to seek out patterns. Then it will "recognize" only those patterns it has been programmed to find.[4] An example of computer pattern recognition is in your word processor. When you use the "Search" command to find a word it will find not only that specific word but also words which have the same pattern of letters within it. This is similar to the brain finding generalized experiences.

On the average, every neuron receives thousands of distinct inputs. At the same time it connects to many other neurons. These other neurons can be (and usually are) in a region of the brain unconnected to that specific neuron. Each of the different sectors of the brain has different jobs to do. This gives the brain a definite advantage when it comes to *accessing* information. So, the brain handles information differently than you might think. Processes which are thought to operate in one region of the brain are actually operating in *different* locations throughout the brain.

4 In humans this is seen in the maxim: People see what they want to see and hear what they want to hear.

One of the most important warnings regarding the brain is that introspection is deceptive. This goes not only for complex but also for straightforward processes. The deception is due to being able to report only a small fraction of the total internal experience. As with the computer, when a series of commands are given there are a succession of internal unseen definitions which produce the result. When you attempt to communicate an experience it cannot actually be done with any real accuracy because of all of the internal processes coming into play in the event. What you get is merely a decoded version of what has transpired.

The basic problem here is that almost any process you can study by observation of overall behavior involves the complex interaction of many different regions of the brain. Each of these regions has its own distinct way of handling the information it receives. You will recognize only the most basic framework of how a distinct region should be identified and categorized. Seldom do you know what process each region is executing. In some instances, you do not even have the slightest idea what is actually happening. This is the main reason that pure psychology, by the standards of hard science, is rather unsuccessful. [i]

The basic difficulty with scientific psychology, essentially from its earliest days as a scientific endeavor, is that it still is attempting to treat the brain as a "black box." The problem with this approach is that unless the box is inherently very simple, a stage is soon reached where several rival theories all explain the observed events equally well. Attempts to decide among them often prove unsuccessful. This is because as more experiments are performed more complexities are revealed. Consequently many psychologists and psychiatrists will adhere to one specific theoretical viewpoint because it's easier to maintain a singular concept than an eclectic picture.

The brain has input, processing and output. On the input side are groups of receptors. These are neurons modified and specialized to transform into electrical signals the various forms of information that besiege it from the outside. Some of these receptors respond to light, others respond to chemicals, and still others respond to mechanical stimulation. It is these receptors which make the contact with the first set of neurons. From then on, the neurons continue passing information on to the brain. At each step of the way, the axons branch to supply a number of neurons in line with their own respective form of information. Each of these axons is in turn supplied by a number of other axons that converge on it likewise feeding it more information. Each receiver integrates the excitatory or inhibitory impulses converging on it from the lower order cells. After a number of steps, the nerve axons terminate on the gland or muscle cells for the output.

Briefly, at first there is input. The input is your only way of knowing about the outside world. Then there is output. This is your only way of responding to the outside world and influencing it. Between those two is everything else: perception, emotion, memory, thought, consciousness and so on, which could be classified under the label of "processing."

Research has even found that there exists connections which are in the reverse: output to input.[ii] This is kind of a feedback-loop. This feedback-loop would give information about the effects and/or results of particular responses.

Internal feedback-loops are important because feedback control of physiological processes, innate behavior and voluntary activities depend on the performance of different areas of the brain. The beginning stages of an inborn act seem to require a blended performance of different parts of the brain while the expendable act appears to be centered.[iii] With the appropriate feedback mechanisms the body can tell if the activity performed is appropriate and correct for the situation and the experience.

As you have seen, every learning experience that you go through to create habit patterns is made up of teaching certain neurons to fire in a proper sequence and time. This creates a neural pathway (See Figure 3-7) so that whenever you learn to do anything you must have the proper ordered neuronal sequence in order to perform that activity properly. Without the appropriate sequences for behaviors you could not perform much of anything.

Some years back research has found that the working arrangement of the cerebral cortex is dramatically modified by sensory experience.[iv] This means that each and every physical experience you have *does* produce an effect in the brain. You need to understand that there will be a change in both the *chemical structure* of the neurons in the brain *as well as* an accompanying change in *the neurons* themselves. *All* learning produces changes in the brain. In the case of stagnation or manipulated control of the brain (and the individual), an accompanying change will occur as well. This change, though, will not be in the direction of neural growth such as the changes of the brain's chemistry and dendritic growth but toward the lack of that growth and neuronal regression. Whenever there is brain stagnation dendritic connections actually recede making less communication potential and more primitive and immature thinking and behavioral patterns.

Anytime a new behavior is learned the same neuronal conditioning procedures are used. If you are just adding to an already learned behavior you are slightly altering the neurons in their firing order. New learning involves a change of released neurotransmitters at the synapse of the neuron. This triggers different neurons and/or the same ones to fire at a different rate or to differing biochemicals. Understanding of these processes is basic to an appreciation of the workings of the brain. For in the brain there are close to one-trillion neurons firing, ready to fire or just finishing firing so something is always happening.

Almost all of the information that you receive is first scanned by the lower brain centers. The essential processing goes something like this: The sensory input comes into the brain going into the Hypothalamus (in the Limbic System). From the Hypothalamus it goes to the Lateral Geniculate Nucleus (LGN) in the Thalamus of the brain where it is organized into a pattern. Then it gets sent to the Reticular Formation in the Brain Stem. The Reticular Formation in the Brain Stem is the main censor for the incoming

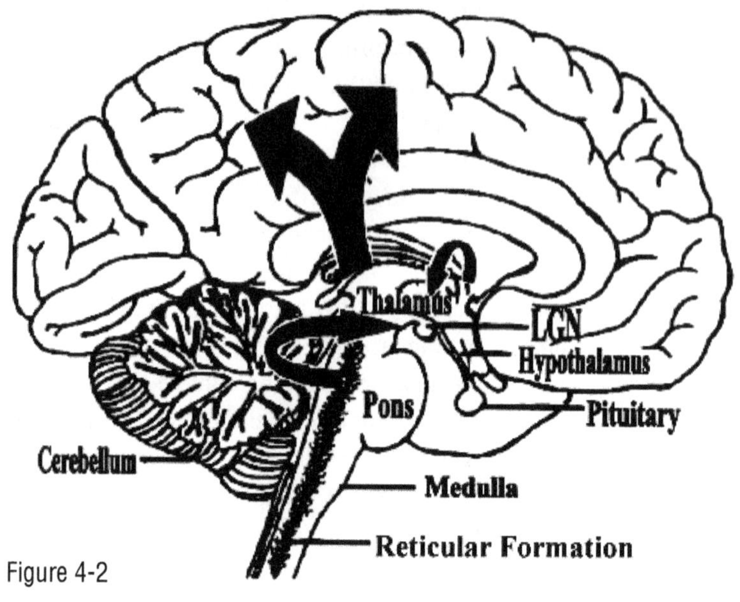

Figure 4-2

stimuli. It decides on the importance of the information and if that information should be sent on to the other areas of the brain for the next level of processing. The information then goes back to the LGN where its pattern is again organized. Then it goes on to the processing areas of the brain where it is relayed back and forth and checked for associations. (Figure 4-2) These associations are termed *neural traces* or *neural images*. These neural images or traces are what are left after an experience. These neural images, by the way, are in the form of *biochemical signatures*.

The term *neural image* is probably the most appropriate term for the mental concept you have after having an experience. The current view of the function of the memory employs images. Research has shown that prior to any body movement or reaction to an experience there is an "image" that is formed in the brain of what is going to be done.[v] This means that the brain automatically decides a course of action and images the outcome of the course of action prior to the actual physical action.

The Brain in 3-D

The current view of the brain is that each neuron has a "picture" of the activities which it does or will do. Many researchers have come to feel that each neuron contains within it a total 3-dimensional holographic representation of the whole and complete experience of the entire brain. In this theory the brain is like a large hologram.[vi] When a hologram is broken each piece of the broken hologram contains an *exact copy* of the total holographic image — only to a lesser degree of clarity. Each neuron is a piece of the brain's hologram and as such each neuron contains a representative copy of the brain's total experience.[vii] Accordingly, since the whole brain is conscious each neuron contains its own consciousness and a representative consciousness of the whole brain. It has been hypothesized that it is all of these consciousnesses acting together that choose your reality.[viii]

The theory of the holographic brain was developed by Emmett Leith and Juris Upatnieks by expanding on Dennis Gabor's holograms. You will recall that a hologram is a 3-dimensional image on a surface such as glass. Holograms are a phenomenon of light waves. The essence of all holograms is that they possess phase and it is the phase differences which you see. These phase differences are a matter of angles.

Like sound, light does not travel in straight lines. Light is *warped.* Warps in the light relay to the eye the specific image which is in transit.

Holographic plates distort incoming waves of light. These distortions appear as a moving 3-dimensional image on the brain. Every piece of the hologram can by itself perform the same function as the total hologram.[ix] A portrait on glass, for example, when broken will be shattered into pieces. Not so for a hologram. If a hologram is broken every piece of that broken hologram will contain an *exact* representation of the complete hologram. All of the pieces will not be in as much detail but they will all have the same image. Consequently, if you could examine a minute piece of the broken hologram you will see the same image in that piece as was in the original only it will not be in as clear detail.

In this context, your brain works much the same way. Whenever you have an experience it will be stored in the brain in a precise 3-dimensional, holographic model. Every experience, thought or sensation is accommodated and held in the brain in a complete 3-dimensional holographic representation. Not only is this in the brain as a holographic image but, just like the man-made hologram, each neuron likewise has this very same holographic image. This occurs because each neuron is either directly or peripherally involved in every experience you have, and in all you think and do. Just as with the broken hologram, it is not in as sharp an image as the whole brain but it is in an exact 3-dimensional copy. It is, then, all of these smaller copies which make up the whole image that you experience and remember. Thus, the whole *is* different than the sum of its parts.

Earlier, a statement was made that one of the main reasons a habit is difficult to break is due to it being imbedded so deeply within your consciousness that it becomes a part of your reality. Now, consider the present discussion: Your brain contains a 3-dimensional holographic representation of your total experience and each neuron contains the same representation, but to a lesser degree.[x] You can then see another reason for the difficulty in upending a bad habit. If each neuron contains a picture of the habit to a greater or lesser degree, then each and every neuron must be altered in order to break that habit. So, it is easier to become comfortable in the habit and many will often choose not to deal with changing it.

Not only does a habit have its own 3-dimensional representation within each neuron but each neuron is conditioned to fire in a precise sequence whenever it is triggered. Whenever the habit is stimulated then these neurons will automatically fire. Because this happens you can see that the habit is imbedded within the neurons and their functioning. Finally, consider also the fact that habit formation is part of the basic human survival system. Since humans do not seem to have many real instinctive behaviors to speak of evolution provided us with the ability to create behaviors (habit patterns) that will help us to survive in our environment. This gives us a huge advantage over animals that operate instinctively. Outside of the environment where a particular animal's instincts operate efficiently it will have a very difficult time surviving. Without the ability to adjust to environmental changes many animals will go extinct. So, the ability to form behaviors specific to an environment and to adjust those behaviors or form new ones when necessary has definite advantages. With this knowledge you can see other reasons why habits are so difficult to break.

Since every neuron is involved in your experience, and since every neuron has a complete picture of the experience of the whole brain then whatever you learn is imprinted not only on the particular neural network, but also on each and every neuron in the brain. If you learn a bad habit, for example, breaking that habit can become somewhat of an ordeal. Not only must there be a change in the particular neural network which directs the habitual stimulus to the brain but also all of the other neurons — being that they have some sort of involvement — must be recalibrated. If you have ever tried to break a habit you know how difficult it can be. In essence, you have to *rethink* almost your whole life to get out of it. You need to cause an effect in each and every neuron of the brain due to its involvement in the original learning experience. It is fortunate that the neurons are malleable and can be changed consequently habits can be overcome — some more easily than others. One major process that needs to be considered here is the rewards that are involved in forming the habit pattern in the first place.

It is a fact that each neuron on one side of the brain has its mirror image on the other. This is one reason that if someone has an accident and walking, for example, is impaired the process of walking can be relearned. In addition, the learning sequence is still there within each and every neuron in the brain and this facilitates the learning process.[5] The only difference between the greater experience of the total brain and the lesser experience of the single neuron is that the greater experience is much clearer. The lesser experience in each neuron is clear as to its exact job and what it does in a specific activity but fuzzy in its job in peripheral activities. This is so because not every neuron is directly involved in each and every experience that you have.

The Mind

The brain and mind are, many times, spoken of interchangeably. They are *not* the same thing. They are both separate and distinct and in *coherent superposition*. This means that the brain and mind overlap in an harmonious manner. The brain is a physical object, the mind is not. Usually when you refer to the mind, rather vague terms such as intellect, memory and understanding are used. All this says is that the mind is an immeasurable and has a separate functioning from that of the brain as a whole. The physical functioning of the brain can be seen but what the mind does is still pretty much a question. What the brain is we know. What the mind is still seems to be somewhat a mystery. Basically, all that we can say about the mind is that: *The mind is something that the brain does*. Since there is no really workable definition for the mind, the idea of a "mind/body problem" would tend to be rather ludicrous. The relationship question would not have anything to do with a "mind/body" relationship, but actually with a "*brain*/ body" relationship. In other words; how do the processes of the brain affect the body? The question of this relationship would then deal with the area of psychosomatic problems, placebos, psychoneuroimmuniology and so on.

Researchers consistently talk about the mind as mechanistic and finite and as functioning in real time. This makes it more of a *process or series of processes*. The mind is not a physical entity.

5 Assuming, of course, that there are no other physiological problems.

The brain is. Since the mind appears to be a series of processes this makes defining the mind quite difficult and somewhat subjective and arbitrary. Consequently, the mind can probably best be defined as a series of processes occurring *within* the brain. These processes construct your worldview as well as your perceptions, behaviors, actions, attitudes and experiences both internally and externally. These processes are based on genetic predispositions, conditioning and internal and external environmental circumstances and conditions. Holding all of this together may be consciousness — another process in the brain.

Intellectual processes as well as knowledge are involved in most definitions of the mind and its operations. Therefore, you need to consider that the quantity of knowledge involved and the rules associated with these everyday abilities makes them quite extraordinary. Knowledge is the key element in intelligence.[xi] Knowledge seems to be a byproduct of natural selection fashioned by competition[xii] even though intuition, inspiration and insight capture the sense of a spontaneous, holistic part of yourself beyond your understanding. Through analogies, recognition, modeling and so forth, you become more aware of what is going on within yourself throughout the day.[xiii]

Cognitive science sees the mind as a *system* for manipulating symbols for information processing. Perception, understanding and learning are, then, not just a matter of following separate rules for a result but an holistic *process* making possible your interaction with your world. What is then involved in the mind is a complete blending of processes. These processes involve: all your past learning experiences including your objective events as well as your thoughts and interpretations of those events; the present environment and its experiences including your thoughts and the interpretations of the present experiences including what is happening physiologically[6] at the present time; and your interpretation of those experiences.

6 This includes all chemical, hormonal, enzymatic, etc. reactions as well as neuronal effects which produce specific and generalized reactions.

Researchers have concluded that the brain is made up of a large number of little processors or agents. These agents or processors are part of what the mind is. Each of these agents makes connections between things and keep lists of what things are useful and in what situations. Each of the agencies has specific goals that they myopically pursue. Their essential job is to learn what signals to send to other agencies in order to get their jobs done.

You have probably noticed that everything that makes up the mind is decentralized. Unlike the computer, there is no central processing unit (CPU). This is necessary because there are many little processes which are needed for a skill that agencies have. One agency is dependent upon another agency because each agency has learned how to exploit other agencies so that all of the agencies maximize each other. This insures that every one of them will get the complete benefit of the total experience and data of the other.

Not only is there not an adequate definition for the mind, there is no consensus as to where the mind is located. Is it in the brain or does it exist outside somewhere? Does it interconnect somewhere in the brain or in the body?[7]

Researchers know that particular mental functions such as sight, language and memory are localized in distinct regions of the brain. They also know that massive brain cell destruction does not wipe out memory in totality.[xiv] There are always memories which are still intact. Even with amnesia there are different forms of the problem, consequently, some memory is still available. Even with the devastation that Alzheimer's disease produces, what researchers have found is that access to memories seems to be where the problem lies.

All knowledge in the mind manifests itself in the connections made in the brain. This is a result of the growth of the dendrites encountered during exploration and learning episodes.

7 It was Descartes who claimed that the mind was connected with the body at the pineal gland.

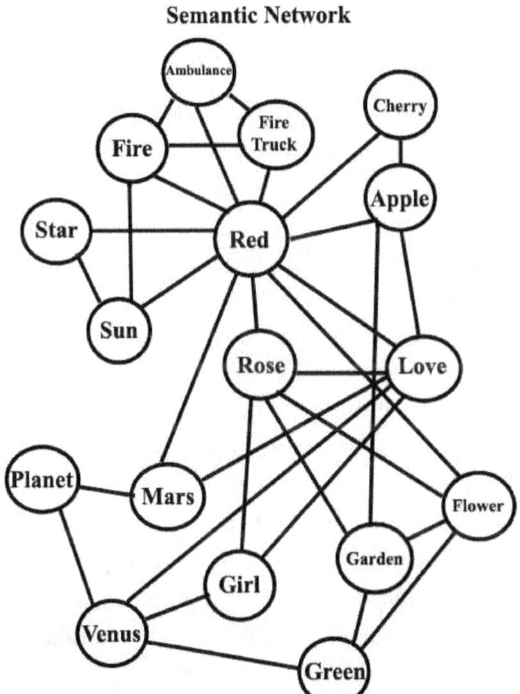

Figure 4-3

Researchers know that the more intelligent brains are the ones with the most dendritic connections and these connections are the direct result of experience with the environment.

Knowledge is dispersed in an intricate web of interacting connections.[8] (Figure 4-3) It is not the agents themselves but *how they are linked* that captures the notion of an object.[xv] Ideas are linked through learned associations and their accompanying neural images and these neural images are left after an experience. It is through these images that associations are made. Each of the agencies of the mind function to report part of the account of the experience and it is the conglomeration of stories which gives you the entire experience. It is from the complete image of

8 This is generally referred to as a semantic network or semantic tree.

an experience where you make other associations and are able to relate and generalize concerning the situation. You can relate to and learn from the experience.

Not only do you have this sort of entrainment of your neurons due to conditioning of physical activities but this same process goes on for each and every thought that you think. With every thought that you think you give yourself input information, do your own processing of that information and make your own decision pertaining to that processing. That is, every thought you think is you putting a group of neurons into action through self-stimulation and that stimulation is being processed *exactly* the same way as stimulation from the environment.

Every thought is an experience and every experience is contained within the brain. Therefore, every thought that you have ever entertained is contained somewhere within your brain. Consequently, every thought is also contained within every neuron throughout your brain to a greater or lesser degree depending upon the neuron's involvement. All this is saying is that every thought that you think affects you on some level. Since the mind affects the brain and the brain affects the body the effect is not only felt in the brain but throughout the whole body. If you spend fifteen or twenty minutes concentrating and picturing yourself as being tired and worn out, it will not be long until this becomes a physical actuality and you will look and act tired.

Every thought is a picture in the brain and within the neurons. Whenever you continually say something like, "I wish ________ would get off my back!" your brain picks this thought up because of the image that the words in the statement project and literally gives you a picture of this individual on your back. As this thought continues, you will assume the physical symptoms and conditions similar to a person who is carrying a weight around on his back. This goes for every symptom that is possible to experience through your thinking processes. Since this has to do with your health, you must learn to accept a definite responsibility for your own illness as well as your well-ness.

Your thoughts exist in your mind as well as in time and space. They *may*, if pondered upon long enough, eventually manifest in the physical Universe.[xvi] So, thoughts can be seen as a form of energy. It takes energy, both electrical and chemical, in order to think thoughts. Consequently, thoughts apparently do have a construction of some sort. They take up space and, hence, curve space. Being that they do constitute and curve space, they probably have some sort of gravitational attraction to them. Thoughts *may* attract to the thinker *the original intent* [9] of the thought. This of course depends upon the strength of the gravitational field: that is, the strength of the thought.[10] The larger size of the curvature, the stronger the gravitational pull. Simply stated, the more often a thought is indulged, the greater the curvature around the thinker.

You think on both conscious and unconscious levels. Both of these levels may not be in harmony much of the time. You may state consciously that something is necessary but unconsciously deny the need for or even the desire to have it. An example is that of visual imagery in healing. It is necessary to have a positive attitude and a *desire* for the healing in order to possibly bring it about. You may be visualizing a healing and denying it or even wanting not to live anymore. Consequently, it will not come about.

Everything you have learned has been installed through several basic processes. The first is having behaviors *conditioned with reward and punishment*. Remember, the basic law of behavioral psychology is, "Whatever you reward you are going to get more

---

9 The general intent of the thinker isn't necessarily what is seen in manifestation nor does it have to do with the thinker's desire. The original state of consciousness along with unconscious drives and motivators will *greatly* influence the perceived outcome. The original intent is often submerged under ego desires and repressed emotions. The original intent has to do with discerning the reason for thinking the thought.

10 The strength of the thought has to do with the intensity of emotion multiplied by the time spent experiencing that thought. In other words: E x T = M where E is intensity of emotion, T is the time focused on the thought and M is manifestation.

of." Rewards do not necessarily have to be something like a candy bar to get a child to do what you want. It can be as simple as attention such as a smile or a certain look. The reverse is also true. Whatever behavior you had gotten punishment for you have a tendency to stop. Punishment, though, may be the attention that a person needs to continue a behavior.

A second process is *imitation*. Whoever you admired most and have thought most highly of you tended to emulate through the acceptance and performance of certain of their behaviors. If these behaviors worked (which is an automatic reward in itself) or if you were rewarded for acting a particular way you repeated those actions.

The third is the process of *identification*. You will identify yourself with those whom you most admire. This leads to, but not necessarily is, imitation. Again, reward is important. If you imitated a behavior and got rewarded for it you will continue it.

The fourth learning process is *modeling*. This includes several aspects such as: 1) identifying with a certain role and so model your behavior after the general consensus of individuals in that role; 2) modeling your behavior and life after someone with whom you admire and/or identify with; or 3) modeling your behavior and life after what you *assume* a certain role entails. Rewarding the behavior increases the possibility of it being repeated.

The last learning process is *vicarious learning*. All that this means is that you will pick up behaviors from different people and places (including the media) and incorporate them into your behavioral repertoire. If they work that can be reward enough to continue them.

On the mental level, these same processes are involved in what you are thinking. One thing that must be remembered: Your thinking is subjective. It is totally internal, private and personal — and it is through this subjectivity that you will make assumptions about what another may be thinking based on your personal experiences and your experiences with that person. The thoughts that you find most rewarding you will usually repeat.

These thoughts do not necessarily have to be positive and constructive thoughts. There are those who find self-defeating and self-destructive thinking rewarding. These problematic thoughts reinforce the negative behaviors, teachings and beliefs that are desired. Remember, you will reward yourself and tend to assume rewarding aspects from another's behavior toward you for the thoughts you think. You will also assume that when you identify, imitate or model yourself after another that you are thinking the same way or possibly even the same thoughts as the other person. In essence, much of your internalized thinking behavior, especially when dealing with others, is spent in making assumptions or "mind-reading." Whatever you have learned objectively can find a subjective representation within each and every neuron. So your assumptions are made on the basis of the experience you have had and you make assumptions from those experiences.

Whenever you were born, you could say that you had no real thoughts, no definite reality except yourself as you were at the moment and only the consciousness for each moment of physical time[11] being in the here-and-now. You were experiencing only the sensations available to you and all of these experiences were being filed away within your brain and in each neuron. The majority of your experience is visual so pictures were being filed away for future reference. This is important to remember for as you matured, experiencing is set aside for conscious thought. Both processes are important to being a fully-functioning human being. In fact, experience and thinking are involved in relating to others. If you have someone who is troubled, when you think on their problems becoming emotionally involved you end up sympathizing with them. If, on the other hand, you experience their concern, you empathize with them. Experiencing is subjective or existing in the mind. Experiencing can be defined as a feeling of oneness *with* something while thinking is more like a feeling of separateness

11 Consciousness shifts constantly. The state of consciousness you're in at a particular time depends on many things including what you're aware of at that time. What you're aware of shows you your state of consciousness.

from something. When you sympathize with another and their problems you tend not to become one with their humanness but separate from them. If you experience their humanness you can empathize with them but you still understand as a human being you are able to choose whichever direction you want to go.

Thinking is objective or external to the mind. This is why private experience is ignored by empirical inquiry as being relativistic and incapable of "factual" verification.[xvii] Thinking is an internalized process which deals with symbols and the manipulation of concepts and precepts. It is a *representational* mental process. It consists of a train of ideas and a problem-solving operation involving mainly creative activities. It comes in many forms, some of which include abstract thinking, associative thinking, illusory thinking, primary process thinking, concrete thinking and magical thinking. All of these cognitive processes are indicative of particular states of consciousness, which are, in turn, indicative of belief systems.

Beliefs

The beliefs which you hold are essentially a set of labels and values that you bring into your interactions. They are formed from your learning experiences. These learning experiences include familial behavioral patterns (often times referred to as "scripts") which you have picked up, attitudes and traits which you have encountered outside of the family and have accepted, conditioning and training procedures which have taught you specific behaviors, acceptance of things which you have been told, and other things which you have just gleaned throughout your wanderings in life. No beliefs are innate to the human being, or any other animal for that matter. You were not born believing anything. You have to be *taught* to believe. One of the ways you experience and perceive the world is through your beliefs.

Your belief system consists of a series of *belief networks*. These networks are models of the way you draw causal inferences about the world. They can become very complicated keeping with the fact that your world, and your understanding of it, can be very complicated. This complexity is due to the fact that any given event can be the result of any number of possible causes thus producing any number of effects. No matter how complex a given belief network is, the process of reasoning with those beliefs will still be governed by the same principles.[xviii] These principles include your attitudes, values, your emotional and physical wants and needs and your expectations. These principles will also influence your experience and perception of the world.

Whatever the belief system is, causality — cause/effect relationships — is at its base. These relationships are *assumed* from associations made between events which appear to or actually do follow preceding phenomena. Causality assumes that every event has some sort of preceding cause or causes. You need to understand that all events in the world cannot possibly influence all other events. So, the flap of a butterfly wing in the jungle of Brazil did not influence the earthquake in Turkey. What you are doing at this time and in this space reading these words has literally no influence over something occurring in some jungle tribe in Borneo or in some modern city in Europe. It also has no influence over someone who is reading about belief systems in another part of the country, or even in another part of your house. In the concept of *limited* or *finite causality* a given event has only a limited number of possible causes. Finite causality does not mean that there is *only* one cause or series of causes with which you are familiar leading to a certain event. It means that there is any number of causes for the event with a myriad of them outside of your experience.

There are several issues to consider in cause/effect relationships. First is the notion of *temporal contiguity*: events occurring in time. Seeing things transpiring at the same time can easily lead you to think that the two events are related. In the majority of instances this is not the case. A series of events which appear to stand out due to the time sequence in which they are occurring do not necessarily have anything to do with each other. Superstitions and superstitious behaviors and religious beliefs begin this way. As an example, someone is walking down a street. Across the sidewalk a ladder is stretched in order for a workman to do some work. Since there is no other place to walk you are compelled to walk under the ladder. A few blocks down the street or even later that day or that week you twist your ankle. Upon getting up from the sidewalk you remember that you walked under the ladder and an association was drawn between walking under the ladder and twisting your ankle. There is no thought to the fact that you may not have been paying much attention to where you were walking. As you can see, temporal contiguity is an insufficient basis from which to draw conclusions.

The next notion that you must consider is that of *spatial contiguity*: events occurring in the same space. Events which seem to occur in the same space do not necessarily occur at the same time. If there are two automobile accidents at the same place several days apart it does not mean they were both caused by the same preceding events. Also, you cannot conclude that two or more events occurring in the same place at the same time (temporally and spatially contiguous) are caused by the same preceding events. There are some events which are spatially contiguous but are non-existent such as illusions or hallucinations.[12] Others can be both spatially and temporally contiguous and have nothing to do with each other. Through the concept of limited causality you are led to the *Principle of Determinism*: every natural event has a cause, and looking hard enough the cause can be found.[xix] With this concept there are no events for which a cause cannot be found. Those which cannot be explained at this point in time and space are not "mysteries." Simply, the appropriate equipment (whether it be

12 Hallucinations are spatially contiguous biochemically in the brain for the person who is experiencing the hallucinations, not for anyone else. Just because someone is experiencing the hallucination doesn't mean that it actually exists in space and time. The experience is only within the subjective reality of the hallucinator.

mechanical, electrical, mental or any other sort) does not exist to explain them. By merely assuming that it is a mystery or is caused by some sort of event which cannot be proven is tantamount to giving up. The human brain, you will recall, has evolved to learn and experience. It is constructed in such a way that the greater the amount of learning, the more connections it makes and the more efficient it becomes. The more efficient it is the more it can learn and the more effective it becomes in relating and adjusting to and experiencing its external environment.

Causes and consequences can be categorized into a few straight-forward rules of inference. One of the main methods of this categorization is by way of *Analogy*. Analogy is the process of making comparisons or drawing parallels. It is a powerful tool of human thought. You reason and learn by analogy and language is filled with analogy in the form of metaphors and idiomatic expressions. Language itself is an analogy. Words only represent the objects and events which they depict and are not the object or event. Whenever you generalize one experience to another or to other experiences you are creating an analogy. Analogy is seen in the social, the governmental, the educational and especially in the religious institutions as well as the social structure and society at large. Countries, religions and your individual self are represented by analogy and metaphor. Hence, analogy and metaphor may be considered the basis for human society. The more ancient and aboriginal societies saw all existence as a metaphor: "As above so below…" Mythology played an immense part in their lives and analogies were drawn from nature and these analogies were used to reinforce their belief systems. The use of analogy is the basis for the superstitious behavior seen in religious institutions.

When humans think, there are some typical patterns which we follow. When confronted with a new situation, we will often recall similar situations in the past and reason by analogy to apply the experience of it to the present situation. In other words, we *generalize* that the two events are similar and can have the same or similar outcomes. In essence, we assume through this analogy that they have the same or similar preceding causes. Belief systems are to a large degree based on analogies assumed from some cause/effect relationship.

The soundest analogies tend to be true even if the corresponding objects are utterly different in appearance or character. What really matters is the roles they play. The best analogies are between shared supporting associations even though their surface characteristics tend to be quite different. Behavior can then be seen as governed by two different set of rules: One concerns itself with access *to* analogies and the other with inference *from* analogies.[xx]

Although analogy is obviously a very important tool in human thought, it is very tricky and dangerous for it can easily be misunderstood. It is easy to mistake the "map" for the "territory" as it were.[xxi] This happens often with language through the experiences that are encountered. You will assume that what is being said is what you understand, or that the experience you are facing is close enough to one (or more) which you had previously encountered that it will lead to the same outcome. Experience has actually shown this not to be the case.

Thinking and Experiencing

Thinking and experiencing are both important aspects of life. Without the thought for a certain thing you could not experience it. The intent is *not* the thought. Thought comes *after* intent and a thought is not the intent of the thinker. Thought is the controller of your experience and thoughts are only the after-effects of consciousness. They tell you what is happening *within* your experience. Thoughts bring to your conscious awareness an intent from your deeper consciousness.[xxii] The same process can work somewhat in reverse. If you consciously think a thought often enough and strongly enough you can bring your consciousness to accept it as being real. Then when consciousness says that it is real, it *is* real — but, as previously stated, may be real in the mind only.

From the time that you are able to begin to physically perceive whatever your Universe is you filed all of the sensations away as images. Whenever you began to understand that the sounds coming from your parents or caregivers have meaning you began associating the symbols known as words to objects that you perceive. From that point you no longer were experiencing the object. Your consciousness begins to gain the limitation of *I* and *non-I*. That is, you began to separate yourself from your creation and eventually from all creation. You began to think of yourself as estranged or apart from everything else in your Universe.

Much of this feeling of alienation came from the conditioning which was placed on you mainly from your parents; then from the relationships outside of the family; then from your society. Instead of allowing you to experience life as it comes along you were told exactly what to do, what to feel, what and how to think and what to be. Although you would like to feel that you do your own thinking that is not wholly true. For as many researchers claim, 90-percent of your personality was formed by the age of five based on your experiences with your family, your society as well as genetics. Since your family is your first introduction to the society, the society influences you to a greater degree than imagined. So it seems that 90-percent of all that you think, do, feel, say and are is influenced by your early environment. Of course, you will not act like a five-year old. You will modify that behavior to fit your chronological age and state in life. But your thinking is private. It is very easy to think like a child but still use "adult" terms and themes. Remember that your brain holds everything in pictures. It would be quite easy to see the performance of some action on an immature level and attribute "adult" terms to it. Much "adult" relating on many levels including love relationships, business and government is, "Since it's my ball you will play by my rules. If you won't play by my rules I'm going to take my ball and go home."[xxiii] This type of thinking is constricting, limiting and extremely immature restricting any sort of honest and open communications.

How thinking occurs has been the subject of much discussion for countless centuries. What goes on to produce a thought has remained quite a mystery — until science has been able to get some understanding of the workings of the brain itself. Remember, when you were born you had no thoughts nor did you have the ability to do any real thinking. All that was available to you was experience. It was all of your experiences which were filed away in your brain creating dendritic attachments from neuron to neuron. You had no ability to really think until you had language. Without the use of language you could not categorize the objects and events that you had experienced. Language is a *symbolic* way of representing your experience. With it you can communicate whatever you have encountered whether internally or externally. But since language is a symbol it can only *represent* what you are attempting to communicate and can never be the actual expression of that communication: The map is *not* the territory. This is where problems with communicating come to light. Symbols do not always represent the same things to everyone.

Even if consciousness is defined as simply a state of awareness, it is easy to see consciousness is not a simple process. It involves the whole brain and the many hundreds of millions of neurons of which the brain is comprised. Also, with each neuron having its own consciousness and being part of the greater consciousness of the brain, the form which is chosen for the reality of the individual is only part of the total available reality. What is chosen is that the experience of reality depends upon the interaction of nature and nurture. The experience of the reality is mainly from nature. The choices of the precise experiences within that incident in external reality are learned: nurture.

From the time you began perceiving your own personal Universe information was being filed away in the recesses of your brain. The majority of this information was in the form of images. When you began to understand that those noises proceeding from the mouths of your parents have meaning, you began associating those word-symbols to perceived objects and events. At that point experience was set aside and conscious thought began to take over. This was when your consciousness commenced a separation of yourself: of the *I* from the *non-I*. You began to isolate yourself from your creation — your personal Universe — and began to think of yourself as "different" and apart from everything else. You began to see yourself as an entity separate from the rest of physical creation. Once you saw yourself as separate and apart you began to have problems. You took on feelings of alienation, insecurity and aloofness. You placed yourself in a position apart from others and saw yourself as an object instead of a person. At that point you felt that it was perfectly fine to obliterate whatever was outside of yourself for you, yourself, are not authentic.[xiv]

The basic structure of your Universe is determined by how you choose to look at it. This includes not only the objects in your immediate environment but also the relationships you have with others. You can look at everything you have in your Universe as a mirror of some aspect of yourself and how you relate to another person or object gives you an indication of some part of your consciousness. The relationships that you have which are the closest to you are generally the ones that are similar to those you have become used to such as one whose attitudes and/or values are similar to yours or your parent's.

How you choose to look at your relationships is determined by several processes:

1. *Your early learning experiences in the family;*
2. *Your early relationships with your family and, later, your peers;*
3. *Your own self-concept, self-esteem and self-image;*
4. *Your present view of your environment and what is happening now;*
5. *All of the effects of the modifications placed on your primary personality or basic temperament;*

6. *Your view of your reality;*
7. *Your physical body and your view of it;* and
8. *Your present level of consciousness.*

All of these items put together show you what you see your environment to be. They all work together and cannot really be separated.

Mind/Body

All that you perceive as nature is nothing more than the creations of your mind. Your brain is only the receiving/processing/reacting unit. It is the mind which seems to do the creating. The brain perceives — the mind senses. The brain analyzes and synthesizes — the mind experiences. The brain reacts — the mind creates. The brain dies — the mind may live on in some other form. There are though, in Buddhist and ancient Egyptian mystical writings a reference to a part of the soul which corresponds to the mind which dissipates at some time after physical death.

What the mind is, no one really knows. Its connection point with the body is also an unknown.[13] What can be relatively certain is that there is some sort of connection between the brain, mind and consciousness. There also seems to be some sort of connection between your body's electrical emanations[14] and your state of health and consciousness. Some of those claiming to be able to see your "auric emanations" say they can tell your

13 There are two current mystical theories concerning this point. Today's "psychics" see this connection as the Pineal gland (Descartes) and the other viewpoint is that of an intermeshing of mind and body with points of connection along the acupuncture meridians. With today's scientific studies of consciousness both the mind and consciousness are activities performed by the brain. There appears to be no singular connecting point of the mind to the body but multiple points within the brain. The mind/body effect is produced from this point.

14 Seen in "Kirilian" or electophotography.

physical, psychological and emotional state. Consequently, there is a definite connection between your state of consciousness and your physical well-being.[15]

It is not necessary to discuss whether the mind controls the body or vice versa. What is important is the fact that the two work in harmony (in coherency) with each other *at all times*. As mentioned earlier, the brain is a literal translator of information. It takes what sensory information has been fed into it and processes it *at face value*, all on an unconscious level. Then when the information begins to come closer to the waking consciousness level it becomes interpreted through association and the aforementioned eight processes.

Your mind and body work together and keep you balanced on many levels. Since your mind does have some kind of connection with your conscious level, if you have the consciousness for a disease (e.g. ulcers) your mind will work in harmony with your body to produce this problem and balance the two out.[16] Thought controls your brain and thought can also affect your mind. This in turn affects your consciousness and this will balance itself with your body's own systems. This same process goes for creating any physical actuality in your universe. It can be said that in order to make changes in any aspect of your life you must change your mind and your consciousness and your reality will change.

All of the events (including occurrences and object-events) in your universe are integral parts of an inseparable whole. Recall that every individual is surrounded by a biogravitational, conscious, self-organizing field and this field probably generated you. For this generation to occur the essence of every possible event had to have been in some way organized and attracted to that field in order for you to become the physical entity you are. Not only are

15 See **The Aura** by W.J. Kilner, M.D. (originally titled, **The Human Atmosphere**).

16 There are persons whom researchers have found who have a *genetic predisposition* to contracting certain diseases such as cancer. How the body fights a disease is genetically programmed as well.

the essences of all of your possible experiences brought to this one point in objective space-time but also the creative direction of the energy that is generated. In other words, you were given an objective point at which you have the possibility of becoming, you were given the creative direction and talents and abilities with which to express that creative direction and then you were let alone to experience, to create and to choose in order to become as much as possible a total and complete expression as the Universe intended. Remember, you were and are an intent of the Universe to express and experience itself.

This then brings up the idea that if you were generated by the attraction of the *essences* of events, then all things (events, ideas, etc.) must "exist" out in the Universe somewhere in some form. This goes along with the philosophical concepts of *a priori knowledge* and Jung's concept of the *Collective Unconscious* and appears to imply *predestination*. The concept of predestination says that you have no choice and that everything that you do is already predetermined. This is not true. Remember, you are generated by the attraction of the *essences* of events, *not* specific events. Remember also that everything is in *potential*. That is everything is on its way to becoming something and can be *anything*. Consequently, many things are *possible* but not all things will happen.

The Grand Universe cannot perceive itself and must somehow create those events which are able to perceive. In this way it can have the experience of itself. So, you are an intent of the Universe for self-perception and self-expression. You are a 3-dimensional finite representation of an infinite multi-dimensional Mind. This Mind has within it the whole concept of the Universe in its 3-dimensions, plus more. In fact, every aspect of the many intents of the Universe has a complete 3-dimensional representation of the complete Universe within it.[xxv] Simply stated, you are part of a complete and harmonious universe and in order to function in that Universe you have within your brain not only a 3-dimensional holographic picture of your experiences but also of the Universe itself for the Universe is a giant hologram where all parts of the hologram contain a complete picture of the Super Hologram.[xxvi] This Super Hologram is essentially all of the minds in the Universe combining to create and experience themselves. It is not something outside of the Universe but is the Universe. You can, by altering your consciousness, experience and perceive events differently within the Universe. Also, you can "tune-in" on ideas, concepts and realities which are in other realms of experience. Further, by changing your consciousness you can change all of the events that you perceive.

One-ness in the Universe

All existences in the Universe are interconnected. Consciousness and the physical world are interconnected and every point in the brain is connected to every point in the Universe.[xxvii] You are in contact with every possible event within the whole Universe. You attract to you only certain occurrences. Whatever is attracted to you, from the initial intent especially, determines the expression of the Universe that you become. Since you do have choice there are other options open. You are not impaled by the energies which you are and which you express, just compelled. You are compelled to express yourself and experience those aspects of the Universe which you represent. You are compelled to create objects which are appropriate for your total expression. You are not forced to do so. By your own personal choice you can negate all of the experiences for which you were organized and intended. You can choose your experiences whether it is along your path or not. When you choose to go against the Universe you begin to run into problems. Some of these are social (e.g. war, greed, poverty), psychological (e.g. personality disorders, psychotic disorders and reality disturbances), emotional (e.g. lack of loving relationships, bigotry, hate, fears, self- and other-punishment), and spiritual (religious intolerance, superstition, religious arrogance and fanaticism and chosen ignorance).

You will follow the path that is easiest for you to navigate the space-time continuum: the path of the highest possibility. You do this because of your consciousness and the experiences which formed that consciousness. The psychologist William James saw consciousness as a flowing "stream" of thought which changed on a continuum. It was a harmony in variety rather than a series of distinct disconnected elements.[xxviii] Einsteinian physics sees consciousness in a "flow" of time which is always in the direction of the highest possibility. This means that *something* directs the course or heading of time. This something is consciousness. Recall that thought is the epiphenomena of consciousness: the after-effect of consciousness. By looking at the stream of thoughts that you are thinking you can gauge the direction of the greatest possibility that you are most apt to experience.

Conscious thoughts may be more or less a mediator with the external environment. There is the possibility of them not even reflecting what is deep in your mind. Remember that you have both conscious *and* unconscious thinking processes. Your conscious thinking tends to be nothing more than a lot of musings concerning mainly what you feel about yourself, your environment and what you desire and feel you deserve from life. In many instances, you do not have access to your inner thinking directly. You can get an understanding of much of your unconscious thinking by paying close attention to the unrealistic demands you place on yourself, on to others and on to the world. These will be reflected in many of the directions you choose and the relationships you have.

Every portion of the Universe knows its correct expression as well as the relationships it is to have with every other portion of the Universe. This is because of the interconnectedness of all creation. The idea of the Universe being a Great Thought instead of a machine gives all of creation a life. No longer are you just swept along with the flow of the Universe but you actually have a vital place in it. You are now seen as an active *participant* in an evolving Universe. *You* create the Universe whenever you observe it for it is you who chooses *what* to observe. Being an active participant gives you great responsibility. You have the responsibility to care for the aspects of the Universe you have created as well as the responsibility to choose *wisely* what you will observe. Remember, your thoughts program your choices. So, take care in choosing by thinking appropriately.

"But," you say, "I didn't choose the mess the world is in." What has brought the world into the place it is in is the consciousnesses of all of those choosing beings in the world working together. It is the same as every neuron in your brain functioning to produce the total experience of your brain. It could be said that the world is an holographic 3-dimensional representation of all of the consciousnesses in the world acting together and producing it. The vast majority of people that have ever lived and are alive now have absolutely no idea that they are choosing the Universe they are experiencing and creating the Universe they have by their choices. The vast majority of humanity does not believe they are responsible for their own existence let alone have anything to do with whatever else is occurring. In essence, the locus of control for their lives is external to them. All of these consciousnesses acting together bring about the experience of the world as it is. This is what may be termed the "mass-mind" or "Acquiescent Reality." Remember, you will follow the path that is easiest for you to pursue the flow of the "space-time continuum"; the direction of highest possibility. Since this Acquiescent Reality is already here, it is the easiest to follow.

The Universe is interconnected and flows in a direction. You are an essential part of the Universe and likewise have a direction. You can remain in harmony with this direction, or reason for being or you can choose not to do so. You are not forced or impelled to follow the flow, only compelled. You do, though, have the choice of the direction and the experience within the "Acquiescent Reality." It does not matter what direction you choose, you perceive the experiences associated with that direction.

Summary

Choice creates your experiences. You choose what you are going to experience. You are an active participant in the evolution of the Universe. All that occurs in your experience is the offspring of your willed intents. Every thought you think, every word you speak, every action you perform was intended by you. Literally, everything has purpose behind it and all that you experience is a product of your intended choices: your desired purpose.

You, as well as the Universe, are in a constant state of becoming. You, as well as the Universe, are in constant motion. You cannot literally conceive of anything that exists as being static. Your senses give you the *impression* that everything is motionless but this is not the case in actuality. Whatever you are perceiving at the moment that you perceive it is not what your senses have understood it to be. Remember, all you perceive is reflected light. So, what you perceive is already in the past and has been altered, unnoticeably slightly, and is not what it was nanoseconds ago. The Universe is in constant motion, in a state of flux and is continually changing. It is your brain alone which perceives the Universe as stable. It is from the experiences that you have had regarding your perceptions which convince you that there is stability. Consider that the age of the Universe is about 14 billion years, give or take a few million. That is infinite compared to the four-and-a-half billion of the Earth and the infinitesimal seventy or so years of a human's life. Something which exists for eons can be viewed as completely stable, infinite if you will, compared to something that exists for a split second in an eon.

The Universe is not what is but — since it is always becoming — *what will be*. At your slowed concept of yourself and your universe you can only experience the past. The idea of a present is virtually non-existent. Even if you could slow time down you still could not have the experience of the present. The present is the past as soon as you perceive it. Consequently, the idea of an "eternal now" exists only in the minds of those who entertain it. In physical reality, it does not exist. It is actually an "eternal past."

All existence in the Universe is interconnected. Consciousness and physical actuality are interconnected. As has been theorized, every point in the brain is connected to every point in the Universe. You are then in contact with every possible event within the Universe. You will, though, attract to you only certain of the events which are possible. Whatever is attracted to you is determined by the choices that you make — or rather, how you choose to view the Universe. This gives you the idea that there are a myriad of possible choices available to you. This is true. What occurs when you make a choice is that you split the Universe[xxix] and from that split you choose what to experience. You have many options that you can choose but due to: 1) your physical nature; 2) your consciousness; and 3) your conditioned experiences you will choose and experience a limited number of possibilities — which ends up being a grand total of *one* experience. This experience is positively related to what you have been taught to accept reality to be. It is your choices which create your physical experience: your physical universe. The Universe is not responsible for your choices. You are responsible for that.

Like nature and nurture intermingle in order to create a functioning human being, the interplay of your choices and their reason to be create your experience. Every move that you make, every word that you speak, every thought that you think has an effect on your universe. You are, on the physical level, an electrochemical, reactive, carbon-based unit. How you perform physically is via electrochemical functioning. Every electrochemical activity has an effect on the field that you are. Remember that you are an organized field for a specific function. You have the choice of direction and experience. It is your thoughts which control your brain and give you your direction and experience. Your thoughts not only aid in generating your reality but also are generated by your experience of reality. Hence, you are a co-creator with the Universe as you co-exist in the Universe and are responsible for the experiences you have.

The Universe intended that you be its eyes, ears, nose, tongue and hands in order to be able to experience itself. Its vibration is too high and its essence is too far beyond any concept which can ever be devised by humans for its own experience of itself. It cannot perceive of itself because the Universe cannot stop or slow time in order to have this experience. The Universe is in constant motion and is constantly becoming. For as soon as you conceive of an idea of what the Universe (or any part of it) is, it is not that anymore.[17]

The Universe is not what is but what will be. At your slowed concept of yourself you can only experience what appears to currently exist. So, in order for the experience of itself, what will be must slow down to the rate of what is (i.e. I will be to I am).

Being an organized field to experience what is means that the expression that you are is affected by all the component parts of what will be. Simply, the whole Universe affects you and you affect the whole Universe. Every move that you make, every word that you speak and every thought that you think has some kind of effect on your universe. Remember that you are an electrochemical entity and all you do is part of your electrochemical functioning. Further, every electrochemical activity of your physical body has an effect on the field configuration which you are. You are an organized field for a specific function. You can choose your direction and your experiences. It is then your thoughts which are the controllers of your brain. This, in turn, gives you your direction and your experiences. Your thoughts not only aid you in generating your reality but also are generated by your experience of reality. You can become what you were intended to be only after you break the bonds of attaching significance to objects. It is then that you begin to experience on more and deeper levels and can transcend physical thought. Consequently, you will be able to take on your responsibility for being a co-creator as you co-exist with the Universe. Then, you can experience the Universe and it can in turn experience you.

17 Remember the Uncertainty Principle.

Endnotes

i Francis H.C. Crick (1979) *Thinking About The Brain*, **Scientific American**, Vol. 241, No. 3, P. 221
Robert H. Kroepel (2006) *Operational Psychology: Introduction*, **Operational Psychology: The Complete Theory**, www.bobwebsite.com, extracted February 27, 2011

ii J.M. Delgado-Garcia (1998 Sep) *Output-to-Input Approach to Neural Plasticity in Vestibular Pathways*, **Otolaryngal Head Neck Surgery**, Vol. 119, No. 3, P. 221-230
http://www.ncbi.nih, gov/sites/entrez?cmd=Retrieve&db+PubMed&list_nids=9743078&dopt=AbstractPlus

iii Benjamin B. Wolman (1973) **Dictionary of Behavioral Science**, Van Nostrand Reinhold Co., New York, NY

iv Debra M. Barnes (11 July 1986) *Brain Architecture: Beyond Genes*, Research News, **Science** Vol. 233, No. 1468, P. 155-156
M.F. Bear, L.N. Cooper, & F.F. Ebner (3 July 1987) *A Physiological Basis for a Theory of Synapse Modification*, **Science** Vol. 237, No. 4810, P. 47-47
J.P.C. Dumont & M. Robertson (22 Aug. 1986) *Neuronal Circuits: An Evolutionary Perspective*, **Science**, Vol. 233, No. 4766, P. 849-852
Lane Leonard (Dec. 1983) *The Dynamic Brain*, **Science Digest**, P. 65-66, 118-119

v Patrick Haggard (8 May 2009) *The Sources of Human Volition*, **Science**, Vol. 324, P. 731-733
Michel Desmurget, et al (8 May 2009) *Movement Intention After Parietal Cortex Stimulation in Humans*, **Science**, Vol. 234, P. 811-813

vi Michael Talbot (2005) **The Amazing Holographic Universe**, www.crystallinks.com/holographic.html, extracted 12/25/2005

vii Michael Talbot (1981) **Mysticism and the New Physics**, Bantam Books, New York, NY
Ivan Dryer (Nov. 1979) **Science, Mysticism and the Future**, *U.S. Psychotronics Conference*, Taped Talk
Norrie Huddle (Jan. 1983) **Interview with Robert Beck, D.Sc.** Taped Interview

viii Fred A. Wolf (1981) **Taking the Quantum Leap**, Harper and Row, Publishers, San Francisco, CA

ix Paul Pietsh (Feb. 1982) *Brain Swapping*, **Science Digest**, P. 76-81, 112

x Ivan Dryer (Nov. 1979) **Science, Mysticism and the Future**, *U.S. Psychotronics Conference*, Taped Talk

xi Mitchell M. Waldrop (Mar. 1985) *Machinations of Thought*, **Science 85**, P. 38-44

xii Roger Lewin (8 May 1987) *The Human Psyche Was Forged by Competition, The Origins of the Modern Human Mind*, **Science**, Vol. 236, No. 4802, P. 668-669

xiii *Op cit*
xiv Paul Pietsh (Feb. 1982) *Brain Swapping*, **Science Digest**, P. 76-81, 112
xv Paul Hoffman (Sept. 1987) *Your Mindless Brain*, Reflections, **Discover**, Vol. 8, No. 9, P. 84-87
xvi Bob Toben (1975) **Space-Time and Beyond**, W.P. Dutton, New York, NY
Fred A. Wolf (1981) **Taking the Quantum Leap**, Harper and Row, Publishers, San Francisco, CA
Gary Zukav (1979) **The Dancing Wu Li Masters**, Bantam Books, New York, NY
xvii J. Arcaya (Fall 1973) *Two Languages of Man*, **Journal of Phenomenological Psychology**, Vol. 4, No. 1, P. 315-331
xviii Mitchell M. Waldrop (Mar. 1985) *Machinations of Thought*, **Science 85**, P. 38-44
xix Benjamin J. Underwood (1966) **Experimental Psychology**, Second edition, Meredith Publishing Co., New York, NY, P. 5-8
xx Mitchell M. Waldrop (11 Sept. 1987) *Causality, structure, and Common Sense*, Research News, **Science**, Vol. 237, No. 4820, P. 1297-1299
xxi Alfred Korzybski (1958) **Science and Sanity** (Sixth Printing) The International Non-Aristotelian Library Publishing Co., Lakeville, CT
xxii Jeff Love (1976) **The Quantum Gods**, Samuel Weiser, Inc., New York, NY
xxiii Alexander S. Holub, Ph.D. (2007) **From Victim to Victor! Defeating a Victim's Consciousness**, Bridger House Publications, Inc., Carson City, NV
xxiv *IBID*
xxv Michael Talbot (2005) **The Amazing Holographic Universe**, www.crystallinks.com/holographic.html, extracted 12/25/2005
xxvi Michael Talbot (1981) **Mysticism and the New Physics**, Bantam Books, New York, NY
Ivan Dryer (Nov. 1979) **Science, Mysticism and the Future**, *U.S. Psychotronics Conference*, Taped Talk
Michael Talbot (2005) **The Amazing Holographic Universe**, www.crystallinks.com/holographic.html, extracted 12/25/2005
xxvii Michael Talbot (1981) **Mysticism and the New Physics**, Bantam Books, New York, NY
xxviii Benjamin B. Wolman (Ed.) (1973) **Dictionary of Behavioral Science**, Van Nostrand Reinhold Co., New York, NY
xxix Fred A. Wolf (1981) **Taking the Quantum Leap**, Harper and Row, Publishers, San Francisco, CA

The universe is change; our life is what our thoughts make it.

Marcus Aurelius Antoninus (121-180 CE)

Chapter 5

How Do *I* Affect the Universe?

The Earth has been described as a speck of dust on the outer rim of an average size spiral galaxy in the visible universe. (Figure 5-1) With a description like this it seems pretty much impossible that anything that inhabits that speck of dust can do much more than simply exist, let alone cause some sort of interference in the Universe. For centuries mystics have been saying that we can and do cause "ripples" throughout the Universe with our choices and our behaviors. This has been considered nothing but speculation and fantasy by the vast majority of people. Then, with the advent of Relativity Theory and Quantum Mechanics this speculation has become more than a fantasy. Physicists have been looking into exactly *how* and *what* effect we individuals have on the Universe.

Interconnectedness

Everything that you do affects the whole Universe. All of your thoughts, emotions, intentions, desires, dreams, actions and behaviors, and things you say cause the Universe to react in some way. You can use the allusion that the Universe is a giant single-cell animal and you, as well as all other things, are very important parts of that animal. As a single-cell animal the Universe reacts to anything which positively or negatively "irritates" it. Like a

Figure 5-1

single-cell animal whatever irritates the Universe will cause it to move away from the irritation. Conversely, whatever pleasures or enhances the Universe will cause it to move in the direction of the pleasure or enhancement. So, what you can see happening here is that there is an automatic balance or harmony which is promoted by the Universe.

Say that you decided to go jogging. As you begin your jog you are moving ahead at a certain speed. This pushes the air around your body causing a certain amount of drag behind and a compression of air before you. Pushing the air in front of where you jog exerts force on all of the air and on all of the things around you. The force, slight as it may be, continues to affect all things ad infinitum so that the effect may be felt throughout the Universe.

Newtonian physics views the Universe through the concept that with every action there is an equal but opposite reaction (i.e. cause/effect). At first look, this appears to be true, but it does not describe the whole situation. Remember, all things in the Universe are interconnected consequently any expansion or contraction in one area influences what is happening in other areas.[1]

As you move along on your jog your forced thrust with your legs pushing down and backward on the pavement moves you ahead at a certain speed. The faster and harder you push your legs the quicker becomes your forward momentum. This is true but it does not describe all of what is going on. To get a clearer picture of everything that is happening you need to look at the effects that you have on all other existences in your space plus the effect you are having on the atmosphere through your forward momentum. So, the simple concept of action and reaction tells a small part of the story.

As you move faster and faster you begin to breathe harder and harder trading more and more oxygen and carbon dioxide. This affects all of the plants in your immediate environment which are doing the opposite. The more carbon dioxide you give off the greater the amount of oxygen is given off by the plants. Your sweating also releases certain chemicals, water vapor and heat into the atmosphere. This in turn is recycled and given back in different ways. The effect then is felt throughout your created universe and whatever affects the small universe (microcosm) affects the Greater Universe (Macrocosm).

1 Remember Bell's Theorum.

Just as minute movements inside or outside the single-cell animal set up a source of irritation which caused it to change direction or size or to do whatever it does at the time, so also does your movement set up a source of "irritation" in the Universe. In the single-cell animal all that usually occurs in order to counteract the source of irritation is a movement. In the Macrocosm whenever there is a source of irritation disturbing the functioning of it then there is a change or reaction of some sort to control it. The Universe functions perfectly and any disturbance to that perfection is dealt with quickly — in Universal time anyway. The single-cell animal will move around until the disturbance no longer affects it. The universe will work directly on and through the affecting organism until it is brought back into some sort of harmony.

The whole cosmos is a unified whole. Every being and every thing in that cosmos is a unified whole. There are *no* separate entities. The only time that anything becomes separated from the whole is when it separates itself. If you feel that you do not belong it is because you have decided, on some unconscious — or even conscious level — that you are different and do not fit into the scheme of things.[2] You are the shaper of your reality through the choices that you make. You decide what it is you will experience and you do all in your power to insure you will experience it. This is referred to as the *self-fulfilling prophecy*.[i] You will recall that the self-fulfilling prophecy states that you will decide something about yourself or your environment and in order to experience that decision you will delete and distort all contradictory information to insure that decision is correct. Much of this is done on the unconscious level, of course.

Take a look at the word Universe. The word does not imply a diversity but a oneness or a unity. Universe means that your perceptual experience is a consolidated whole. It means you and everything else are part of that oneness and, consequently, you are

2 This can be through either positive ("The world revolves around me") or negative ("Nobody loves me; I'm worthless") narcissistic attitudes.

one with it. You cannot be disconnected from it. In essence, the Universe is not something "out there." It is all around you; it is in you; it is you.

As much as some groups and philosophies would like you to believe, the controlling element in the cosmos is the perceiver not some incorporeal entity either causing or allowing you to experience the events that you are experiencing. Remember, you are an active participant in the cosmos. You create what you perceive and you make sense out of what you perceive through the choices that you make.[3] These choices reflect your worldview and beliefs that underlie your worldview. If you see a world filled with "sin and evil;" a world that is quickly heading toward destruction and oblivion it is because you have chosen to see that world and if you are a world leader with this idea you will do what you can to bring that destruction about. If, on the other hand, you see a world populated by interesting things to experience, a lot to learn and the enjoyment of learning and a myriad of ways to express your talents and abilities, that, too you shall experience.

Volitional choosing organisms have a degree of control when it comes to responding to the possibilities for their future. Because they are always in the process of relating to the environment with their own special measure of freedom to drive them toward personal fulfillment, there is in nature a constant tension between order and chaos. It is produced by the mind being taken out of the head and placed in the world. This means that the processes which are the mind are viewed as things which occur "out there somewhere" instead of processes naturally occurring within. When mind appears to be controlled from the outside then there is no order, only confusion. You will look for and see that someone, or something else has the key to your life and that person or thing knows what is good for you.[ii] They can live your life better than

3 These choices include the philosophies, ideas, values and beliefs that you choose to accept.

you can. They can make better choices for you than you can. Their experience is *the* experience and the only one worthwhile; not yours.

The idea of the Anima Mundi or the Soul (or Mind) of the World, a soul which permeates not only the Earth as a whole but every individual part of it, fosters the idea that the Earth is a living entity. This is echoed in the "Gaia" concept. With this idea the Earth is a living organism which takes care of itself. Any harm which may be inflicted on it will be dealt with by the Earth. The Earth heals its own wounds and will constantly and eventually bring itself into a natural balance with all of the living things on it. The Earth and every living thing on it has an awareness of itself, its place in the scheme of things and other living entities which exist in the same time and space. Each particular event, including each person with his own thoughts, feelings and intentions, reveals a "soul" in its creative manifestation. One consequence of this view is that you begin to experience your partiality with other beings on a level that contacts the core of how you experience yourself to be in your most insightful moments of inspiration and self-knowledge. It is part of the process of simply being alive. As you have seen, in order to perceive anything you must have the consciousness for its existence. Without that it would not exist in your reality. Further, the perceived must have the awareness of the perceiver as well. What is being described here is a feedback-loop and an innate understanding of potentialities and possibilities. This implies a sort of "knowing" by the Earth and the Universe.

Consciousness is centrally connected with all of the processes in all living systems. Knowing was created first by the Universe and second by humanity. You do not take knowledge from the Universe. You are the Universe knowing itself![iii]

According to the present concepts of the Universe, wherever there is mass there is curvature. Wherever there is curvature there is gravity.[iv] You will remember that you are a self-organizing field and being such you generate matter. Since you were formed out of the curvature of space and since you have mass you have gravity or an attracting force.[4]

On the Macrocosmic scale this concept means that at a point in space where there is a warp or fluctuation in gravity or in the gravitational field that one body has on another, mass can form. Dust can collect in the pocket formed by this fluctuation and an object can eventually be formed.

On the microcosmic scale this means that you were formed or organized due to a fluctuation or warp[5] in the gravitational pull of this planet and possibly in space and time as well.

Since you are a rather minute part of the Universe you were organized by a rather small gravitational pull. With this concept you can see that the matter which formed in this curvature of space is an expression of the size of the curvature or fluctuation. Whole worlds and solar systems were formed in large areas of gravitational fluctuation. In fact, astronomers have found in galaxies where stars have gone supernova new stars and planets are reforming in almost the exact same area of space as before. This implies that gravitational fields seem to remain pretty much stable.

Transforming Matter

Matter is an expression of the curvature of space[v] and has been defined as gravitationally trapped light.[vi] There are what may be termed "natural" areas of curvature which formed suns, galaxies, planets — and you. You were not left here just by being coagulated into a little point in space. You were given the ability to create curvature and this curvature will attract the proper mass to it. For the smallest part of the Universe in its potential reflects the largest part.

4 Make no mistake; this has *nothing* to do with the so-called "law of attraction." The "law of attraction" is a metaphysical metaphor not a scientific reality. For something to be a scientific law it must stay the same under the same scientific conditions. It is based on research and experimentation, observation, and analysis.

5 I guess that some are a little more warped than others.

It seems that curvature may be formed in a certain region of space for some specific reason. We will probably not be able to understand the reasoning behind the workings of the Universe, so let us simply say that everything exists for a reason or it would not exist.[6]

As the Macrocosm creates curvature so also does the microcosm. Space-time can be warped in order to form some object or event. Since the Macrocosm is less like a machine and more like a great thought, the conclusion is that thought can cause curvature in space. If the Universe is like a great thought, the question arises as to who is doing the thinking?

Thoughts control your brain. Your thoughts are also affected by your reality (and vice-versa) and your consciousness. For consciousness is at the basis of everything. Without a certain level of awareness you could not perceive the reality at that level.

Your thoughts tell you exactly what your reality is. They tell you what to expect and what not to expect. They tell you who you are. They give you an indication of what you think your place in the Universe is. Thoughts are the programs that you put into your brain and which come from the previous programming that is already there. Your brain does the processing and the output is the reality which you perceive.

Your thoughts behave like quantum wave functions and the quantum wave functions obey the laws of cause and effect. They exist in your mind as well as in time and space, and may eventually manifest in the physical Universe as perceived realities.[vii]

Thoughts, then, are a subtle form of energy. This means that they are a reality of some sort. Being a reality and a form of energy they have some kind of construction. Having construction they take up space first within your brain as biochemicals and later as object-events created from your intents. Since they take up space they curve space, and it will be remembered that wherever there is curvature there is gravity. Consequently, thoughts attract

6 The main reason, as we've proposed, is for the Universe to perceive of itself.

to the thinker (you) the original intent of the thought.[7] This all depends on the strength of the gravitational field. The larger the size of the curvature of the space the stronger the gravitational pull. In essence, the more you indulge in a thought the greater the curvature of space around you and the stronger the attracting force of the thought.

Remember that you do not simply think on the purely conscious level alone. There are two different parts to your thinking processes: conscious and unconscious, and the two are not necessarily in balance. You may recall that you follow the path that is easiest for you to traverse the space-time continuum[8] due to your consciousness and the experiences that formed that consciousness. The "flow" is always in the direction of the highest probability.[viii]

What you think consciously may not reflect what is deeply within your mind. Your conscious thoughts are more or less a mediator with your external environment. Your unconscious thoughts contain a lot of repressed materials concerning mainly what you feel about yourself, your environment and what you feel you deserve from life. Further, there also seems to be an automatic servo-mechanism hidden deeply inside your unconscious mind which relates to other consciousnesses with whom you are in contact.[9] This servo-mechanism "judges" your appropriate or inappropriate behavior toward others and relates it back to you in different ways. The fact is that the Macrocosm knows exactly the correct thing to do at all times in order to maintain a balance within

---

7 It isn't your belief that becomes reality rather it is your focused intent.

8 Einstein postulated a space-time continuum going from past to future. Look at the space-time continuum as going from lowest to highest *probability*.

9 Psychologists have noticed that very young children have an empathetic reaction to others when they are distressed or happy and will react to another's emotions appropriately. Researchers have also seen the amygdale in the brain reacting to another's emotional facial expressions. They have further noted that our brain contains "mirror neurons" which can help us understand another's emotional reactions. These mirror neurons seem to be the automatic servo-mechanism

its construction and does it. Even though you do have a similar mechanism you have the aspect of conscious choice and this can, to a degree, override this built-in system. Since the Universe operates in total harmony at all times, once this servo-mechanism is tripped by the unconscious judgment of your behavior you "irritate" the Universe and the Universe begins to compensate.

Remember, your mental life is not limited to conscious experience. Conscious perception is the product of unconscious inferences based on your knowledge of the world through and with your past experiences. Your conscious mental life is determined by unconscious ideas, impulses and emotions. Most of your mental activity is automatic or unconscious. On the basis of the analysis of stimulus input, responses are generated. Consciousness then becomes a matter of time rather than activity.[ix] That is, consciousness becomes a process based on when instead of what. It has to do with what is in the present (the when); the knowledge, awareness, thoughts, perceptions and emotions of the here and now.

You create your own reality; social and otherwise. You do this by influencing what you observe; influencing your own reality as well as that of others. When you fail to take into account your participation in this creative process, you will misread and misinterpret behaviors, situations, statements and so on. (Figure 5-2) Another aspect of the self-fulfilling prophecy[x] describes falsely defining a situation.[xi] This in turn evokes a new behavior which makes the originally false notion seem true. This action perpetuates error for the prophet will cite "actual" cases or events as "proof"[10] [xii] of being correct about the situation from the beginning.[xiii]

10 The "proof" most often is either manipulated facts with unwarranted assumptions or anecdotal evidence which is not evidence at all.

Communications Feedback Loop

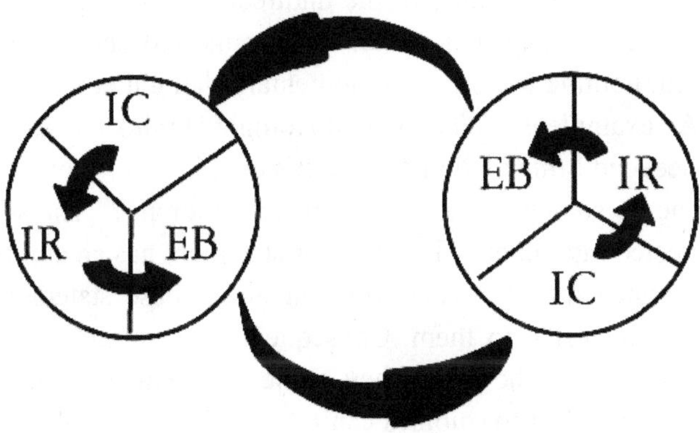

IC = Internal Computation
IR = Internal Response
EB = External Behavior

All communications is a feedback loop. We can only respond to another from the information that the person gives us. The communications process progresses in this manner:
Person #1 perfroms a certain action or says a specific thing.
Person #2 perceives that activity and this information goes into his/her Internal Computation where associations from past experiences and projections into the future are compiled. From the Internal Computation the information plus future projections go into the Internal Response mechanisms. From the Internal Response this information goes into an External Behavior.
Person #1 perceives the External Behavior of Person #2 and this goes through the same processes as was done by Person #2. As long as there is positive responding by both persons, the relationship and communications will continue.

Figure 5-2

Dealing With Self-talk

A very important part of making the changes that you want is what you are saying to yourself. You are talking to yourself constantly. The dilemma is that the majority of time you have so much chatter going on inside of your head that you really cannot hear yourself think. The problem comes from the fact that you tend to spend more time paying attention to the chatter than to anything else. There are two kinds of self-talk. The first type is an undirected monologue. In the undirected monologue there is statement after statement which is disconnected and appears to deal with nothing more than a momentary thought at a particular time. An example is: "What will I do tonight? I think I'll call John. This weekend I think I'll just relax. It's cold in here. Why doesn't someone do something about this air conditioning?" The second is a directed monologue. This type of statement has an emotional charge attached to it. Whenever you make these statements to yourself you listen to them. Consequently, the more you make these statements, the more they come to mean to you. Some examples are: "I'm so stupid! I can't do anything right! I wish that she'd pay attention to me. I must be the ugliest thing on the whole planet! God knows I've tried! I couldn't make a success of my life if I was handed $50 million dollars!"[xiv]

You may have heard that the language that you use is an indicator of your intelligence. The fact is that your language, both externally and especially internally, is directly influencing your consciousness and vice-versa. So, the words you choose, the things you describe, the labels you use all set up your experience and motivate and direct your behavior. That is, language sets up the experiences that you have and focuses your attention either toward or away from certain parts of your environment.

An important thing to remember is that nothing — no words, no input, no experience — has any meaning until you attach a meaning to it. This meaning is a label and you learn this label from past experiences. Once something is labeled it automatically has a value judgment placed on it and it has been projected into the future so from that point on all it will always be is what it had been labeled.

This labeling process is part of the problem that you have when it comes to dealing with life. Labeling is limiting. Whenever you label anything it limits your ability to experience it and any part of your life related to it. Do not get the idea that labeling is "bad." It is neither bad nor good. The main purposes for labeling are to help you construct a consistent experience that is predictable as well as to aid in communications with others. So, whatever labels you attach to things will tell you how you are going to deal with it.

Words are labels. They are meaningless vibrations in the atmosphere until they stimulate your auditory sense and become neural patterns in your brain. They do not become recognizable sounds until they reach the association areas of the brain. It is there where meanings are associated to them and you begin to make sense out of the experience through the labels you have for the experience. As you make sense out of the experience you assume that certain outcomes are possible and others are not (predictability). You will then act on those assumptions.

The words you use are models that you utilize in order to describe your experience. They are not the experience but a kind of "meta-experience."[11] This is so because as you learned the meanings of the words you attached images and emotions to them. So, when you use the words in specific sequences you bring into your experience (or the experience of another) the configuration that those words represent.

You will recall that in order to deal with your self-talk you need to: first of all pay attention to your self-demanding statements. All of those woulds, shoulds, ought tos, musts, have tos, need tos, can'ts and "I can't stand its" are your first targets. Remember to catch all of those little demands, stop them and confront them immediately. This is the best way to keep those little demands from becoming over-blown, out-of-proportion demands that are more difficult with which to deal.[xv]

The second part for dealing with your self-talk is to listen to yourself as you are talking to yourself about yourself. Many times as you talk to yourself in the confines of your mind you come down on yourself worse than you would your worst enemy. For some reason most of us tend to be much harder on ourselves than on anyone else. What do you say to yourself when

11 That is, an experience of an experience.

you are thinking about how you are living your life? What do you say about yourself after you have made demands on yourself? Just how closely do you listen to your self-downing self-talk? The fact of the matter is that you listen to the emotionally charged self-talk (directed monologue) on the unconscious level all of the time and that is the self-talk you act on continually.

As you were growing up you were told many things about yourself. You acted upon what was consistently repeated. These became the labels with which you identified yourself. So, if you were told you were stupid often enough you began to believe it and began to act stupidly. You found you were not able to learn well; you were not able to make any useful decisions; you were not effective in how you approached your life and your relationships. As an adult you still tended to operate from that childhood model of experience. Many of the things you are telling you about yourself are left-overs from that childhood model. Most of it, though, tends to be in adult words. Instead of, "You are so stupid. You can't do anything right," you will say to yourself, "I'm such a dumb asshole. I'm a total fucking failure." The point is that you have taken on an identification that was given to you when you had no idea what it really meant and you assumed it to be correct. Once you had taken on this identification you automatically acted on it. It then became a nasty circle where you looked outside of yourself to prove that the identification was correct. In order to prove the correctness of the identification and reinforce the position what you tend to do is to take the portions of your environment that fit the assumption and accept them without question. As the identification is reinforced it proves itself and you are driven to continually look for more proofs. This goes on and on. The problem is that as you are looking for these proofs you will totally disregard any contradictory identifications that demonstrate the singular identification you have accepted to be wrong. These contradictory identifications are portions of yourself that will be disregarded as part of your conscious identification. These personal contradictions cause confusion and with this confusion you are not able to make changes in the areas of your life enveloped by the confusion.[xvi]

This idea naturally leads into the third part of dealing with your self-talk: paying attention to your identifications. Simply put, whatever you attach "I am …" to you are. That is your label and those are your limits and the filters through which you see your environment. You cannot possibly act any way other than your label. The problem occurs when you have assumed this identification and you have not performed the activities associated with the identification for years. What you have set up is an anxiety state where you are *expecting* yourself to engage in those activities at any time. This becomes most frustrating if you do not want to engage in those previous behaviors. In this instance, either you are that identification or you are not. If you have not performed as the identification directs in years, then you are not the identification. The quicker you stop identifying yourself as that thing the sooner you can get on with your life without the constant unconscious anxiety associated with the internal conflict. With that internal conflict removed you can be free to act more appropriately without those unnecessary expectations.[xvii]

From here we go into the fourth and last part in dealing with your self-talk. That is, doing semantic restructuring. One of the most valuable tools that you can employ is semantic restructuring of your thinking. You will recall that the language you use is motivating, directing and limiting all at the same time. Your identifications, as you found out, can limit your experience and your ability to act and interact. By changing what you are saying to yourself and how you are saying it will begin to change your limits and your experience. So, if you are no longer performing a particular action making a statement as if you still are is counter productive to changing it. To admit that you have a problem is one thing. To continue to affirm that problem still exists even when it does not increases the possibility that you will continue to have the problem or return to its performance. You will be constantly acting *as if* from that point. Acting *as if* the problem still exists means that there will be internal forces motivating you to continue the behavior. If the problem is one that really got in your way and you have truly decided that you did not want to be involved in those behaviors any more you could make a concerted effort to quit the behaviors. Without alternative behaviors to replace the previous behaviors what you will end up doing is exchanging problem behaviors. As adamant as you were about holding on to the previous behavior that is how adamant you will be when it comes to defending and protecting your new behavior. The new behavior, by the way, ends up being nothing more than another version of the behavior that you are out to eliminate.

Admit that you are no longer active in that particular activity and state it as it is in the past: "I used to …" "I had that problem …" etc. The more you identify with the behavior that you want, the behavior that you are, the quicker you will be acting it out.[12] Remember, the words that you use are motivating and directing. By choosing wisely what and how you are talking to yourself you will motivate yourself to act in accordance with the way that you want to be. So, whenever you think about that bad habit, see it in your mind's eye as something you used to do, as a temporary problem that you had. Soon you will find the urge subsiding. Then the image you had of the way you used to be and the way you had acted will be seen getting smaller and smaller and dimmer and dimmer, looking farther and farther away in the past behind you.

All language is ambiguous. This means that language can have a multitude of meanings. Take for example the words this and that. Make the statement, "I'd like to see *that* movie." Now make the statement, "I'd like to see *this* movie." To most people the word *that* is more dissociative: the idea is placed away from you. The word *this* brings it up close and has more of an association. What happens when you think *about* an experience? Compare it to thinking *of* that same experience. Simple changes in semantic structuring can mean the difference between peace of mind and

12 As long as you're not affirming consciously and denying unconsciously.

motivation or frustration and stagnation. Another case in point: different suffixes can also have a directional or static component. The –ion, -sion, and -ed words have a static feel about them. The –ing words have movement. Think about the difference between something that is a frustrat*ion* and something that is frustrat*ing*. How about an ascens*ion* of stairs and ascend*ing* stairs? If you are recover*ing* it is an ongoing process that apparently never comes to an end. If you have recover*ed* you have completed the process and you can get on with your life. If you are *doing* something it is a process that is currently consuming much of your time. If you have *done* that same thing you are able to go on to other things. Think about that: Do you want to continually have your time being consumed on one thing? Or does this appeal to you: That you have completed that thing, you have learned from it and you are on to new things which are more enjoyable and life-affirming, now?

Communications is a funny thing. Whenever you say anything to another person, he or she will act out a response in accordance with their understanding of your communications. (See Figure 5-2) How often does it happen where you tell someone something and the response is totally different than the statement had directed? You have to say, "That is not what I meant." You felt you were being clear. Apparently you were not clear enough. Maybe you began to wonder what may actually be going on instead of blaming the other person for being stupid.

All communications, whether verbal or non-verbal, has two properties: 1) There are inherent assumptions within the communications; and 2) The communications are basically ambiguous. Since communications are basically ambiguous they can mean anything. Hence, as we've seen any form of communications really has no meaning until a meaning is attached to it. Consequently, communications can signify anything you choose. A semantic ambiguity occurs when there is a difference between what is stated on the surface and with the meaning on deeper levels. This makes for confusion in the processing of the information and the brain chooses a meaning to which it can respond. So, one statement can mean many things the same as many words having more than one definition.

This goes not only for communications with others but also with what you are telling yourself. In the confines of your own mind you spend a lot of time talking to yourself and not paying much attention to your own internal reactions to it. You do not consider that your brain may not be responding all too clearly to what you are saying to yourself. You may even be wondering why you were acting as you do (e.g. "Why does this always happen to me?") and not consider that you are acting on your own internal dialogue. The famous family therapist, Virginia Satir, stated, "The meaning of the communications is the response you get." Look at the response then go back to the event that appeared to start it. This will lead you to the internal dialogue that motivated your actions in the first place. If you look more closely at Satir's statement you can see the first property of communications as well: All communications have certain assumptions within them. These assumptions are essentially expectations concerning something in the environment, a way to respond, an outcome, a way to feel or think and so on. You will act on these assumptions with the full expectation that the assumptions are meaningful and factual. Your brain will translate into action the meaning of the assumptions within the confines of the communications. How you are responding gives you clues as to how your brain is processing the information.

One thing that is important to remember is that words are motivators. They set a direction and provide convenient labels for things as well as for your experiences. This labeling process gives you a meaning to your experience and you will act out accordingly.

Words are only representations (symbols) of the experiences that you have had. As Alfred Korzybski, the developer of General Semantics, put it, "The map is not the territory." In essence words are descriptions: nothing more than a means of communicating an experience. Consequently, they will convey, along with images and emotions, their personal meanings[13] and assumptions. These images and emotions are also assumed. So, you will assume that the images and emotions you get using a set of words are the same as another person's. As far as your own internal dialogue, you are assuming that the words you use to talk to yourself are conveying to you exactly the same meaning this time as when you first had the experience. The problem is that the experience is subjective and the words are objective. Consequently, the meaning of the words at the original time of the experience may not be the same as now. This happens due to other experiences that you have had which can change their meanings.[14]

Assumption is an important part of your communications with yourself. Paying close attention to the words that you are saying to yourself will help you to find some really important self-motivators. Words do set a direction. Look at the statement by Satir again. You will see that whatever you are telling yourself will result in moving toward some outcome. The outcome that you receive tells you the meaning of the words you use; the meaning of your self-talk. So it is very important that if you really want to make changes in your life that you begin by paying attention to your self-talk. You need to build an understanding that the language that you are going to use conveys the meaning that you want so you will get the outcome you expect.

Language is a product of a combination of three processes: 1) your perceptual processes; 2) your cognitive or thinking processes; and 3) your affective or emotional processes. As a perceptual process you will perceive and express your world through the language that you use. As you perceive your world you will classify or label the things in it and when you express your perceptions you will express them with the labels with which you

13 Personal meanings are not necessarily the accepted meanings for words or phrases.

14 We need to also consider the fact that there can be vast differences between the objective meaning of a word and the subjective meaning. Hence, the meaning on the conscious level is different than that on the unconscious level.

are familiar. As a cognitive process, without a language you cannot classify your experience. In fact, many levels of thought itself involve language. Without language all you have is experience. It is through language that you express your experiences. As an affective process language gives you a means for classifying, expressing and reexperiencing your emotions. Without the ability to do this all you have is a biochemical reaction in your body with no understanding of what it is. Language is your way of thinking about, classifying and organizing your world and your experience. The words you use are a result of your internal processing and this internal processing shapes your language and your language shapes your internal processing. So, if you change your language you will alter your internal processing in some way and it is through language that you can detect the internal processes that create your responses and your behavior.

All too often you will engage your self-talk and pay no attention to what you are saying. You take for granted the statements you say and disregard their potential and motivational quality. We see this in the demands you place on yourself (e.g. the "have to haves"), the repeated ideas and comments (e.g. "I'm a failure") and the parental dictates (i.e. would, should, ought to, need to, must and so forth) that build up into problems the more you use them. It is also seen in the use of ambiguous words and universals (i.e. the nefarious "they" or "it" and always, never, cannot, and so on). All of these move your mind into a direction that allows for either a specific experience (e.g. failing at whatever you do) or unfocused experience due to the universal being forced into some sort of definition by the brain.

Attached to the self-downing statements become demands (e.g. "I'm bored … and I have to have stimulation and excitement"). Other demands come in the form of parental dictates with ideas like, "I should have known better … and since I didn't, I must be stupid." With universals assumptions are stated, "I'll never be successful … since I'm not, I'll be failing at everything I try to do." In other words a simple statement that you make to yourself is not always a simple statement. There is more you're telling yourself on a deeper semantic level.

The words you use and how you use them reveal what is going on inside as well as influencing your model of the world. Not only do words motivate you they give you internal images of your experience. These internal images whether clear or not, are prime directors of your behavior. They show you what is going on and project into the future the outcome of the present situation.

What you say to yourself directs your thinking, your behavior and your experience in the world. Every statement sets a direction and you will experience the results of that direction. Your self-talk reorganizes the incoming information in such a way that you will experience only the model of the world that has been defined. Your model of the world is assumed from the language that you use and the language that you use assumes a particular model of the world.

Everything you do comes from a set of choices many of which are unconscious. The words you use are part of the unconscious set of choices. Words can never accurately represent an experience. What words do is create a set of generalizations about your experience. Words, as you've seen, are labels. Labels define the object or experience. Definitions are generalizations. Generalizations create boundaries which direct your behavior and filters through which you view your world. The key to how strongly the words motivate your behavior is where your attention is placed. The ideas that you dwell on most will influence you the most and you will tend to act out on those more often. Ideas like your identifications (e.g. "I am ..."), your demands on yourself, the generalizations you use and so on are the things you will find most motivating in your life.

The Homeostatic Universe

The Universe is made up of innumerable bodies of differing sizes, weights and forms. All of these bodies exist in complete and total harmonious interaction with each other. Each body "intuitively" knows its exact position, situation and relationship with every other body. There are those which totally exist without free will or conscious choice and in an exact place with little or no shifting (e.g. planets, stars and other heavenly bodies). Then, there are those such as the majority of existences on this planet (e.g. plants, animals and so on) that exist for a short time and disappear. Finally, there are those life-forms who, like human beings, appear to have some degree of conscious choice and free will.

All that exists knows its exact position in the Universe and the fact that it is to express itself as a functional aspect of the Universe. In other words, everything exists in the form and location in space-time for a reason or it would not exist. Instinctively you know the portion of the Universe that you are to express and are directed toward that expression. If you choose to interfere in some way with your own direction and expression or if you in some way interfere with another's direction and expression, the Universe, desiring to experience and express itself perfectly in every form, compensates.

Every aspect of the Universe knows what its correct expression is and knows the relationships it is to have with every other aspect in the Universe. It knows this because the smallest part of the Universe reflects the whole Universe and your brain is a metaphorical representation of, and is connected to, the Universe. So, being that you reflect the construction of the Universe, if you get yourself out of line in expressing that perfection you will be given the opportunity to get back into alignment. If you continually stay out of alignment then, as a planet which falls out of orbit is pulled into the most powerful gravitational field, you will also be pulled in a similar way into a more powerful field.[15] Remember, you will always follow the path that is easiest to traverse the space-time continuum. In other words, by continually remaining out of

15 This is when a person can be taken in by those who set themselves up as authorities in one way or another and by cults. This occurs especially when a person thinks that there is something lacking in themselves or in their life.

your proper path to your appropriate expression, you let yourself open to those ideas, persons, philosophies and groups which draw in your energies and never release them. You will allow yourself to be controlled and manipulated. You will let others tell you how to think, feel, be and believe. You will not allow your talents, abilities or yourself appropriate expression. You will not perceive yourself as an expression of the Universe but as an object with a title that limits your thinking and your reality.

Everything that occurs in your universe is the offspring of all of your willed intentions. Whatever you do to or for another brings with it certain ramifications. All of your activities, and even your thoughts, have energies behind them.[16] For example, if you do something for another and have in mind that you will be given a reward, there is a Universal principle that governs the fact that that deed was performed for personal gain or satisfaction. Maybe you did receive something in return. You will notice that the reward will be temporary and other things must be done in order to bring about the harmony that altruistic service would have originally done.

You express the greater part of the Universe which you are by being of service.[17] When you think that another has something that you feel you should have you begin to pull yourself out of the alignment in which you originally began. You will begin to interfere not only with your own expression but the expression of others and set up an "irritation" that the Universe must correct. When you continually look at another expressing him or herself and claim that it should be yours you are blocking the Universe in its perception and expression of itself and blocking any good that is yours from reaching you. The Universe, being a Homeostatic System, senses that something is wrong. This sensing is done thorough the perceivers involved in the blocked Universal expression. The Universe, then, wanting to express itself perfectly

16 Those energies can be biochemical or electrical or mechanical.

17 You will notice that everything on this planet exists in a synergistic harmony including those designated to be parasites.

and bring itself back into harmony, will begin to compensate and seek other ways to express its perfection: The stronger the need for expression, the stronger the compensation. Remember, every façet of the Universe is highly important.

Anthropomorphically, look at it this way: An apple tree does not perceive a peach tree as having something it should have. It just accepts its expression as an apple tree and accepts its importance in the functioning of the Universe. Human beings, on the other hand, who appear to be endowed with some degree of free will and choice, consider expressions other than their own as being theirs. By accepting all that you are now, all of your talents, abilities, assets and liabilities, all of your total expression, you can begin to become the fully-functioning being which you were intended. By understanding the difference between what you really need and what your ego wants you can begin to grow and express yourself. By accepting all that you are and all that you have right now you can start the process and what is not right for your Universal expression will be made right by the Universe.

Your free will, your conscious ability to choose, is what sets you apart from the lower forms of life on this planet. You can choose to express yourself and your talents — or not. You can choose to follow the intentions of the Universe — or not. You can choose to interfere in some way with the functioning of the Universe — or not. It is all up to you as to your life's experiences.

Consider a corner which was covered with asphalt such as a parking lot or gas station. After the area is cleaned up and all of the asphalt is removed, within a matter of weeks there will be green plants growing. Within a few months that area will look like an untouched field. In the Universe the seeds for life are everywhere. After a star goes supernova or becomes a brown dwarf, there is a natural process where balance is maintained. Currently many scientists are speculating that it is within this balance where life involves in order to evolve.

You need to also consider the part personal responsibility plays in your life and your behavior. You are totally responsible for everything that you experience in your life.[18] You are responsible for the way that others in your immediate environment behave toward you for you give them the behavior from which they will react. (See Figure 5-2) Responsibility becomes a two-way street when dealing with both your actions and those of another. Another cannot react to you unless there is something in those behaviors from which the other's reactions can be expressed.[19]

Some persons feel that if another does something which they consider impedes their life in some way that they should do something in return to them or that displacing their aggressions is a proper reaction. These persons will sit in judgment over another's behavior assuming it to be wrong or evil while their behavior is fine. What is not understood by many is this: If you simply leave the Universe alone it will balance itself. It will do so much quicker and sooner than if you attempted to control, manipulate, coerce or otherwise try to direct it.

The same goes for your own feelings toward another's behavior which you have judged as wrong in reference to your own. By giving in to resentment, hatred, anger, envy or any other motive with hostile intents you do not permit the Universe to do its work and allow for the inevitable change that is present to occur. By your feelings of resentment and hostility you are actually blocking the intents of the Universe for you are throwing an energy in front of another energy and only redirecting the original returns. Further, you end up doing yourself more harm than you could do to another. Your resentment is your choice. It is you blocking your own source. It causes you emotional, mental, psychological and, eventually, physical problems. It forces your consciousness and your reality to remain the same and to stagnate. Your perceptions

18 All that this means is that it is *your* experience, not someone else's. Sometimes outside sources can cause your life to be totally disrupted. By accepting what you're going through as *your experience* you will be able to traverse what is happening in a better manner.

19 It is also important to consider the responsibility for allowing something to happen; especially if it is a continual occurrence.

and your relating to the rest of the Universe then are altered to admit only a limited experience in a limited expression. Your behavior will follow the limited consciousness that you have and in turn the behavior of those around you will reflect your limited consciousness and perception of reality.

Another major problem with resentment is the fact that much of your resentment has been etched deeply into your unconscious. So deeply, in fact, that it becomes increasingly more difficult to find and bring to the surface. Much of your resentment of yourself primarily, and of others, was conditioned prior to the age of six. You will hate another for what they may have, or assume they have, because you were told that you could not, should not, or would not have it. You will be envious of another for their universe because you were told this is the way yours should be. You will spend much of your time resenting, hating, envying and fearing another and their objects that you lose track of the fact that you have your own life to live and that you need to get on with it. You want to create a reality which is not yours or try to prevent another's reality from reaching them and do not realize that it is only your ego driving you. Without the burden of the ego, you can learn, experience and express. Knowledge of life comes from the negating of the ego. Nothing can be more egocentric than hate, anger, resentment, jealousy, anxiety and fear. Once these energies are accepted you assume that the whole Universe revolves around you and that the Universe is there to do your bidding. You will think of yourself as being better than another due to having these emotions. You will see yourself as better due to the energies which are assumed to be outwardly directed when in fact they are inwardly directed. So you think that you have the whole Universe revolving around your personal limitations. If these emotions were truly outwardly directed the effect would be felt by those to whom the energy was directed. They are not. You shoulder these energies yourself bringing upon yourself mental, emotional, psychological and physical aberrations which are personal and private.

Resentment, hate or envy of another or what they may have

prevents what is yours, by way of the Universe, from reaching you. You will recall that the only true constant in the Universe is change. Resentment or any other inwardly spiraling energy causes stagnation of consciousness, a limited and distorted view of reality and a blockage of what is to be yours to aid you on your way to experiencing and expressing the Universe. It is very unfortunate that humans have devised religions that teach hate instead of love, resentment instead of acceptance, envy instead of joy for another, fear instead of confidence, and most of all, ignorance of fact for the truth. When negating forms of thought instead of affirming forms are taught there always are deeply selfish and totally ulterior motives involved.[20] It restricts growth by restricting free will and limits expression and experience. When you are not allowed to question and seek answers or not allowed to experience and be a true child of the Universe that you are, you have no rights, human or otherwise.

Another aspect of the Homeostatic Universe that many fail to comprehend fully is that of the rights of each and every individual that exists in the Universe. Gauging the appropriate behavior in relating to another is important to this Homeostasis. You are constantly relating to all other forms that exist due to the fact of your own existence. Appropriate relating between the different parts of the Universe assists in this Universal Homeostasis.

As simply put as possible, your rights end where another person's begin.[xviii] When you impose yourself on another for any selfish or egocentric reason you are violating another's individual right for expression of his portion of the Universe. This imposition can come in a multitude of ways. Discussion had previously centered on the negating forms of thought such as hate, envy, resentment and anxious fear. These are all impositions on another's as well as your own rights. Further impositions on another's rights come

20 Often people are taken in by the negative teachings of many of those preaching. Those taken in don't realize that those espousing hate have ulterior motives which involve their being in power, controlling others, their lives and, quite often, their money and *being worshipped* by their followers.

from personal actions and attitudes which seem to be innocent but actually are a means of control and restriction. Anytime that you restrict the free choice of another you are violating their rights. From the simplest act such as continually asking the same question(s) or holding up a conversation even after all has been said, to the proselytizing of ideologies and whole and complete philosophies that restrict Universal expression of individuals or multitudes, these are all impositions on individual rights. In other words, anything done with an ulterior motive instead of an altruistic intent, the care of another's well-being and freedom to be violates individual rights.

Understanding the concept of imposing on another's rights is relatively simple, but that of imposing on your own rights tends to be a bit more difficult to understand. By its very nature the Universe seeks to perceive and experience itself and it is always in a constant state of becoming in order to do this. Any restriction of this expression is an imposition on the whole Universe. You are a major thought for the Universe's desire for self-expression. If you, by accepting any limiting ideologies, philosophies or concepts block your own expression, you are imposing on yourself and consequently on the Universe. By assuming a limited level or range of responses in your existence you are narrowing your expression of yourself. By limiting experience you limit expression. Negative thought forms are an imposition on yourself and your free expression. You are then getting in your own way and not allowing yourself the rights that you need to be who you are.

This is not an affirmation of anarchy, the "lasiez-faire" attitude of "do your own thing." It is an affirmation of the positive construction of the Universe. Anarchy breeds total chaos for human beings will probably never reach the level where they will allow themselves and others to be the personal expression of the Universe for which they were intended.[21] Nor will human

21 In spite of Gene Roddenberry's positive view of the Earth in 300 years and the "Alpha Quadrant" in the Milky Way Galaxy in "Star Trek."

beings ever be able to assume full responsibility for or regulate their personal behavior. Only through the assuming of total responsibility for your choices will you be able to achieve greater expression of yourself and your Universe.

Summary

The experience of non-ordinary realities through altered states of consciousness can remind you that the world you experience is a construction of your mind. This can be done by reestablishing a connection with the Earth. The challenge is to encourage creative responses to the practical challenges you confront in every field of endeavor and every aspect of life.

A worldview is always supported by a world, and the worldview structures the world you perceive. This is why you can change your personal world by changing your convictions about it.[xix]

Many will claim that this is not so; that you will still see the exact same world you have always seen. The fact of the matter is that if you change your convictions about your world, yourself and your life you will then see life from a different perspective. As the conditions around you begin to change you will be forced to conclude that the world is different. You may still see the same trees, the same cars, the same people and the same political problems but you will see them differently. Remember, it is your convictions about yourself and your world which shape the direction for your experiences. The experiences themselves will not change. It is your perspective of them that will. This will help you to find workable solutions to your problems and make different choices for your life. You need to also consider that what you view as external reality is not only part of your consciousness but also part of all of the consciousnesses of everyone that exists today. This "Acquiescent Reality" is an intermingling of all of the convictions, attitudes and motivations of everyone. Therefore, we are all basically responsible for the condition of the world. You need to accept that and begin to change your perspective of your world. Your worldview is influenced not only by the conditioning that you have encountered but also by the worldviews of everyone else living as well as those who have been here before. The frustration and anger you experience comes from the helplessness you feel when attempting to make an unrealistic worldview — your expectations — fit into what you are really experiencing. If you try to believe in something that does not work and does not satisfy or fit into your actual knowledge structure you will attempt to get others to follow what you claim to believe or to destroy those who refuse to believe or act as you expect. The more devoid of meaning the philosophy the more you will attempt to identify with it and the stronger will be your desire to get others to follow suit. If another does follow you, the more you will be convinced that you were right. If they do not the more convinced you will be that you have to try harder the next time. You will then satisfy yourself with the rationalization that others are the problem. There is something wrong with them for you know that you are right! At least, that is what you have been told.

When you do finally get down to changing your convictions you will begin to see changes occur in your worldview. As you view your world changes, you see new facts of yourself and new opportunities come into focus. You begin to think and act differently, and the energies of life organize themselves differently in you.[xx]

What you perceive as reality is a combination of your own consciousness as well as all the consciousnesses existing today with those of the past as well. Consequently, you and everyone who is alive today are actively involved in creating your experience of reality as you know it. Perceived Reality (the "Acquiescent Reality") is the creation of all conscious beings combined.

The corrective construction of the Universe is not being discussed much today. We still have a world of hate, envy, fear, resentment, hostility, jealousy, ignorance and superstition. If humanity would learn that we restrict ourselves by our own limiting choices, that we impede ourselves by attempting to limit others, that it is in service to each other where we can reap the greatest rewards, that we are a direct expression of and the desire of the Universe to experience and express itself, and that the Universe always takes care of itself then we can begin to take our place among the gods.

Endnotes

i R.K. Merton (1948) *The Self-fulfilling Prophecy*, **Antioch Review**, Vol. 8, P. 193-210

ii Jennifer A. Whitson and Adam D. Galinsky (3 Oct. 2008) *Lacking Control Increases Illusory Pattern Perception*, **Science**, Vol. 322, Pp. 115-117

iii Thomas J. Hurley, III (Spring 1987) *Beyond the Modern Worldview*, **Noetic Sciences Review**, Vol. 2, P. 19-24

iv Bob Toben (1975) **Space-Time and Beyond**, E.P. Dutton, New York, NY

v *IBID*

Gary Zukav (1979) **The Dancing Wu Li Masters**, Bantam Books, New York, NY

vi Michael Talbot (1981) **Mysticism and the New Physics**, Bantam Books, New York, NY

vii Gary Zukav (1979) **The Dancing Wu Li Masters**, Bantam Books, New York, NY

viii *IBID*

ix John F. Kihlstrom (18 Sept. 1987) *The Cognitive Unconscious*, Articles, **Science** Vol. 237, No. 4821, P. 1445-1452

x R.K. Merton (1948) *The Self-fulfilling Prophecy*, **Antioch Review**, Vol. 8, P. 193-210

xi Michael Shermer (June 2009) *Agenticity*, Opinion [Skeptic], **Scientific American**, Vol. 300, No 6, P. 36

xii Jennifer A. Whitson and Adam D. Galinsky (3 Oct. 2008) *Lacking Control Increases Illusory Pattern Perception*, **Science**, Vol. 322, Pp. 115-117

xiii Edward E. Jones (3 Oct. 1986) *interpreting Interpersonal Behavior: The Effects of Expectancies*, **Science** Vol. 234, No. 4772, P. 41-46

xiv Alexander S. Holub (2007) **From Victim to Victor! Defeating a Victim's Consciousness**, Bridger House Publications, Inc., Carson City, NV

xv *IBID*

xvi *IBID*

xvii *IBID*

xviii *IBID*

xix Thomas J. Hurley, III (Spring 1987) *Beyond the Modern Worldview*, **Noetic Sciences Review**, Vol. 2, P. 19-24

xx *IBID*

A huge gap appeared in the side of the mountain. At last a tiny mouse came forth.

Aesop (c. 550 BCE)

Chapter 6

At-One-Ment

Before you can begin to make changes in your life you need to have a unity of mind, body, emotions, intent and purpose. Most metaphysical systems that claim to assist in making change and achieving goals work strictly from the mental, emotional and physical levels. With these systems you do your visual imagery, get the feeling of already having what it is you want, and act *"as if"* you already have it. That is fine as it goes but it is too simplified. In order to accomplish your goals most effectively more needs to be done. Before you even begin it is necessary to clear away what may come between you and your goal. If you are consciously affirming one thing and unconsciously rejecting it at the same time you can be sure that you are not going to get it. The question becomes: How do you know that this is happening? One way you can tell is by looking at the things you have worked on that *did not* happen. If you were working on the basic necessities of life and have not been able to achieve them most likely you have an unconscious denial.[1] For example, you may be going toward your goal and may have an unconscious command that says something like: "Money is the root of all evil,"[2] or "People who have money

1 Of course, if you're living in a country where the government or fanatic religious armies are preventing the basic necessities from getting to you, it becomes much more difficult to deal with. Just attempting to keep a positive attitude is about all you may be able to do.

2 The actual axiom is; "The *love of money* is the root of all evil." 1 Tim 6:10

are never happy," or "Life will always be a struggle," or "Once you have money you have to have more." Any of these commands can easily block your ability to achieve your goal.[3] Other blocks can come from fears.

Fears

Probably the most basic and primal emotion that gets in your way of making changes and achieving goals is *fear*. Everyone is familiar with the fear caused by some life-threatening experience.[4] The great majority of people have no awareness of the other kinds of fears: the more subtle fears which exist. Recognizing and verbalizing these fears gives you power over them as well as the ability to make the changes that are necessary.

Fears confront what is going on in the present based on your past experience. Essentially, what is happening is that something is going on in the present (e.g. an argument with a loved one) and based on what had occurred in the past you will automatically (habitually and unconsciously) overreact through hidden expectations (fears). Take, for example, being rejected emotionally. This overreaction may cause you to reject your loved one before you think the loved one will reject you or to act in a passive aggressive manner (stubbornness), physical abuse, name-calling, or any number of actions. All that you are doing is repressing and covering your fear.

One thing that is necessary to understand is that you are experiencing fears daily. The problem is that the experience is

3 Also see **From Victim to Victor! Defeating a Victim's Consciousness** by Alexander S. Holub to find out how many of these blocks came to be and exercises that can help you to overcome them.

4 It is so unfortunate that there are governments and religions who in their self-righteous indignation, promote hatred of others through torture and murder thus preventing those to whom the anger is directed from achieving what they can be. The most valuable asset that a country has is its people. The people will help the country to become prosperous, not foreign aid. So often the foreign aid ends up only in the hands of those in charge and never reaches the people for whom it is actually intended.

not recognized as fear-producing. These fears are small internal reactions to what is going on in your life.[5] It is these smaller, more subtle fears that end up becoming crippling and keeping you from achieving your goals.

Fear is a part of the survival systems of all mammals, including humans. Fear produces the fright-fight-or-flight response. Even the most subtle fears can produce the same responses you get from a major fear — only to a lesser degree. When these subtle fears build up that is when the problems begin. Being able to recognize and conquer these subtle fears is a major step toward getting out of your way and achieving your goals.

Human survival does not only imply life and death situations. Since humans are at the top of the food chain in most areas of the Earth physical survival is not the issue. It is a matter of social, psychological, emotional and mental survival where these subtle fears enter. Your body has a mechanism which keeps it operating harmoniously. This is known as *homeostasis*. Whenever your body needs a certain vitamin or mineral, it will tell you through what is termed a *specific hunger*. If potassium is needed you will be motivated to seek out foods that are high in potassium such as bananas or potatoes.

Primal emotions are the major controllers of your behavior because they are focused on basic survival. Survival is the most important duty of all living things. You express your survival differently than most other animals. You have the same basic needs and drives as the other mammals except on top of those drives are learned habit patterns. These learned habit patterns are there to aid you in ways of relating to your environment at a particular time. These habit patterns make it easier for you to deal with the environment by having some behaviors which are automatic so that others requiring thoughtful consideration and conscious decision can be engaged. An example of this is the drive to fulfill hunger. This is a natural drive but when food is scarce

5 This is called "anxiety."

the choice may be to either overeat to create a store of fat or to find some other method of storing food. After generations in an environment a tribe of humans would have the experience as to which approach would work best and a genetic pattern would be formed.

Your mind works much the same way. Whenever you have an emotionally frustrating experience you will automatically react with specific thoughts or actions. These thoughts or actions tend to give you an appearance of psychological harmony. Freudian psychology calls these automatic reactions *ego defenses*. Basically, they are essential human survival drives which have been redirected through social contact.

Your daily fears are the most important to contact and confront. A lot of money has been made by people who have presented workshops designed to assist people in conquering their fears. What virtually every person who has laid out money for these courses has dealt with was their major fears (e.g. fear of intimacy or fear of success). It was assumed that if the major fears were confronted then the more subtle fears will automatically be conquered. The fact of the matter is that the major fears are built upon more subtle fears; fears that were never really dealt with when they came up. Consequently, the most important fears to confront are the daily fears. The problem is that you usually do not recognize these daily fears. It is in these daily fears where you undermine your efforts to achieve your goals.

Recognizing these fears can be somewhat difficult because the actual fear characteristics tend to be repressed. What is it that you are not dealing with when you are putting your energy into accomplishing a goal? What is it that you want someone else to take care of that you do not want to do? What is it that you are not saying that needs to be said? Who are you not confronting that needs to be confronted? In what areas of your life are you holding yourself back and not truly getting involved? What is a priority that you have taken the importance away from? What is it that you would prefer to continue doing rather than extend yourself and taking a risk? What in your life are you wanting the "magic wand" to take care of rather than taking full responsibility for doing? What behaviors are you constantly rationalizing and making excuses for rather than challenging and changing?

If you are not taking care of the things that need to be taken care of there is generally a fear involved. Not seizing the opportunity to change, not meeting daily obstacles head on and resisting making change indicates fears. Whenever there are psychological blocks to any sort of achievement this indicates you are not really dealing with your present experience. Getting in touch with these subtle fears[6] creates a direction for change.

These subtle fears take you out of the running and keep you from going after your goals. It is not until you take your power back and deal with those things you need to deal with that you will be able to make the changes you want. You must be willing to face the issues no matter how small and be willing to look at them for what they are.

Fear is worst when it is left as an unrecognized underlying feeling that gets covered with layer upon layer of other emotions. Stating what emotions you're feeling when you're feeling them and giving the reason(s) for the feelings gives you control over them. Not saying anything about them makes them *appear* worse because the locus of control for them gets placed outside of you. Once you begin stating your feelings you will be able to see them from a different perspective and not look at them the same way. Then you can start doing something about those fears and you will find change beginning. By focusing on the things you can do and can change you will be able to do something about those things that you feel you do not have control over.

The solution is to look at what it is you are avoiding, putting off, keeping at a distance or not dealing with in your life. By looking at what primary aspects in your life are not going the way that you hoped for you can begin to focus in on the basic problem. Look at how you are not putting the appropriate energy, thoughts,

6 Generally, any subtle fear is known as *anxiety*.

effort and willingness into dealing with these primary needs. You have to deal with your primary needs before you go on to anything else. If you are not, there is an underlying fear. Notice your internal feelings, bodily changes, breathing changes, changes in muscle tension and so on and ask yourself: "What am I afraid of? Why am I acting like I'm afraid?" If something in your life is stuck and not moving or is not moving in a positive direction, fear underlies it. Fear indicates that you are not focused on being in the present. Fear, by definition, indicates that you are still dealing with what *had happened* in the past and projecting to what *may* happen in the future. It is more like you are dealing with the symptoms of fear and not the fear itself. Until you are able to deal with those fears you will not be able to move ahead. If you feel that you do not have control over a situation that is helplessness. Helplessness is when you are afraid and do not realize that you are afraid. How you begin to deal with those past fears is to confront the daily fears and overcome them. As you confront the daily fears you will notice that you will be running into less and less obstacles and less larger fears. It is like removing the bricks from a building starting at the bottom. At some point the building will crumble. As you are confronting the daily fears you are removing the bricks that hold the feelings of hopelessness, helplessness, vulnerability, anger and so on that restrict you in place. These are old habit patterns that worked at one time but are now getting in your way. They get in your way of expressing yourself more fully, of having better relationships, of enjoying life more and of achieving many of your goals. What if those feelings that held you back disappeared, what can you achieve?

Another way to get into the subtle fears that are holding you back is to go through a listing program of specific words geared toward finding with what the fear is dealing. Think of the goal that you have in mind. Then, go through these words in this manner: "I am *ready* to achieve (to be or do) (state your goal)" and pay very close attention to the feelings that you are having in your body or to your thoughts. If you are getting a "cringe" or "butterflies" internally while making any of the statements, there is a fear. The word list is:

Ready	Willing	Able	Desire
Accept	Allow	Let	Permit
Want	Deserve	Open myself to	Give myself the freedom to

Some of the words on the list may seem the same. Understand that the unconscious *knows subtleties*. You may react well to the word *let* but when you change the word to *permit* you may get a different reaction. Knowing where you are fearful can help you to change a liability into an asset. You will do this by questioning yourself and confronting those fears.

A small phrase that many use without even thinking of its effects is "*What if...?*" "*What if* I do this and it doesn't happen?" "*What if* I do this and this happens?" "*What if* I can't do this?" "*What if* he does that?" *What if...* indicates anxiety. Anxiety is a fear; a fear of the unknown. When you become anxious about one thing you tend to generalize it to just about every area of your life. Consequently, you become blocked throughout your whole life. Another way that the *What if...* is stated is through a "*yes, but...*"response; "That's true, *but* it may not work out." When you stick your "but" into your goals you're going to find them unachievable. Confronting the subtle fears also means confronting the *What if...* and "*yes, but...*" in your life.

Changing Reality

Along with your consciousness, your thoughts are the co-creators of your reality. If you have a fear consciousness, no matter how small it may be, you will experience the results of your consciousness. Whatever you perceive on the physical plane was once a thought which had worked its way into your consciousness until it had become a physical manifestation. As soon as it became manifest it was able to be perceived by your physical senses.

All that you perceive in life becomes a direct extension of your consciousness. Whatever your consciousness can accept, you will perceive.

Realities can be created in your life through many means. The main procedures which can create these realities are: 1) your ***creative imagination***; 2) your ***intention***; 3) your ***self-talk***, and 4) ***visual imagery***. All of these will produce effects which will or will not harmonize with your life. Those which harmonize with your life it would best be flowing with. Those which do not, the events that get in your way, are those which you would be better off taking another look at and from which you need to learn.

Your ***creative imagination*** is the architect of reality formation. It was said by Quintilian[7] "For it is feeling and force of imagination that makes us capable."[8] If it was not for creative imagination, that is, imagining something and saying, "Why not?!"[9] then going ahead and bringing it into reality you would not see the incredible discoveries that the whole world is experienced in the 20th and into the 21st centuries. Thanks to great minds like DaVinci, Newton, Descartes, Poincaré, Einstein, Durac, Bell, and Hawking as well as the futurists such as H.G. Wells, Jules Verne, Isaac Asamov, and even Gene Roddenberry you would not be looking at a future that places humans in the stars and among the gods. Imagination is a most powerful tool for change. For imagination to work best it must be tempered with reality. Untempered imagination is fantasy and fantasy tends to be nothing more than an egocentric desire to place yourself into a position of power and control. For imagination to be most effective there needs to be guidelines to follow. These guidelines are:

1. ***Imagine by using all of your senses***. Remember that your brain does not know the difference between a physical

7 Marcus Fabius Quintilianus born c. 35 C.E.

8 "Pectus est enim, quod disertos facit."

9 As George Bernard Shaw stated: "Some men see things as they are and say 'why' — I dream things that never were and say 'why not'." Later John F. Kennedy echoed these same words.

event or one that is going on in your brain so make sure that you bring all of your mental senses into play. See yourself in the most compelling and motivating way immersed in your goal. Hear what you will be telling yourself about your achieving of your goal. Feel what it feels like to be successful and achieving what you want to achieve. This is what has been referred to as acting "*as if*" you have achieved your goal.

2. ***The goals that you set need to be realistic***. Many people who get little or no response with their achievement program often have unrealistic goals. Why? Because they do not have the skills, the education or the knowledge, or they have no goals at all nor the motivation to achieve their goals. They expect the universe to somehow magically manifest everything for them without doing anything. An example encountered by the author was a young man who announced that he was going to become a world famous rock star. When questioned if he knew anything about music he said, "No." He was then directed with the comment: "If you want to be a rock star you had better start there." This young man was expecting something to happen "out of the blue" so that he could somehow achieve his fantasy. He apparently had no concept that in the music industry it is necessary to have a working knowledge of music nor did he have any plan for achieving his objective.

There is a big difference between what you really need and what your ego wants. Often you will hear someone say or you may say that you want to do a specific thing, to become a well-known personality, or to gain a lot of money and give some seemingly altruistic reason for the goal. In virtually every instance the reason given for this achievement is nothing more than a rationalization. Most often those who want to have fame and fortune is because of an inferiority complex. It is felt that if there were millions of adoring fans or the power that money supposedly gives that would be all that is necessary in order to feel good about one's self and be a worthwhile person. This is not true. If you need "things" on the outside to make you feel good about yourself then you are identifying yourself with the "things." Once you have done this you have effectively made yourself an object. As an object you have no feelings. How you will deal with others is exactly the same way that you deal with yourself. Others will be objects to be manipulated and discarded whenever their use is completed.[i]

The ego wants things. It wants objects with which to identify itself. What you, or anyone else for that matter, really need is to be comfortable in life. This means to be respected and cared for by others and to respect and care for others and to have enough money coming in that you do not have to concern yourself about any large problems and still have enough to pay all of your bills and be able to enjoy life. It is your ego that wants obscene amounts of money, adulation, large mansions on the hill and expensive cars.

On a smaller scale, consider the difference between what you really need and what your ego wants. As an example: there are many college students who just *have* to get their degree at a particular time. For some reason they think that they are going to be missing something if they get it later. The added stress encountered by forcing themselves to work harder tends to cause them to make mistakes and not learn as well as they could. What is the difference if they get their degree at one time or a semester or two later? Only a few months, that is the difference. Why do they put themselves through such aggravation to satisfy some egocentric ideal? What generally happens is that this stress and pressure will continue long after the graduation and this stress can be taken into the family and into the job.

For our purposes here the ego will be defined as all of those "I ams…" that you identify yourself with and to which you are emotionally attached. In essence, it is ***any emotionally-charged identification where you feel that if you would lose it you would feel that part of you has been taken away***. Some people are emotionally attached to their car. This car is an extension of them. Others are emotionally attached to money. Still others have attached themselves emotionally to their job. With these people if ever they would lose that object they would lose their identity. They would have no idea anymore who they are and they might sink into depression or would emotionally strike out at anyone or anything that is near. This kind of attachment sometimes occurs in families. Parents sometimes become so attached to their children that they live their lives vicariously through the children. Then, when the children leave home the parents sink into a depression. This is called the "empty-nest syndrome." If you find yourself feeling angry or fearful or depressed or "empty" whenever you think about the loss of that particular object, you are emotionally identifying with it. With the emotional attachment you are the one who has lost control. This thing now controls you.[10] With the ego wanting more and more your real needs become secondary. This is because of the identification that the ego makes with the object. It is a *"have-to-have"* identification in order to serve the ego. Once you have lost control virtually all of your choices will be based on an incomplete view of reality. Many people build the rest of their reality around a fantasy that is part of the emotional attachment. So the person attached to money, for example, will do *anything* to acquire more money than could ever possibly be used and act *as if* everyone is an object to be used toward their own ends. As you can see, egocentered emotional identifications create the objectification of others and this objectification reduces the guilt that can be experienced when another person is purposefully abused to get your own ends.

3. ***For a goal to be realistic it must be achievable and something that you are capable of doing***. Do you have

10 How many people are so attached to their cell phone that they *have to have* it with them and switched on constantly because they just *have to* be in touch with *all* of their friends *all* of the time. There's a big difference between needing the cell phone due to business and the social need that most cell phone subscribers have.

the skill, education or training and experience necessary to achieve your goal? High achievers, researchers have found, take stock of their abilities and so on and do whatever they *need* to in order to reach the level of success that they desire. This means that the high achiever will take responsibility to take charge of his or her life in order to get what is wanted *without* interfering with anyone else. They will gather all of the necessary information before making a decision and make the decision based on the future. The low achievers are the ones who will abuse, manipulate and take advantage of others to get what they want. They will take the big risks because they're looking at the present: "What can I do to get what *I* want *now*?"

4. ***Positive action makes things happen***. This is one step beyond positive thinking. To accomplish your goal you need to *really* want it. Your intention and motive for wanting your goal will strongly affect and influence the end result. Attach to this the desire and passion that you have for loving what you are doing and you are fueling the action process and promoting the successful achievement of your goal.

An important aspect of positive action is *motivation*. This means that one activity leads to another, which leads to another, which eventually leads to the accomplishing of your goal. Consequently, every activity becomes a motivator for the next activity until, in a step-by-step fashion, you succeed. This is called *chaining*. To accomplish this you have to stay focused on your goal keeping it *clearly* in mind.

Wanting to do too many things can cause muddled thinking and confusion. In order to accomplish something you need to know *precisely* what you want. In order to achieve your goal stay focused on that goal *only*. With a lack of clarity in your thoughts you tend to get exactly what your thoughts have expressed.

There is a difference between what you *want* to do and what you would *like* to do. Whenever you want to do something you have that little urge that compels you to go on and it feels good. Wanting to do something has its own innate emotional counterpart as well as motivators and is clear, focused and consistent. This is because it is based on a loving response. Liking to do something is temporary and unfocused and has little or no emotion, a somewhat negative emotion, or the wrong emotion around it. It is not something that you would stay with for long and unconsciously you realize this. In fact, it is not even a means to an end. It is just a passing fancy — more appropriately, a fantasy. Consequently, you change your mind even before you have made up your mind and completed seeing your intents begin to gel.

The late mythologist, Joseph Campbell, put it this way: "Follow your bliss." Your bliss is the desire and passion, that deep inner *urge* that comes not from doing things for yourself but from the joy received from using your talents and abilities for *serving* and *giving* to others. Your bliss is what you can *give* and it is through this giving that you receive. There is a wonderful example of a young person who is following his dream, this bliss, in the person of Tiger Woods, the golfer. As a young child he loved the game of golf ever since his father first put a golf club in his hands. His drive, his urge, his passion was playing golf. His love of the game is so great that many of the seasoned professionals have commented on how Tiger Woods has breathed a breath of fresh air into the game. Tiger Woods' attitude toward the game is that it is important just to be playing it. The money is secondary — although he does enjoy that money affords him the pleasure of doing and contributing to the Tiger Woods Foundation. This love and enjoyment for playing golf was seen when at the age of 21 Tiger Woods became the youngest golfer to win the Master's Tournament title with a record score and several years later had won six straight titles placing him among a small number of professional golfers to do so.

If you are following your bliss you will be doing and being what you *love* to do. In reality, not everyone is going to be famous or rich. Not everyone's "bliss" has to do with notoriety or wealth. Your bliss may be that of being wonderful parents. Maybe your bliss is to be an excellent cook or excellent automobile mechanic or excellent teacher. Your bliss is created by being and doing something you *love* and when you *love* something you will do it so well that it is a gift to the world.

5. ***You need to have a systematic pattern to reach your goal***. What this means is that it is important to have a plan for achieving what you want to achieve. Expecting things to fall in place is unrealistic. Look at what you need to do in order to achieve what it is that you want to achieve. What steps do you need to take? What things do you need to do? What talents and abilities do you have now that can help you to achieve your goal and what ones will you need to develop in order to make your goal a reality? What time limits have you set? These are only some of the questions necessary for you to consider when setting goals.

6. ***You need to be able to clearly define your goal***. That is, you must know exactly what it is you want to achieve and what it will be like having accomplished your goal. In order to do this list all of the things that you will be seeing, hearing and feeling with your goal accomplished. Doing this gives you direction and motivation.

If you are truly interested in accomplishing a specific goal it is necessary that you invest the time and energy into setting yourself up to accomplish it. In order to have this change occur you need to work scientifically. One of the most important abilities you have available to you is your ability to focus your mind on one particular thing. The brain does this naturally, but only for brief periods of time. You can control that natural process. Whenever you are daydreaming, or reading a book or the newspaper, or watching a film or program on television or watching your child play and during this time you are undisturbed, you are focused. Like the scientist, as you are focusing on your goal you exclude from your thoughts those things which can interfere with the accomplishing of your goal. Consequently, the most important thing to begin with is a clear idea of your goal so that you know what your goal is and what it is not. In this way you can focus the appropriate thought/ emotion energy in the correct way on your goal.

Interestingly enough, the scientific method for doing research is a very good pattern to follow for achieving goals. There are seven steps in the scientific method. The first step is that of ***observation***. The scientist will observe the objective reality to find out what needs to be clarified or understood. In your life you will observe to see what is happening that is going well and what is not going well. Your observation needs to be, just as the scientist's, objective and unbiased. From this observation it would be wise to make a list of the things that you want to change. Then you need to prioritize the list and find what is of immediate importance. The second step that the scientist does is to ***define the problem***. This is a statement of what was observed. What you will do is precisely and clearly state what is to change. For example, if it is money state precisely how much money is required to do what you need to do: Be careful to keep egocentric attitudes out of it. The third step of the scientist is to ***hypothesize***. An hypothesis is a statement of cause/effect. Here you state what it is that you want. Be exact. If you are too general you can in many instances have a problem. If, for example, you are seeking a loving relationship, list all of the desirable traits of your desirable mate. Get your ego out of the picture and look at the type of individual who will *harmonize* best with you, not boost your ego.[11] The fourth step is doing ***research***. The scientist will look into previous studies to find if anything else was done in the field and from it will be able to modify the present study. What you will do is to look at yourself; your talents, skills, abilities, education, strong and weak points and so on. List them and find which can be utilized most effectively and efficiently in the accomplishing of your goal. Look also at what you have

11 Obviously you're not going for the "trophy."

accomplished before and how you did it. This can give you an idea of what inner capabilities you have that work. The fifth step is to ***design the experiment***. The scientist needs to take into account all of the previous experiments that were done as well as any variables that can interfere with the experiment and in finding a clear answer. You will take your talents, abilities, skills and so on and list how they will help you accomplish your goal. List also in a step-by-step manner what you are going to do to get to where you want to be. Design your visual imagery, your affirmations and the emotions that you will use and exactly how you are going to use them. Remember, time is important. You need to include the period of time that you will be doing your experiment. The sixth step is to ***conduct the experiment***. Bring all of the data together with your experimental design and conduct your program for the period of time that you will have decided to do it. Do your visual imagery, your affirmations and imbue all of this with the emotional counterparts you are using. This will give you an idea of what works and what does not. In the last step the scientist will ***look at the results and theorize*** about how well his experiment worked and what it means. What you will do is to look at how far you got with the techniques that you used; looking at what worked and what needs to be modified and making the appropriate changes so that you can get what you want. Remember, any goal-directed working is an *experiment*. You have no idea what will work nor how well. If you get what appears to be no results an important check is to look inside at your intents. Look to see how strongly your ego is involved in your goal.

The Seven Postulates

You will notice that goal achieving is not simply positive thinking. Positive thinking is part of the process and it does have some advantages. When correctly done it can *direct* you to pay closer attention to the things that are working in your life. Another advantage is that positive thinking can keep you focused on a goal that you want to achieve and you can be more accepting of others, yourself and the experiences that come your way. Positive thinking is a way to begin to form different attitudes toward those things that previously caused problems.

Every time that you commit yourself to making a specific change you set the wheels of nature in motion. The important point here is that you *commit* yourself. Without that commitment you are blowing smoke into the wind. Commitment involves intent and every true intent is an act of will-power. It does not matter what it is you want to do, once you stick to your commitment you have empowered your will.

Nature is constantly changing. By taking advantage of this natural process of change you can connect yourself to the ebbs and flows of life. Then, as you apply your committed will power you can affect that change into the direction you desire. To do this appropriately you need to consider certain facts:

1. ***You will accomplish only those things that you have the talents, abilities, skills, and knowledge to accomplish***. If you are attempting to gain something that is beyond your potential you are going to be quite unhappy with the results. You may gain the goal but you will be extremely disappointed in it and, most likely, in yourself.[12]

2. ***By using your talents, abilities, skills, and knowledge you can get into the flow of the direction of highest probability in the Universe***. This means that you will be able to accomplish whatever you set out to do using your talents, abilities, skills, and knowledge. As an example, not everyone who plays a sport in college can become a professional. You can still work in the sport by coaching and teaching others. Your knowledge may help some younger player achieve his goal and your example can be an inspiration for others.

---

12 There's an axiom that says: "There are two times that you become disappointed in life; when you don't get what you want — and when you do!"

3. ***You can only use your capabilities***. You can build on what you have by using the skills you have doing one thing and applying them to another. This comes from the ability of the brain to generalize and transfer that training. A simple example is the transferring of the skill of driving a five-speed transmission truck to driving a ten-speed eighteen-wheeler truck. It is the same principle. All you need to do is know where the gears are and how and when to shift. When it comes to gaining your goals, if you have a system that works to help you get one kind of goal (e.g. money), use the same (or similar) techniques on another goal (e.g. success) and check your results. It is in this way that you are using what you know.

4. ***A great advantage for accomplishing any goal is to know how much of your egocentric desires are involved***. The greater the ego involvement, the less likely you will be satisfied with the outcome. People who are dissatisfied with what they have will do one of several things: give up and go for nothing, or strike out at those whom they believe have what they do not, or want to have more without regard of how is was gained.

5. ***Any energy in the Universe is capable of being transformed into any other kind of energy***. One law of physics states that energy can neither be created nor destroyed; only transformed. Since there is an inexhaustible supply of energy available you can take advantage of it. As in the previous example, if you were not able to become a professional in a particular sport you take that energy and redirect it into another area. You may become a teacher in high school or college and coach the sport, or you may volunteer your time to coach Little League baseball, Peewee football, or any other form of the sport.

6. ***You are limited only by the choices that you make.*** Your choices are directed by your beliefs, your values and attitudes and your personal identifications. These are things that you learned from others. In order to allow yourself the freedom to make changes you will find it advantageous to confront your beliefs, values, attitudes and identifications. They will show you the limitations that others have placed on your life. After you have dealt with those limitations, confront your fears. This will help you to break those patterns of self-destruction, self-doubt, self-sabotage and immobility.

7. ***Everything that you do is an*** **experiment**. Many people have the mistaken idea that whenever they set a goal that it *must* happen. If it does not, either there is something wrong with them or that the Universe (or God or whatever) deems it inappropriate for them. If you realize that all you are doing is what a scientist does, you will have *feedback* from which to work.[13] This feedback is the most important part of your goal-setting. It tells you what works and what does not. It gives you direction for future goals. It tells you what to change, when and what goals are achievable. It will also give you valuable information on what you are doing that can interfere with what you are doing. In essence, feedback can tell you *how* to get your goals.

These seven postulates are what the ancient mystics and medieval alchemists and magicians learned after many years of study and experimentation. This is what modern scientists, both cognitive neuroscientists studying the brain and theoretical physicists studying the action of atoms are finding out using modern technology. This is what you can use as well. By applying yourself you can achieve worthwhile goals.

---

13 Richard Bandler, co-developer or Neuro-linguistic Programming has stated: "There is no such thing as failure; only feedback."

Your ***intent*** is the blueprint for the creation of your reality. You will recall that intent, not belief, is the initial step toward accomplishing your goal. Intent is a directed act of will. It is more than focused attention although it involves focused attention. You have most likely had the experience of wanting something or wanting to accomplish something and achieving it. It may be a minor thing but that does not matter. What was the process that you used? There is a high probability that you did not just say, "I'd like to have this," and it came about. You most likely followed a completed process and this process led up to achieving your goal. The final step was the statement. The first step was the intent. In between you put together everything that was necessary in order to insure success.

Your intent is not the same as your belief. Although there are some similarities, they are not the same thing. Beliefs invariably include unrealistic, untenable and irrational ideas, concepts and philosophies. Beliefs are no more than **opinions which are acted upon *as if* they are real**. They are, in most instances, *fantasies* that you *hope*, through faith, will manifest.

The opposite of belief is not unbelief or disbelief. It is knowledge. When you have knowledge of something you do not have to hope for its manifestation. It is real. Knowledge of the existence of something gives it the power for manifestation. The difference between belief and knowledge can be seen this way: Consider the color blue. What do you believe about the color blue" You may answer something like, "I like it. It is relaxing." Or "It energizes me," or "I feel down when I see it." These are all subjective *opinions* based not upon actual knowledge or on facts. Knowledge of the color blue involves *facts*. The color blue being part of the electromagnetic spectrum is a fact. It is also a fact that the color blue is 500 millimicrons in the visible spectrum. A further fact is that the color blue is one of the three primary colors. These are facts about the color blue. These are all part of the reality of what makes up life. Beliefs, like opinions, are formed when, few, if any, of the facts are in. They are based on limited, and often no, experience. If you have a limited experience of or have not fully analyzed something in order to try to make sense out of it beliefs will be formed. These beliefs then become part of the *assumptions* made about life.[ii] Remember, Alfred Korzybski, the founder of General Semantics, said: "People form beliefs when they do not know what is real."

Mental representations are *realistic* ideas and thoughts which have been constructed and contemplated upon. The more they have been considered the greater their capacity for being manifest. Unlike beliefs, which can be about anything, mental representations have a basis in reality and direct sensory experience. They are those things which both the conscious and unconscious minds realize have the actual potential for manifesting. Mental representations are not those things that you "just know." Those things that you "just know" are beliefs. Unless something can be proven on a physical level you do not know it. Essentially, if you have a belief about something you really don't know.

Self-talk is the third method to assist in creating reality. It is the mortar and nails for the formation of your experience. What you say to yourself helps build the mental representations that you already have. The more that you tell yourself something the greater the chance for it to become manifest. You have seen that there are two types of self-talk. The first type is that of *undirected self-talk*. These are the meandering thoughts that have little or no meaning and most often have no emotion behind them at all. The other type of self-talk is the *directed self-talk*. These are the statements which form the basis of your perception of reality. They are the statements which have an *emotional attachment* to them. These are the statements that you listen to and make manifest in your life. If, for example, you were told that you were a failure and would never succeed, after a long period of time of being bombarded by that idea you will come to accept it as a reality. Then, every time you had the opportunity to succeed you would undermine your success and would prove the statement correct. The major key to the power of the directed self-talk is the emotional attachments to the statement. Further, just changing your self-talk and the emotions does not at all change the experience from the past. What you need to do is to look into your past purposely looking for examples that prove the opposite and begin to build from there with a different emotional experience and different mental representations for the future. Only then will you be able to make the changes you need in order to succeed.

The last way to recreate reality is through ***visual imagery***. The building blocks for reality formation are seen in visual imagery. Every statement that you make indeed every word that you say carries with it visual images. By paying close attention to the words that you use you can redirect your visual images. By changing what you are seeing your future to be you can redirect your words changing your experience. For many years metaphysicians and mystics have been saying that the brain does not know the difference between a real or imagined event. Only within the past forty or so years has this been shown to be true. With the advent of CAT and PET scans and MRI has science proved this to be true. It is no longer a belief; it is a fact that *functional visual imagery* affects the brain *as if* it were actually being experienced. The thing to remember is that even with functional visual imagery both the conscious and unconscious know when something is realistic[iii] and it is this knowledge that will bring about the manifesting of your conceptualization.

Finding Synchronicity

Ideally, your behaviors should harmonize with your living experiences. Quite often, they do not. When they do not they are *getting in your way* and prevent you from having a positive relationship with yourself and your life. When your behaviors are out of harmony with your life you develop psychological, emotional, mental and eventually physical problems. You, then, on the level of the physical reality, experience frustration, emotional pain, mental anguish and other physical symptoms (e.g. stuttering or excessive "heart-burn"). At this point you are out of alignment with your original intent and with the expression of the Universe which you are.

Whenever you have the consciousness that there is something missing from your life all of your experiences will verify that consciousness. Your perception of reality will be one of constant lack and you will attempt to compensate for that lack by one (or more) of several means: 1) You will accept it and *generalize* the lack from one area of life to many or all areas of your life; 2) *Give up* and claim that it is your lot in life (or in the stars or some other rationalization) to be lacking; 3) *Become angry and hostile* toward anyone you believe is not lacking and strike out at them; 4) You may *attempt to remove yourself from the problematic situation*; or 5) *Become determined to overcome your limitations* through constructive methods. Some people have to go through the first three of these operatives before they come to the realization that it is they who is interfering with their life — not someone or something outside of themselves, before they finally do something about the situation.

If you accept your lack and limitation and assume that your whole existence lacks, you set up a pattern for the constant experience of the statement of lack. Whenever you attempt to make changes in your life you will see every one of them fail no matter how hard you try. It is an interesting point to note that trying then becomes your excuse for failing: "Well, I tried." In most instances, you will pursue your attempt no farther than is necessary to fail and will rationalize your conclusion of failure to the degree that you need in order to bring your ego into harmony with your experience. Your reality of constant failure and lack becomes so deeply embedded into your consciousness that your perception of yourself and your life is based on your inability to make positive gains. Created, then, are all of the experiences you need to continue your conception of a disharmonious life.

By striking out toward another due to your own concept of lack you are bringing yourself deeper into the acceptance of the consciousness of lack. The main areas of this striking out are: 1) *Society*, you blame it for your problems; 2) *Philosophies other than your own*, this is an overcompensation of your own lack and fear of another knowing and having something more and better than you and that you do not really believe the ideology you're espousing in the first place; 3) *Others with greater wealth and position*, you blame them for your limitations as if they are holding something back from you; and 4) *Other races, cultures, or groups*, you see them as having more opportunities or possessing something better than you.

Through hostile striking-out you set up the conditions to continue this behavior and its accompanying reality. Once you begin to do this you will always find excuses to continue. You will take your feelings of lack out on other people mainly through illegal and antisocial acts. This can be through pimping and prostitution (so-called "victimless" crimes), to embezzlement, accepting bribes or "special favors" or "perks" as politicians do, and all the way to assault and murder.

There are other acts which have hostile intent and are also a means of striking-out such as purposely taking advantage of, intimidating and manipulating others for personal gain and position, or constantly setting yourself up for an emotional fall. The latter may seem unlikely to be a hostile act, remember, all emotions are inwardly directed and that *any* hostile act is hostile toward oneself.

The most positive and constructive method of dealing with your feelings of lack and limitation is to begin by reframing the idea of lack: What may be a lack can be a means of gain in another area. You can always learn from your experience. For each "failure" brings you one step closer to success — if you look at the "failure" as *feedback* and reframe what was called "failure" as simply *being unsuccessful*. You have the potential to become a fully functioning human being but it is your acceptance of the limitations placed on you as being permanent which blocks this potential. When you put yourself into a position to grow from what seems to be failure you then open yourself up to the many possibilities of expression available.

You were born to become great — but great in your own way. You were raised in such a way as to see your own limitations. You were told who you were, what you could do, why you were here and what to expect from life. Then, all of your experiences gave you verification for those teachings.[14] From this training you would perceive your whole existence as based on your accepted experience.

Your reality does not have to be what you see at this present time. By viewing reality in this manner you limit yourself to certain experiences when the Universe is unlimited in its expression and potential. The problem then becomes one of getting into a more positive relationship with the Universe. Put into a question the problem is: How can you get more from life without getting in your own way or imposing upon another?

What you are attempting to do is to set up what is termed *positive synchronous patterns* which will direct and bring you to the right place at the right time. You have been trained to experience a lot of negative synchronicity and this shows in where you lack, that is, if you can see it and not just complain about it. Most people will see the lack and limitation and not go beyond it. Both positive and negative synchronicity involves what many call *coincidence*. Coincidence can be used to direct you into the proper area. Positive or negative these events can be meaningful — if you work with them.

You are an expression of the Universe and are here to express that part of the Universe which you are. You are compelled to express yourself in a certain way but are not forced to do so. Your *existence* is blueprinted — but your free will varies that pattern.

This is not predestination. The doctrine of predestination states that you have your whole life predetermined and that no

14 This verification came from the fact that all you expected of yourself was what you were taught and that is all you saw being reflected in your life. Anything to the contrary was not noticed or discarded.

matter what you do or what happens, this is all part of that plan. No concept of free will or personal responsibility is considered in predestination. You have the potential to express that aspect of the Universe which you are but in most instances you do not. The first culprit which limits your expression is being born. As soon as you were made flesh you took on limitations.[15] Simply by looking at the limitations of the senses you can see this. Your body slows down the potential of the Universe to an unimaginable rate. It is something like watching a three-and-a-half hour motion picture one frame per minute. This makes it extremely difficult to try to figure out what is happening. The constant change in the Universe is almost imperceptible due to the innate limitations of your senses.

Second, you are limited by your early family conditioning. You will tend to stay in the same social patterns and have marriages which are similar, by virtue of the behavior of yourself and your mate, to your parents'. Your thinking is based and biased by your early conditioning in the family.

The third limiting factor to the expression of experience of the Universe is the society itself. This includes the laws and regulations placed on the members of the society and all of the social institutions involved and incorporated in the society. Each of these controls of your behavior also limits your thinking, your experience and your expression.

The forth limitation is that which is placed on your free will and probably the free will itself. Your free will is a free expression of your existence based on your physical being. It must be understood that as long as you have a physical body of any sort free will is limited. The limitations placed on your free will are a combination of all of the aforesaid limitations. Consequently, you may talk of free will and the freedom to choose but these freedoms are limited.

---

15 Assuming, of course that the body places you in a position of limiting your experience of the Universe.

The fifth culprit which limits your expression is your consciousness. Your consciousness is mainly molded from your experiences of yourself, your environment and your previous training and that is the reality which you will perceive. Consciousness is at the basis of your whole existence and consciousness is the director of your reality. Since you are consciously aware of only a small number of things at a time what you are conscious of limits being conscious of other things at the same time. Much of your experience of consciousness is based on what you choose to perceive at a particular time and your present choices are based on your past conscious choices.

Either you or someone you know has had the experience of nothing seemingly going right. In these instances statements like: "Why does this *always* happen to me?" or "Why do I *always* do this?" or "I knew I *shouldn't have* done it" are heard. A period when things are going wrong; you seem to be running into the "wrong" people, and nothing seems to be in harmony, is generally called "bad luck." More precisely, it is termed *negative synchronicity*.[16] Through this process you are being told that you are not following the blueprint of your Universal expression. During this time you do a lot of rationalizing and making excuses and blaming others but tend to not look into yourself for the reasons why.

Probably the greatest reason for negative synchronicity is your own *ego*. Once you get into the process of placating your ego you begin to lose track of your real self. You will then attempt to satisfy ego wants over true needs. You will control, coerce, intimidate and, in many ways, impose yourself and your egocentric desires on to others. Maybe some material gains will be made at the expense of your self-concept, which you will modify to suit your choices, but deep inside you know that the behavior was inappropriate. You know this because in spite of material gains you experience unhappiness, loss and failure in other areas of your life. It could be in health, emotions with relationships, or mental

16 This is a reframe.

with anxieties and fears. In other words, you are getting in your own way when you are experiencing negative synchronicity. The longer you continue the egocentric path the more uncomfortable become your experiences.

Another reason for negative synchronicity is your belief system. If you believe yourself to be only one thing you will continue to experience all of the experiences related to that belief.[17] Much of what you believe about yourself is a direct extension of your early training with, of course, later learned modifications. Unfortunately, much of this early training is negative in concept and construction. Consequently, your experiences due to these early years will have negative patterns with emotions attached to them.

You can get into patterns of positive synchronicity. You can experience the so-called coincidences which are termed "lucky." By paying close attention to the negative patterns you can begin to see a positive direction. Remember, these coincidences are there to aim and direct you. You can, as a matter of fact, set up your own synchronous patterns. You can attract to you the people and conditions which are positively directed and more in harmony with your blueprint for life. Having something in mind which does not follow this blueprint brings about negative synchronicity. If you follow this blueprint precisely, or as closely as possible, you will not get in your way or impose yourself on to any other person's existence. You will generalize positive direction in all areas of your life not just in some areas.

Negative synchronicity will be seen whenever you gain in one or two areas of your life at the expense of other people or at the expense of your own feelings of self-worth. This negative synchronicity can come in as simple a form as that of feeling that you *have to have* certain things, having to manipulate and control

---

17 Most people are unable to separate the action from the actor even in themselves. So, when someone says, "I am a teacher" he/she fails to understand that the statement just made was an identification. "Teacher" is something that a person does. It is not who he/she actually is.

others and conditions to get what you want, the fear of making choices, stubbornness, arrogance, narcissism, intolerance and a myriad of other daily behaviors that cause yourself or others problems.

The first step into setting up more of life's harmonious experiences involves a bit of soul-searching. Initially, you need to go back in time, in your mind of course, to when everything was going well. There are instances which you will have experienced that are examples of moving in a positive direction. Analyze them by asking yourself these questions:

1. What was happening?
2. What was the direction that I was going?
3. What was my state of mind?
4. What were my attitudes toward myself and my life?
5. How was I approaching each new experience?
6. What is (are) the reason(s) I was doing what I was doing?
7. What was I seeing myself to be?
8. What were my identifications of myself?

If you have a problem finding a time when everything was going well then you need to build up an experience. This you can do by asking yourself these questions:

1. What do I do that gives me a feeling of accomplishing? Am I successful in a sport or in the ability to learn or in drawing and painting or some other art form?
2. What about that gives me the feeling of accomplishing? Is it the planning of the project, executing of it or completing the project that gives me these good feelings?
3. What is my state of mind when I decide to do a project?
4. What is my state of mind as I am doing a project?

5. What is my state of mind as soon as and after I have completed a project? How do I feel days, weeks or months after a project has been completed?
6. How do I feel about myself during each portion of a project: beginning, during, completing and after completing it?
7. What do I see my life to be like before, during, completing and after completing a project?
8. How do I identify myself before, during, completing and after completing a project?

After you have finished doing the questioning what you need to do is to take those positive feelings and identifications and attach them to the present. In this manner you will be bringing the successful feelings into what you want to do now.

The next thing to do is to get into the reasons for setting up synchronous patterns:

1. What are the reasons that I want what I want?
2. Do I know what my real needs are?
3. Do I know what my ego wants?
4. What does my ego want?
5. What do I want from myself?
6. What do I want from my life?
7. What do I think I deserve from life?
8. What do I believe about myself?
9. What do I believe myself to be?
10. What is reality to me?

These are some of the necessary questions to begin to straighten out the disharmonious patterns being experienced. The first and most important thing is the negating of the desires of the ego. It is the ego which blocks most of your expression and your ego is the most difficult aspect of your self that you must overcome.

Another good method of looking at yourself is by keeping a dream diary. Dreams show you what is going on inside of yourself in a symbolic form. It is an excellent aid for self-discovery. When it comes to understanding the meanings of your dreams, those dream dictionaries are of literally no use because researchers have found that the majority of dreams seem to deal with every day matters. What you need to do is to ask yourself questions about your dreams. These questions include:

1. What was the dream that I had? Describe it in as full detail as possible.
2. What were the major symbols in the dream? List them.
3. What do the symbols mean to me? State them.
4. What do the symbols mean in the context of the dream? Replace the symbols with my meanings for the symbols.
5. What is the dream telling me about myself and/or my life?

After you have gotten sufficiently deeply into yourself and your life to see the games you are playing with yourself, your life and with others you can begin to understand the difference between what you realistically need and what your ego desires. You will then be able to set about to affect your present experience.

You have been trained to look at and for the most negative things that you can find and experience. Now it is time to turn that around and begin to see the most positive aspects in your life. Initially, when you begin to look for the most positive things you will notice the negative even more. With a little self-trickery you can begin to notice the good things which occur.

From Asia there are a few things that you can do to direct your day. One of the ideas which predominate throughout many ancient cultures and philosophies is that there are negative energies which become active at night. When the sun rises, these energies are banished. This is obviously a hold-over from the time when small bands of early humans gathered around the camp fires for protection from nocturnal predators. In the morning these animals would go back to their lairs to sleep. Certain simple rituals can be performed in the morning in order to remove the "influence" of these "energies." The first one is quite simple. All that is necessary is immediately upon arising laugh heartedly. The ancient belief is that the laughter "scares" the influences of these energies away and, of course, there is the old adage that laughter makes the heart lighter. Today we know that laughter releases both endorphins, which are natural mood elevators, and t-cells, the natural protection killer cells enhancing your immune system.

Another very old method is that of deep breathing. Among the Chinese it is believed that as soon as you wake up in the morning you should take 100 slow, deep breaths. This will give you a long life and make you strong and healthy.

From India comes another breathing exercise for the morning (and anytime during the day for that matter). This is out of the breath control system known as pranayama. There are many ways to do this but the simplest can be the most effective. This method involves an inhalation, a retention and exhalation of the breath done with a 1:2:1 ratio of inhalation, retention, and exhalation. What you will do is inhale saying to yourself a mantra or affirmation to a one count;[18] retain your breath using your mantra or affirmation for twice the inhalation; then release your breath using your mantra or affirmation for the same count as the inhalation. This breathing exercise is done for about twenty to thirty minutes at each sitting. You may want to do what is called "alternate nostril breathing" along with this. One round of breathing is a 1:2:1 in each nostril. Using the alternate nostril breathing exercise balances the left and right hemispheres of the brain.

---

18 If your affirmation is short your "one count" may be six (more or less) repetitions of the statement. That would equal the one count.

Another way of positively charging your day is through meditation. This can be done simply by getting out of your bed and sitting in a straight-back chair, closing your eyes, taking a deep breath and *vibrating* a simple mantra. To vibrate a mantra means to place it about an octave lower than your normal speaking voice. In this way you will feel the vibration of your voice throughout your body. The most popular is the *OM* (pronounced AUM).[19] Feel your whole body vibrate with the mantra but the areas of the greatest vibration should be felt in the center of the forehead, the solar plexus and the base of the spine.

There is also something that can be said for morning and evening prayers or affirmations (affirmations will be discussed more fully later). The concept behind morning and evening prayers stems from the ancient belief of negative entities becoming active with the setting of the sun. The morning prayers are believed to chase their influences away in order to conduct a positive day and the evening prayers are for protection from these influences while asleep.

Prayers and meditations are the same. Both are designed to place your mind into a greater state of awareness and a higher level of conscious awareness. With prayers, unemotional repetitions of pre-written words are wasting your time. For prayers to have meaning and to get any kind of results it is best if you: 1) make them up yourself; 2) state them with feeling; 3) be positive throughout; 4) forget about bargaining, coercion or manipulating of any sort; 5) feel positive after you have finished; and 6) be accepting of whatever transpires. From this point you can control your life and thus not be ruled by externals.

In reality, as an enlightened person you do not believe that there are these negative entities and energies of which their influences come alive at the setting of the sun. Many of these old ideas came from a time when many believe that there were influences outside of the self which control life. Misfortune had to be caused by something outside whether good or evil and obviously the evil

19 AUM (אום) is one of the 72 names of God according to Hebrew mysticism.

wondered around at night for everything, even the most familiar things, take on an eerie appearance in the dark.

As you can see, you are starting from the very basic concepts that you have accepted and began breaking them down and reconditioning yourself to having a new reality. To begin this new reality probably the most important part is to commit yourself to the change and stick to that commitment. This is probably the most important part. Much of your experience of "bad luck" stems from the lack of any real commitment or being committed to the wrong things. Beyond that, you lose out due to the fact that you are not paying attention to other possibilities and outlets for expression.

So far, you are cleaning out the cobwebs of your mind in the morning with one or more methods. Now you have to keep it up during the day. It is not as difficult as it sounds. Probably the easiest method is to keep a diary or journal.

Many people keeping a diary or journal put in it all kinds of useless and unimportant information (e.g. problems they encounter, what someone did to them, something that happened to them, and so on). In this diary there should be placed *only* problems that you happen to work through and experiences that you dealt with effectively. Things such as how well and differently you handled a situation which usually would have caused frustration or anger, creative ventures which worked out well and those which did not — as long as the reason was known for their not working out — positive changes in relating to others, things done at work and at home that had a positive outcome and what was done to achieve that positive outcome, and positive things and coincidences which occurred. The only time that you place some negative experience in your diary is when you list things that you can do to insure change the next time something similar happens. Once you start this process you will notice that positive synchronous occurrences seem to be happening more often.

Another simple method of continuing the morning process is to have a good detailed picture of yourself surrounded by loving persons and being and doing that which you desire. Whenever a negative experience occurs immediately flash this picture in your mind and the negative influences will soon disappear. Another similar method is to use a positively charged statement that can be invoked whenever a negative situation or feeling happens.

With these little tricks you are setting yourself up to see the best in life. You are also setting yourself up to experience the most positive synchronicity that can direct you toward your total self-expression. In many instances, you will not even pay attention to the things that happen to you or shrug them off as "mere coincidence." When this occurs you are cutting off the direction to your expression.

The discussion always seems to turn to the reality of coincidence whenever synchronicity is mentioned. Is there coincidence; some occurrence at the same time or very near the time that you are thinking of or working toward a certain objective which coincides with that objective, or not?

The term coincidence implies that its occurrence is without basis; that it just "seems" to happen. Take for example Elvis Presley. His mother died at the age of 42 and he said that he would not live beyond that age. In August, eight months after his forty-second birthday, he died. Do events simply happen or is there some sort of reasoning behind them? Whenever you meet a certain person at a certain time, is there some meaning to that meeting or not?

Coincidence is the principle of non-causal or acausal events. It represents an acausal principle in nature.[iv] Nature is seen fundamentally as irrational or governed by chance.[v] Consequently, any event which upsets this irrationality would definitely be something of which to be aware.

There are two kinds of connecting principles in nature: 1) Ordinary causality which the sciences study and is structured linearly in time as cause and effect; and 2) Acausal principles which are structured at "right angles" to causality and structured in space. (Figure 6-1) Synchronous events are related within the logic of the deeper mind,[vi] for it is within the deeper mind where these events take on meaning and from which they are directed.

THE FOUR-DIMENSIONAL CONE OF SPACE-TIME

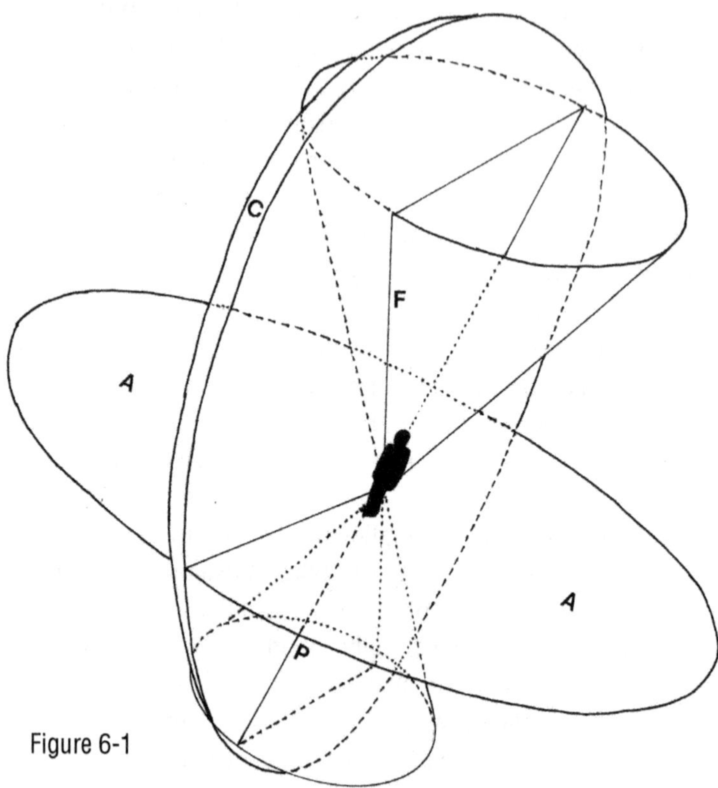

Figure 6-1

Four-dimensional space-time is divided into four regions: 1) The Future (F); 2) The Past (P); 3) Causality (C); and 4) Acausality (A). Causality is seen when the Past and the Future converge at the same time in the Present. Acausality is a thin, flat region lying outside of space and time.

Physicists see synchronicity in terms of quantum potential. It is the interaction between quantum mechanical events that exist outside of space and time. It is a signal given by particles to inform other particles that the probability has been fulfilled. It is an information exchange from the particle level upward. It has been described as a *Superluminal Information Transfer* between particles and events.

There are several things to be considered when discussing

coincidence. First of all, you will remember that the Universe no longer seems like a huge machine but a great thought. All thoughts have some sort of objective or they would not exist. The objective of the Universe is twofold: 1) to express itself, and 2) to experience itself. All physical realities and existences have this at their basis.

Second, the Universe, being a great thought, is a unified whole. All physical existences in the Universe are also unified wholes and reflect the complete Universe.

Third, the main objective of all physical existences in the Universe is to survive and express itself to its fullest and to experience as much of the Universe as it possibly can.

Fourth, in order for the Universe to express itself to the fullest the Universe creates life and it is these innumerable life-forms which do the expressing and experiencing. Each of these life-forms has a specific energy, form, and substance. Each of these forms has its own innate reality and consciousness and they all perceive the Universe in different ways. This specificity is the basis to the blueprint of expression that each form in the Universe has.

Fifth, the Universe aims or directs you toward expressing yourself to the fullest so that it may experience itself to its fullest through you. This direction is the synchronous events which occur in your life. Positive synchronous events say you are on the right track; negative synchronicity says you are out of harmony. Coincidence is, then, not just a perchance happening but an attempt of the Universe to unify itself. Further, there are also a few items to consider within yourself which allow synchronous experiences to occur.

Consider first your consciousness. Whatever level of awareness you have you will express it on your physical reality. Then you must remember that change is the only true constant in the Universe. Anything that forces you to think one way or to remain the same goes against the operations of the Universe and will be dealt with by the Universe. For example, if you get yourself wrapped up in some sort of philosophy which refuses to allow you to think outside of its teachings, to change and to express yourself, you will generally meet with a lot of negative synchronicity. You will assume that you are "meant to suffer" and this is your "trial to prove your faith." This is not true for the intent of the Universe is toward self-expression and experience and not to punish even the most minute part of itself. Besides what reason could there possibly be for the Universe to punish itself? Self-punishment detracts from self-expression and self-experience.

Summary

You need to always allow for change. Nothing remains the same. Nations rise and fall. Empires rise and fall. Religions rise and fall. Gods rise and fall. This is due to the fact that they are all constructions from the mind of human beings. Synchronous occurrences are there to remind you that change is inevitable and that you must change in order to grow and to grow with that change. It gives you the chance to more fully experience and express the Universe and yourself. One thing that even all of the great teachers of meditation have told their students is that a specific mantra and meditation procedure is to be used to take you to a point or level of experience. After that, the mantra and technique must change in order to allow the student to grow. As growth continues, mantras are changed in order to assist in that growing. Consequently, growing and changing become constant.

Since you were blueprinted for success then all you need do is to follow the coincidences which occur in your life. To begin this process, you must clear yourself of the mental, emotional and psychological blocks which hold you back. This will affect your consciousness. Your experience of life is a direct extension of your state of consciousness. Consequently, this sets up your synchronous experiences and coincidences. Whenever you have something in mind which follows your blueprint, you are in the right place at the right time. Whenever you are growing psychologically, emotionally and spiritually you always seem to meet the people who are on the same level from whom you can learn.

Together consciousness and your thoughts co-create your reality. If you have a certain thought in mind which follows the blueprint then positive synchronicity follows. You become directed and motivated toward expressing yourself more fully. Attracting synchronous events is nothing more than the ramifications of your current thought processes. All that you experience is a direct result of your consciousness.

Consider cause and effect. Cause and effect was stated earlier with the Newtonian axiom that with every action there is an equal but opposite reaction. On the Macrocosmic level this is true. It must be remembered that this concept stems from the idea that the Universe is one huge machine. In order to more fully grasp the very basic principles which govern the Universe it is necessary to understand that the concept of equal but opposite action/reaction does not fully fit. Scientists are beginning to understand that on the very mundane level of traditional physics this happens but in the level of particles and energy, concepts of classical physics just do not quite work. In fact, a whole new type of numbering system had to be devised in order to better conceptualize particles. One of the most unsettling findings is that there is *no* pattern or order for what happens at the particle level.[20] Things just happen. So, the order that you perceive is *not* from the Universe at all but from your own consciousness, your beliefs, the way your senses work and the way your brain is organized and perceives its input.

When considering the level of thought you are dealing with very subtle energies: Energies that at this time cannot wholly be measured. But they are energies. There is cause and effect through them. Your thoughts are the controller of your brain and your reality. Your life is a direct extension of your consciousness. It is your thoughts which, if listened to, tell you what your consciousness is.

Whenever you put a thought into your mind for any length of

20 This includes fractals.

time it has certain energies attached to it. As long as you think the thought the energies accumulate behind it. The more you think it or the stronger the thought the more the energies accumulate and the greater the probability of manifestation.

Another thing to remember is that everything, including a thought, is in potential. This means that it can be any number of things. Consequently, each thought has the potential to manifest in innumerable ways. What makes a thought become a particular manifestation is your choice to continually think it into physical actuality. This thought process thus limits its potential.

One of the major facts of nature is that all things or energies eventually return to their source. This goes for plants, animals, minerals, and thoughts. So the energy from the thought will return to the thinker. On its return trip it will have gained in strength and will return with greater force. Science has noticed that this occurs on the atomic level as well. The faster an atom is accelerated the more mass it gains until it approaches the speed of light. Then, as some believe, it will return to energy as it surpasses the speed of light. Not only will it gain in strength on its way out but on its return will gain in mass. Further, the movement of the thought will be directed by the amount of thinking done with regard to the thought.

The Universe is its own cause and effect and you are part of that cause and effect. In order to be able to comprehend its totality the Universe affected perceptible objects all of which affect each other to varying degrees. You, as a small universe, also can affect your existence in order to more fully comprehend your totality. You exert force on your life through your thoughts. There is cause and effect in your daily existence. You can make things happen in many positive ways if you so desire and if your consciousness is geared up for it. Whenever you are moving in the direction that places you in harmony with the Universe then synchronous events occur more often — as also do thinking (causing) and realizing (effect) events, for both to work harmoniously. Cause and effect events depend on your consciousness as does your reality. You cannot affect anything which is foreign to your consciousness, as you cannot perceive anything which is outside of your consciousness. Cause and effect are the result of your consciousness, your thoughts and your intent or will. Synchronicity is the result of the Universal blueprint. Both can be in harmony or they cannot. That is your choice.

Endnotes

i Alexander S. Holub, Ph.D. (2007) **From Victim to Victor! Defeating a Victim's Consciousness**, Bridger House Publications, Inc., Carson City, NV

ii Jennifer A. Whitson and Adam D. Galinsky (3 Oct. 2008) *Lacking Control Increases Illusory Pattern Perception*, **Science**, Vol. 322, Pp. 115-117

iii Anna Abraham and D. Yves von Camaron (Mar. 2009) *Reality=Relevance? Insights from Spontaneous Modulations of the Brain's Default Network when Telling Apart Reality from Fiction*, **PLoS ONE**, Vol. 4, No. 3, e4741

iv R.A. Wilson (Jan. 1982) *Mere Coincidence*, **Science Digest**, Vol. 90, No. 1, P. 82-85, 95

v Gary Zukav (1979) **The Dancing Wu Li Masters**, Bantam Books, New York, NY

vi *Op cit*

The actuality of thought is life.

Aristotle (384-322 BCE)

Chapter 7
Changing Perceptions

How many times have you heard the expression, "You change your mind and you change your life?" Most likely the phrase has lost its meaning because by this time you have changed your mind about quite a few things but your life is still the same. Changing your mind obviously involves more than just saying "no" when you usually say "yes." For change to have any meaning you need to have a deeper understanding of not only the brain and its workings but also how you construct your reality. For this understanding you need to be familiar with the nature of the self and its relationship to different states and dimensions of reality.

Many Realities

You live in many realities at the same time. It is often difficult to understand this for all you perceive is the 3-dimensions of the 5-sensed physical reality that you deal with every day. Science recognizes different realities and calls them *dimensions* or *universes*. From this point we will use the term dimension to describe any one or number of these realities.

You are familiar with the dimensions of length, width and height. Length, width and height are the controlling aspects of your physical sense world. Science goes beyond these realities and adds to them the dimension of *space-time*. The dimension of space-time, the fourth dimension, lies at a right angle to the three-dimensional world. (Figure 7-1) Consequently, those who view the Universe through the eyes of 3-dimensions see such a small portion of their existence. Adding a fourth dimension broadens the whole spectrum of possibilities. One of the reasons for the considerable use of symbol and allegory in ancient text, story, legend and myth is an attempt to get a better understanding of the dimensions beyond those of the physical senses. There are realities which are beyond even the fourth dimension.

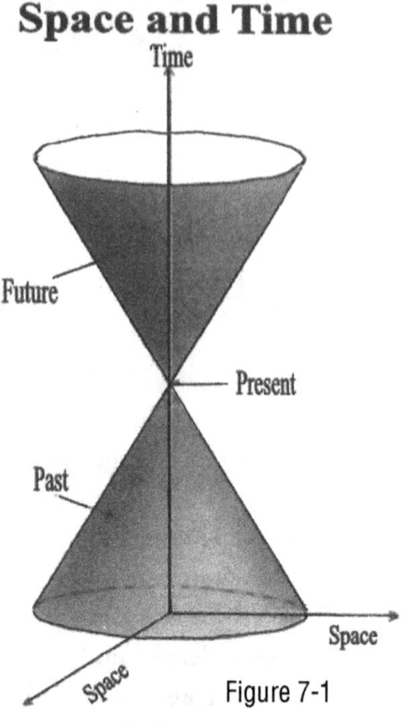

Figure 7-1

These, for the most part, remain unnamed mainly because they are totally unfathomable to us. In the current Chaos studies this incomprehensibility is seen as natural, uncontrolled formations referred to as fractals. You have seen fractals in the evening newscasts. Whenever the weather is forecast and the image appears to fly down across the local area, these images are created with fractals. Whenever a space probe sends back radar images of a planet's surface and you see the mountains, valleys and crevasses those images are fractals. A fractal is a way of measuring the degree of irregularity or irregular patterns of real objects. This degree of irregularity remains constant. That is, the real world is regularly irregular. There are computer programs that can generate fractals.[i] What these programs do is generate images based on the highest probability. It is actually no different than your own programming. You think certain thoughts, you visualize images,

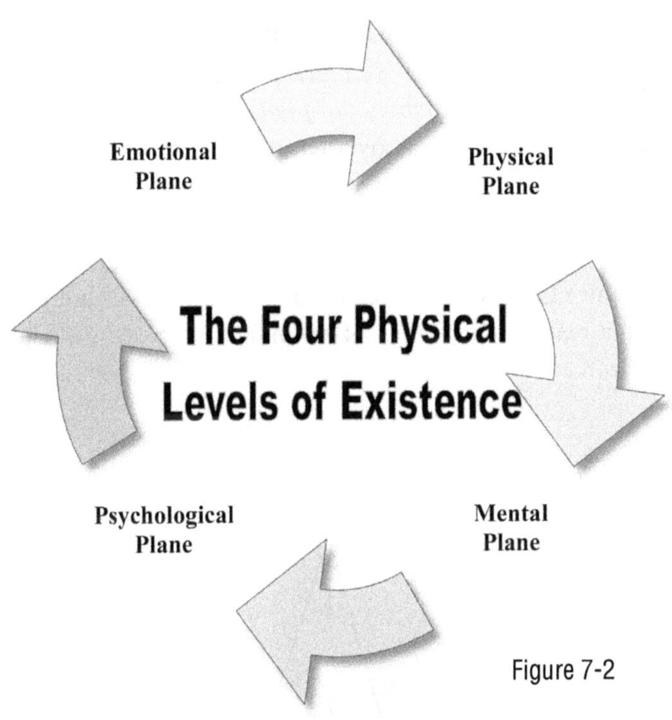

Figure 7-2

ideas, and landscapes and you affirm specific ideas over and over. If all of these go along with what you have been consistently working with you have created a pattern of highest probability. It is this pattern of highest probability that you will experience as your 3-dimensional world. Essentially, it is your choice which creates a multitude of universes or dimensions and these universes or dimensions fractionate or dissolve into fractals each proceeding to an end and you are unaware of all of them except one. That one dimension is the one which corresponds to the choices that you have made. The choices that you have made are based on your total past experience and other previous choices.

On the purely physical level you exist on different planes. (Figure 7-2) The *physical plane* itself gives you your perception of the 3-dimensions of all of your physical sensations. The *mental plane* gives you the perception of your conscious thoughts and the realities associated with your states of consciousness. The *psychological plane* gives you the perception of your mind's well-being. Finally, the *emotional plane* provides you with your feeling states. These levels overlap in many areas but they still have aspects which are totally indigenous to themselves.

Each of these levels or planes is also related to your individual self. They may all be thought of as one of the aspects of the self. (See below) Each self is a reality of its own but all are part of a greater reality where you as an individual exist. As Gestalt

Figure 7-3

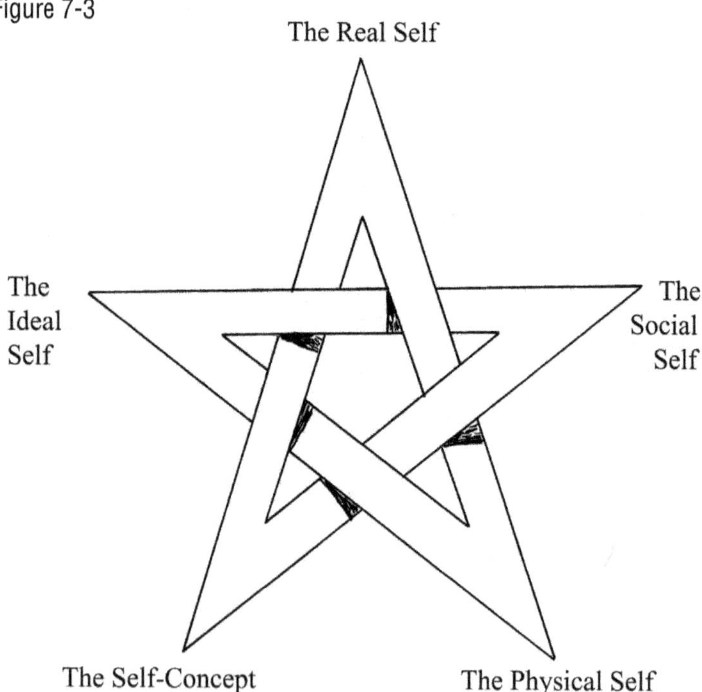

The self is made up of five components. The Ideal Self is the self as you would like to be. The Social Self is the person you show in public situations. The Self-Concept is your evaluation of yourself. The Physical Self is your physical being; your body. The Real Self is who you actually are away from the influences of your environment.

psychology states; "The whole is different than the sum of its parts." The reality which you are is an intermingling and mixture of all of the realities on which you exist.

In the theory of the self-concept, you have five basic selfs. (Figure 7-3) The first is the ***physical self***. This is your physical being; the body and all of its parts and appearances and your feelings toward your body and being in your body.

Second is the ***social self***. This is made up of the roles you play in social situations. Included also are the games that you play and the roles you take in social contact and your feelings and image of yourself and your place in any social context.

The third self is the ***self-concept***. This is your own personal view of who you are. Much of this part of the self is given to you from the way that other people act in your presence. So, this is very closely related to the social self and to self-esteem. Remember that another can only act toward you from the information that you give him by your actions and attitudes.

The fourth self is the ***ideal self***. This is the self as you would like to be. You find this self in your daydreams and your personal and private wishes, hopes and desires. This is the self where you never fail and are always loved and admired by all. The size of the gap between the ideal self and the self-concept shows up in emotional and psychological problems: the wider the gap the greater the problems.

The final self is that of the ***Real*** or ***True Self***. This aspect of the self combines your constant flow of thoughts, emotions and behaviors. It is your total experience. It is who you really are stripped of your learned emotions, all of your conditioned behaviors and without any social roles and games. Your Real Self is you in total potential without your ego to defend.

Each self is made up of a complete reality all its own. Each one of them is different but still related. Together they combine and form the dimensions of your total personality. It may be said that combined with your outer world your complete self forms the overt expression of your inner consciousness.[ii]

Not only do you exist in your own realities both conscious and unconscious, you also exist in the realities of other object-events. In order for an object to be perceived two consciousnesses have to combine for the expression to become perceptible. So, whatever reality you perceive likewise perceives you as a reality in return in a feedback loop.

Beyond the physical, there are existences and Universes unheard of and completely unknown. Each one is a separate reality with other realities contained within. There may have been times during your life when you have glimpsed realities beyond your own. But for the time being, let us stay with the five-sensed human realities because that is what you want to change.

One of the realities which many find quite fascinating is the reality of dreams. Whenever you go into a dream state you are shifting your consciousness and going into another dimension. You may, as many believe, be glimpsing into the fourth dimension for in this reality you can do anything and go anywhere with just a thought as there is no sense of time or space in a dream state.

In the fourth dimension, the space-time dimension, there is, ironically, no space or time. It is a reality where causality violations can occur easily. In this dimension all things are possible. You can contact those who have gone on and hold conversations with them. You can get in touch with your real consciousness. In fact, the symbols (archetypes) you experience in your dreams are expressions of your inner consciousness. Gaining an understanding of the symbols in your dreams gives you a deeper understanding of your consciousness.

Dreams are not the only way in which you can get in touch with your consciousness or gain access to the fourth dimension. There are methods and techniques which can affect your consciousness in such a way as to change your physical reality.

As a child maybe you had been reprimanded for daydreaming, especially in school. Reprimanding a child for this has a tendency to thwart one of the most valuable innate tools which he possesses. This is the art of *creative visualization*. In nearly all instances when

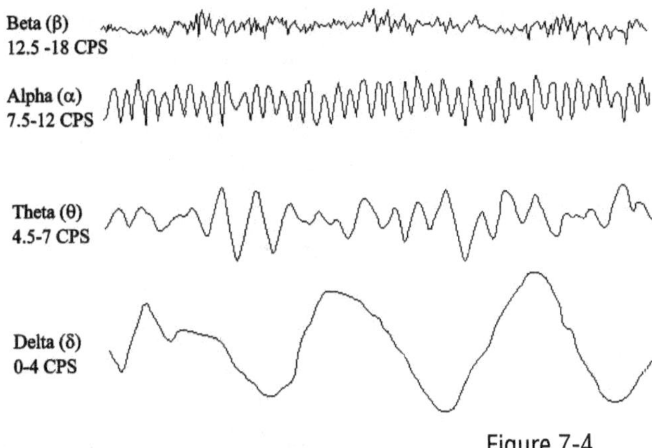

Figure 7-4

a child is scolded for daydreaming in school the teacher blames the child and not him/herself. There are two very important things to remember about school-age children: 1) If the child loses interest it is mainly due to the teacher either going too slow or too fast or it is due to the child's home-life where there is a negative attitude toward education and learning; and 2) The majority of a child's life (under the age of twelve) the slower brain wave patterns associated with the opening of the unconscious part of the mind dominate. (Figure 7-4) These patterns are very favorable to learning. A lot of learning and social behavior patterns and studying behavior is conditioned during the first six to twelve years of life.

Daydreaming for most children, as with most of us, is an escape from boredom or life's problems. It is a way to shut-out all kinds of external stimuli and think of something else, to be somewhere else or even be someone else for a while. This is the closest that you come to an actual night dream state without being asleep. One major similarity that the daydream and the night dream have in common is that they seem to occur in a slow brain wave state. Another similarity is that they both can be controlled. The night dream which is a bit more difficult to control for confronting emotional, mental and psychological problems in symbolic form; and the daydream for bringing about changes in your reality and your state of being. Both night and day dreams are realities. They appear to be a step into the space-time dimension. In the ancient mystical beliefs this reality was referred to with terms like the æther, akasha, the primordial matter and heaven.[1] As much as many of us would like to put off our dreams, both day and night, as flights of fantasy, they are dealings with realities of a different kind. By invoking conscious control over them you could manipulate reality to suit your desires.

Many times you can daydream quite vividly and in many instances, quite profoundly. The problem is you spend your valuable daydream time in unrealistic fantasies. You see yourself in unrealistic, unattainable places and situations and in scattered thoughts. By taking command and control of these daydreams and using them as an actual projection for a realistic objective, you can accomplish goals.

Now consider what is realistic and what is not. To begin with, what is realistic is *attainable*. You should not even attempt to aim for something like becoming a brain surgeon when you do not even have a high school education and are eighty-seven years old. Striving to gain a college degree in a chosen field when you have the appropriate previous training is realistic.

Second, what is realistic is *not egocentric*. It is based on your true needs and on the direction given you by virtue of your position in the Universe. Included here is the fact that there are no ulterior motives involved in your desire. Ulterior motives are egocentric and self-serving. Once the ego is removed the reality of the desired objective comes into focus.

Third, what is realistic *makes full use of your innate talents, abilities, skills and strengths*. You must be pretty well on the road toward self-actualization and have a pretty good understanding

1 Carl Jung referred to it as the Collective Unconscious.

of who you are and where you are going. When you do you will make rational, realistic choices.

Fourth, to be realistic means that *you do not go around telling everyone about what you plan doing*. It is nobody's business but yours. If you talk about what you plan to do you are looking for approval because you are unsure of yourself and your choice. Besides, people will be more than willing to tell you that you cannot do what you want to do.

Fifth, realistic means that *you have made plans and goals and can carry them through*. You have set your goals at a reasonable level so that they can be achieved and one goal naturally leads to another so that you become "doing oriented" and success-full.

Controlling of and repeating the *same daydream* over and over impregnates it deeply into your consciousness. Remember, you are in a relaxed brain wave state when you do daydream so the more this is done the greater the chance of changing your reality.

If something which you daydream is pure fantasy (unrealistic or unattainable) your brain knows it and works directly against its accomplishment.[iii] This is one of the reasons that many of your dreams never manifest. Another reason they may not manifest is that you really do not want to have your dreams become realities. The fact is that accomplishing dreams brings with it responsibilities. Most people do not consciously consider this when wanting to accomplish their dreams. Look into what responsibilities there are inherent in having your dreams. It could be that on the unconscious level there is something that you are not happy with having to do or to be or that you need to give something up in order to have your dream. If there is a reasonable chance for achieving of your goal and you are consciously and unconsciously willing to accept the responsibilities accomplishing brings, it has a good chance of being achievable.

Your daydreams are a doorway to your inner life and being. By controlling them you control your deeper self. You are controlling what is going into your consciousness and consequently you will see the results of your work objectively because of that upon which you gave your consciousness to work. You purposefully limited the stimuli into your consciousness and your reality changed in accordance with the information given.

Another very powerful tool that you possess is your ability to do creative visualization. This process has been known and used for countless centuries but science is just beginning to find value in its use. Similar to the daydream, visualization is a bit easier to accomplish and control.

Visualization is a moving picture in the mind. In the healing arts, for instance, the picture can be of whatever symbol an ailment presents itself as and the healing comes from picturing another form coming in and destroying it. As mentioned in an earlier chapter, before you make even the simplest movement of your finger it is first an image or picture in the brain then it is instantaneously transferred from one reality to another.

In the accomplishing of desires, you will picture yourself being and doing what you desire. In many of the occult or esoteric arts other types of visualizations, in many instances these visualizations contain specific archetypes, are employed for well-defined purposes. An example is the use of specific archetypes in meditation. In many meditation procedures, such as Christian Monasticism, a certain archetypal image will be held in consciousness and emotions which come with it are experienced. From these emotions spiritual growth can be monitored. The higher level the emotions being experienced the greater the spiritual development.

You are also dealing with other dimensionality whenever you visualize as well. Consequently, you are not bound by even space or time here either. In your physical world you are limited by length, width and height and all of the physical laws which control them. In visualization there are no limits. In the physical world you can perform an act of kindness and receive a thank you or a small honorarium of some sort. In visualization you can, for that same act of kindness, receive a cashier's check for $1 million tax-free.

In the physical world if you have decided to take a trip you are bound by however long it takes to get to your destination. In the visualization you can get to the farthest planet near the farthest sun in the farthest galaxy in any universe you desire instantaneously. Some will call it ridiculous or fantasy or impossible. But the point is that both realities are valid realities to the brain.[2]

One of the differences between the visualization and the daydream is the ability to control emotion within its context. To be more effective, certain types of visualizations need certain degrees of emotion. In some instances, a daydream does not involve emotion at all. The inclusion of emotion involves more of your complete being. In this way it makes the picture more believable to the brain.

Often what you see in your visualizations does not aid you in accomplishing much of anything. You will see yourself as one who is unsuccessful at whatever you attempt. You will picture yourself as someone else and be dissatisfied with who you are. You will spend a lot of time seeing yourself still as a child trying to please your absent parents. You will picture a positive thing for yourself and deny it with another picture. You will see what your ego wants over what you really need. You will see life as a constantly frustrating struggle from which the only way out and accepting your "lot in life" is by doing one of the following: 1) nothing; 2) displacing aggression on to those who have nothing to do with your lack of success; 3) giving up by going to prison, going on welfare, illness, crime; and 4) even suicide and death. The essence of all of this is that you were taught to see yourself the way you are and you have accepted it. Your external environment becomes and is directed by your inner visualizations.

An interesting point is that each of the basic selfs which make up your total self-concept is a visualization. You see yourself performing and being a certain type of individual as a visualization

---

2 Recall Bell's Theorum.

prior to showing it outwardly. Your beliefs were initially a picture in your mind which you came to accept not doubting it as existing in reality. Whatever identifications you make can all be narrowed down to the visualizations you have of yourself. Every perception that you experience and every name and label you have of yourself was learned. These labels are your "I ams…"—your identifications. You cannot see yourself any different than the accepted picture you have of yourself. The obvious identifications you have are as a male or female and a name. This is purely physical. Then you will identify yourself as attractive or not, coordinated or not, and any other titles with which you refer to your physical being. You will then make note of your abilities on the mental, emotional, psychological and social levels. From that you will identify your position and whatever else seems to be appropriate.

You will notice that virtually every one of the titles that you give yourself is associated with the words, "*I am.*" If you desire to find out exactly who and what you think yourself to be you need only to list your "*I ams…*" along with a supplemental explanation as to the reason for being that. You will then find the supplemental explanation is your visualization of yourself.[3] Consequently, if you desire to change anything about your identifications, your *I am*s, you must change your visualizations associated with those identifications. This means seeing yourself away from the behavior which gets in your way and with a behavior that assists in relating to yourself and everything in your created universe.

Your brain is a sensory receiving, processing and expressing system. Not only do you get sensations from your external world but also from your internal world: All of which are processed in the same way and become expressed in much the same way. Whatever you perceive on the physical realm as a reality you naturally accept as "real." Whenever you visualize anything you generally have a tendency to disregard it as being nothing but flights of fantasy, or

---

3 See Exercise 1 in **From Victim to Victor! Defeating a Victim's Consciousness** by Alexander S. Holub, Ph.D.

lacking real substance or form. Your brain, though, finds it totally impossible to tell the difference between an objective experience and visual image and consequently treats both of them exactly the same. This is one reason you can get emotions from a visual image as well as that of a physical experience. The more often and more clearly that you visualize a certain objective the greater is the chance that you will see it manifest on the physical plane.

To illustrate how the brain sees a picture from your inner world as a total experience, consider this situation:

Imagine, picture if you will, that you were just pulled over by a traffic officer for a minor infraction of the vehicle code. In your view you did not make a mistake. The officer is a rather stubborn individual and you are trying to explain your view of the situation without becoming angry and/or hostile toward him. Go through this whole scenario in your mind's eye and feel the sensations involved.

It is next to impossible not to feel something in this sort of visual imagery. Notice also how your body begins to tighten up in certain areas: the jaw, the forehead and the chest and that you start to become rather uncomfortable just *as if* the situation were actually transpiring on the physical level.

This same process is the basis for the sensory exercises used in teaching "method acting." Here you are taught to go into your sensory experience and visualize a scene which had a particular emotional association attached to it and go with it to get the appropriate response in the present role. You cannot possibly get the appropriate response and feelings without visualization or reliving the situation in as clear detail as possible with all of its sensations. If the brain did not treat your inner experience as a reality this could not be done. This also goes for whatever events you may contrive.

There are some people who do not have very good visualization abilities. This can stem from many situations most of which occurred in youth. Just like anything else, in order to improve, this skill must also be practiced.

Improving Imagery

With all the following exercises, only do it for about twenty minutes at a time and no longer than an hour at a daily sitting. Once you have developed your technique the exercises will become easier to do. The whole purpose of all of these exercises is to make it very easy for you to bring to mind any sensation and experience, anything you so desire whenever you so desire and you will have a much greater use of your mind than ever before.

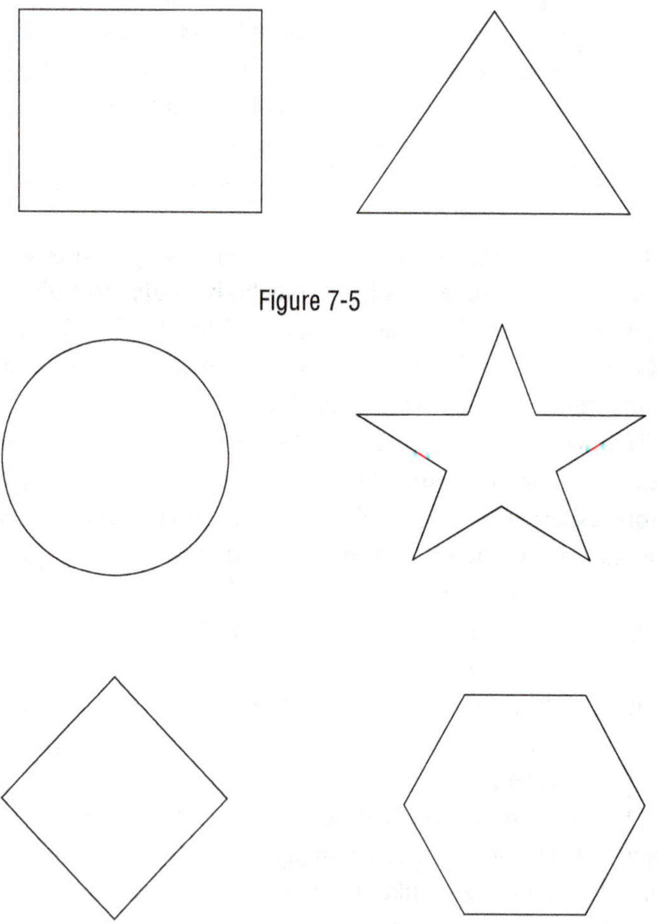

Figure 7-5

It is always easiest to visualize objects with which you are familiar. You can start with simple 2-dimensional forms such as squares, triangles, ovals, rectangles, trapezoids, stars and so forth. (Figure 7-5) Take each one and draw it out on a whole sheet of paper. If you would like you could darken the background. It is best if you draw the form instead of using a printed one. When you draw it out you will get more of your sensory input involved. This will make the visualizing much easier. Then take your time and study the form so that it becomes embedded deeply within your consciousness. Now, close your eyes and visualize it as clearly and distinctly as possible. Do that with each of the forms one at a time until you are able to picture each one clearly[iv] for several minutes at a time.

After you have completed this exercise sufficiently then go into 3-dimensional shapes. Get more sheets of paper and draw out cubes, pyramids, interwoven stars, balls (shaded circles), pillars, columns and so forth. (Figure 7-6) Study each form again and close your eyes and visualize each one very clearly[v] for several minutes at a time.

Now that you have increased your visualization ability with simple forms, go to color. You may begin doing this by getting sheets of construction paper or any other sheets of color paper as you will be working with one sheet at a time. Then place the colors in front of you in this order: red, orange, yellow, green, blue, violet and white. Bring into your mind one color, then the next, the next and so on going from beginning to end and back again. Hold each color as long as possible in your imagination. After this, surround yourself in all of the colors as if you were engulfed in a rainbow keeping you in this blanket for as long as possible.

The next thing that you may work with is adding color to your shapes. It may be wise to begin with the 2-dimensional shapes seeing each of them in color. After you have been able to do this clearly see the 3-dimensional shapes in color.

At this point you will then change from simple visualizations

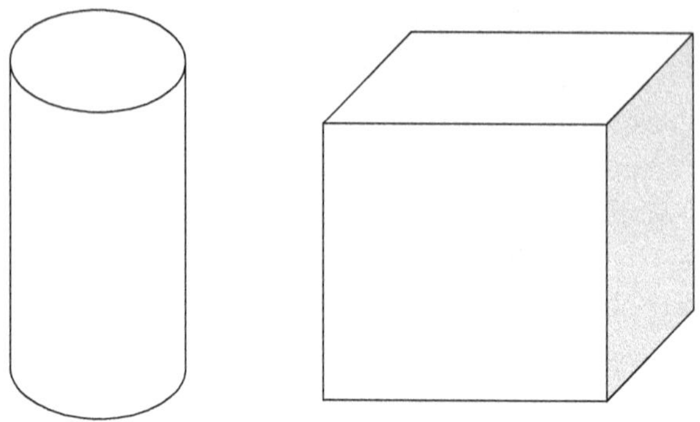

Figure 7-6

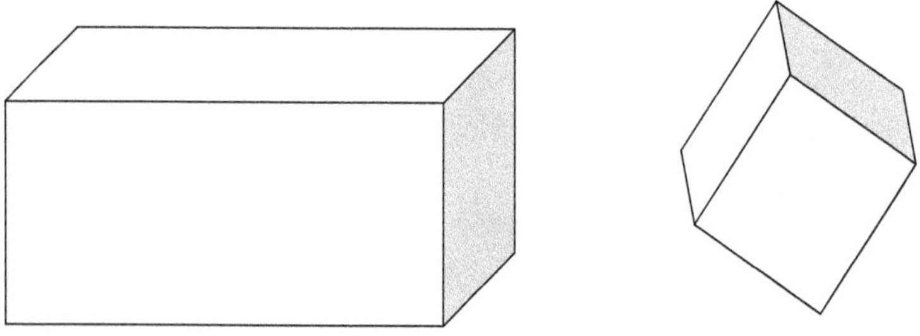

to more complex ones. Take three objects and place them on a table in front of you. (Figure 7-7) Study only one closely. Now, close your eyes and see it as clearly as possible. With this, as with all of the exercises whenever you lose your visual image, simply open your eyes study the object and go back to your visualization. The use of three objects aids you in focusing your attention to a much greater degree by eliminating the other two. It is also necessary that as you become more proficient that you continue to change objects three at a time. Do not simply pick another from the same group of objects. Get three new objects.[4] [vi]

4 See also Concentration Exercises (Chapter 11) in **From Victim to Victor! Defeating a Victim's Consciousness** by Alexander S. Holub, Ph.D.

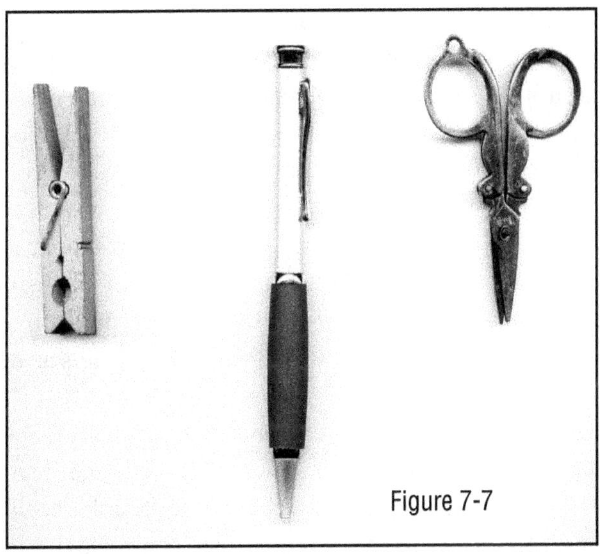
Figure 7-7

After you have completed the previous exercise you will need to visualize other objects. For this exercise you will need to sit comfortably in a chair facing a blank wall. Now, with your eyes closed visualize first the wall, then a simple object, such as a clock on the wall. At first begin with the usual wall clock then go to an older "grandfather" type pendulum wall clock. See it clearly with the pendulum swinging back and forth and watch as the second hand goes from second to second. After you have visualized this object proficiently then get into more complicated objects such as shelves with objects on them, pictures in frames, relatives, friends, animals and so on.

After completing these visualizations with your eyes closed do each one over again starting from the very beginning *with your eyes open* — kind of like a controlled daydream. Doing these exercises this way will aid you in keeping the desired picture in front of you whenever you want to see it.

After the visualizations you then graduate to the auditory sense. Sit in a quiet place and focus your attention on a specific sound such as a bird's song. Pay very close attention to it. Hear its meter, timbre and all of the subtle nuances of the song. Then turn your attention away and reproduce it as accurately as possible in your mind. Do this with as many sounds as you can. After this you will then focus your attention on the sound of a close friend or relative's voice and reproduce it. You should get to the point that you can reproduce another's voice saying whatever you so desire. Now you need to get to the tactile sense. Get an object and put it in your hands. Caress it and get all of the feelings and sensations possible from it. Put it down and reproduce all of the tactile sensations again. Do this with as many objects as necessary to accomplish this task.

Lastly, you may consider conditioning your olfactory and gustatory senses in order to produce fragrances and flavors. First begin with familiar scents such as your favorite cologne or favorite flower. Then go into the more unfamiliar scents. Do the same with tastes. Learn to reproduce them easily and accurately. Working with scents can have a powerful effect because the olfactory bulb, which sits right above the nose, has all of its nerve endings connected directly to the limbic system. The limbic system, you will recall, controls virtually all of your emotional reactions. So, reexperiencing a scent, even if it is mentally reproduced, can trigger an emotional response.

After all of these exercises have been completed (and it should take some weeks or months to do them properly) it is time to combine all of them into a single visualization. Initially choose something with which you are familiar such as a pet. Begin with your eyes closed. See, hear, smell and feel your favorite pet. Then with your eyes open reproduce it as accurately as possible. From your pet on to other familiar objects which are not too complicated, then go on to people. The final step is to place the people and objects into a complete situation which combines all possible sensations. Don't think that you can accomplish all of this in a few days or even a few weeks. If you are doing the exercises properly it will take several months. Too often many people don't want to take the time to insure that this skill is properly in place. All that not doing the work insures is that their goals will have less of a chance of coming about.

With this skill very highly developed you can begin to see things happening the way that you would like to have them happen. You can see yourself being, doing and experiencing the best that there is in life. You are dealing with a reality and to the brain a reality is a reality.

Remember that reality was defined as all of the sensations available at a certain moment in time and point in space. The more sensations that you experience with a situation the more your brain is able to accept that situation as a true objective reality.

In visualization it has been said that the stronger the picture the greater the effect. This is due to your nature of not accepting many of your visualizations as a reality unless you come away with the conscious thought that you had just physically gone through the situation. What is necessary for your visualization is that you accept your visualization, no matter how fleeting, as a reality. You must do this without question, for then you will see your visualizations begin to become clearer and stronger. You will also see more of your visualizations become physically manifest.

After completing all of the above exercises it is time to move on into visualizing for an overt effect. Start with something on which you are working: something that you know you can attain. Visualize the task already completed perfectly. See what you will be seeing, feel what it feels like being successful as feelings of accomplishing engulf you, and hear what you will be telling yourself upon its completion. Quite often people will not be congratulating you because of the job that you have done. Consequently, what you will be telling yourself will be more important than what others will be telling you. See yourself receiving your reward (if there is one). Perform this complete visual image several times during the day: usually once in the morning for about fifteen or twenty minutes, once or twice a day for about five minutes and once in the evening for about fifteen or twenty minutes. Results should be forthcoming and possibly sooner than expected. One thing that tends to be overlooked when doing visual imagery is to see *others benefiting* from your success as well. Many well-known inventors made this image a major part of their mental work and this is a part of visual imagery which is highly important. Seeing others benefiting from your success is an imagery used in order to accomplish more than a simple visualization. See yourself totally completed in your objective. See yourself and others benefiting from your work. It is of necessity to remember that you always go to the end result in your visual imagery. You must see everything in total completion.[5] The visualization must be precise, strong and held solid for a period of time. If not, it can result in a haphazard and sketchy outcome. Be and do that which you desire through visualization. Keeping the picture uppermost in your mind helps you to stay in the appropriate consciousness for its realization.

Most people are completely unaware of how the brain works to produce an image. Researchers talk about *top-down* and *bottom-up* processing. Top-down processing is from the *big picture* to the details. Bottom-up processing begins with the *details* to build the big picture. (Figure 7-8) Visual images are more accurately built with a bottom-up process. This is important because working with a top-down technique makes it much more difficult to achieve results. Most systems that teach visual imagery tell you visualize your final outcome *in complete detail.* This means that you are seeing the *big picture*. This is top-down processing. It is much more difficult to visualize a complete picture and to look for details within it. The simplest way to use bottom-up processing is to begin with a sheet of paper. On each line of the paper write out one detail of your outcome building an image up step-by-step. Doing this will help you to clarify for yourself exactly what you are wanting to achieve. Then, whenever you are doing your visual imagery all you need to do is to visualize one line at a time. By

5 The completion always involves others benefiting from your success. Because of this you can understand why egocentric purposes can block your accomplishing of any goals.

Processing in the Brain

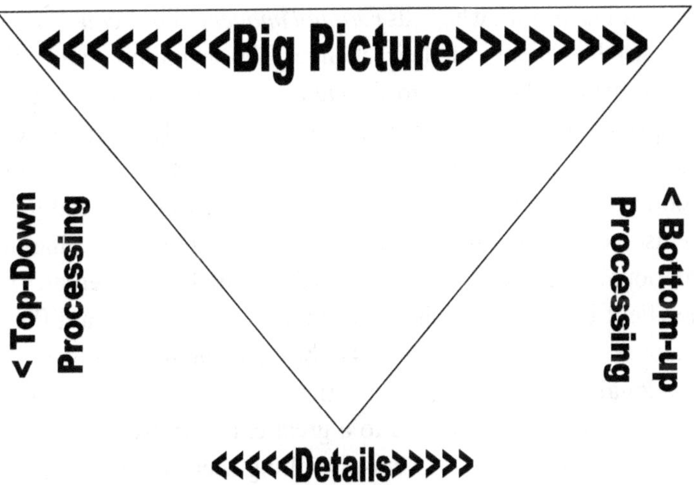

Figure 7-8

the time you get to the bottom of your list you will have built up a clear, precise and intense image of your goal.

An important thing to remember about visualization is that at some point you will have to let go of or release your picture or visual scenario. If some sort of results, even just a calmer and more relaxed attitude, do not come about quickly then check it as well as yourself for your intent. You may have forgotten something in your scenario and have to add to it, or your intent may be selfish, egocentric or manipulative or you may be going too far ahead of yourself.

You are probably familiar with medicine using visual imagery as an adjunct to healing. Many psychological therapies use it to aid in a client's adjustment. For example, Carl Jung's Analytic Psychology wrote extensively about the subject and suggested that patients keep journals which would aid them in their therapy. The technique of *active imagination* was used to have the patient gain information from his symbolic visualizations. Further, certain archetypal images could aid in an understanding of your inner life if visualized.[vii] Albert Ellis in his Rational-Emotive Behavioral Therapy teaches what he calls *rational imagery* or *projected fantasy* to assist his clients in their change. The techniques are rather simple having the client go through a situation where there was an emotional over-reaction *as if* they were actually reexperiencing it taking the emotions all the way to the original outcome. On the second pass through, the client is instructed to do something to themselves that is different and take that all the way to the new emotional outcome. This outcome will definitely be different. Then the client is asked, "What did you tell yourself to get a different outcome?" This technique helps to bring about more choices in an emotional situation where at one time there seemed to be none.[viii] Visual images are employed to a great extent in Neuro-linguistic Programming (NLP). Anxiety-provoking scenes are played back and the opposite is then invoked. Both are "anchored"[6] and the client can choose from a number of responses. The theory is that anxiety is caused by the feeling that you have no choice in a certain matter. Further visualizations include the reviewing of a problematic situation from different perspectives and in different ways. The process known as *systematic desensitization* incorporates visualization techniques as well. A hierarchy is found in an anxiety-provoking scene. This hierarchy is then used to desensitize the response. You are taught to relax one part of the body at a time when visualizing successive approximations toward the anxiety-provoking stimulus. *Aversive training* also makes use of visualization. A noxious stimulus is introduced when you clearly picture yourself performing the habit that you desire breaking. When the pleasure of the act is felt the noxious stimulus is brought in and discomfort is exchanged for pleasure. Flooding the mind with visual stimuli associated with an anxiety-provoking scene is the basis of *Implosion Therapy*. Seeing the worst that can

6 An anchor is not much different than a post-hypnotic suggestion. A touch, a word or sound, a visual or maybe even a smell will be used to produce a specific response.

happen in your fantasy life with regard to a situation can satiate you to such a great degree that you will pass through the anxiety without much of a problem. Finally *EMDR* (*Eye Movement Desensitization and Reprocessing*) makes extensive use of visual imagery. A client is instructed to visualize a problem situation bringing in the emotions. At this point the instruction is given to have the eyes follow a stick as it moves back-and-forth. This seems to help some types of emotional problems.[ix]

Down through the centuries most relaxation and meditation techniques made use of visualization: "See yourself in a comfortable spot beside a lake on a warm summer day just relaxing." This type of instruction is given to a person in order to get him into the proper physical and emotional state. If you have trouble sleeping you are told to "count sheep." If you have a physical pain you are told to think of something relaxing. Relaxation and anxiety cannot exist in the same body at the same time. If you are cold you are told to see yourself in a warm place or see yourself as a bright, burning flame. If you are too hot you are told to visualize yourself immersed in a cold mountain lake.

Hypnosis makes extensive use of visualization. From the above simplified relaxation technique to different processes done in state, hypnosis' main process is visual imagery. Instructions to the subject are given in statements referring to seeing or feeling yourself as something or somewhere. Many of the things done under hypnosis seem rather wondrous to most people but they are nothing more than normal, intensely focused attention and visualization. As we've seen, the picture has to be there before the action occurs.

We're living in a world that seems to have lost its imagination. With the advent of television the art of visualization began to slowly subside. When radio was the main means of family entertainment it was necessary to picture the scene in our mind as it was happening. This same process had come down through the centuries from the stories told of the hunt, to the storyteller relating tales of the gods, goddesses, heroes and heroines in myth and legend, to the bard with his poems or the minstrel singing his songs, all the way down to the parent reading a book to the whole family. It was necessary to be able to obtain visual images of the experiences while the tales were being told.

Television has greatly aided in subduing your imagination and expecting everything to happen quickly. Now, in order to help yourself to get the best from life you have to take the time to see yourself in that position. You must begin to work to effectively manipulate your inner world. Your thoughts control your brain and your thoughts are pictures more so than words. Controlling the pictures that go into your brain is one of the keys to reprogramming your consciousness and affecting your reality. You are constantly seeing yourself in certain specific ways that are left-over mainly from your childhood. By identifying them and visualizing yourself unencumbered by these behaviors you can then not get in your own way in relating to life.

Many of the techniques mentioned in this chapter are very old. They were modified to get the most effect as quickly as possible. They are built upon each other. By taking the time to work with each of the techniques until you've mastered them you will become a more effective and efficient person in your life. You will assume greater control and be more responsible. With these techniques you will be able to think and make worlds appear.

Summary

To change your life you need to change your mind — your thinking. To do this you must have a more complete understanding of how the brain works and how you construct your reality.

We live on many realities or universes at the same time. Seeing the world in only three-dimensions keeps you from experiencing more in life. Adding a fourth dimension, space-time, broadens the spectrum of possibilities. There are computer programs that generate images based on the highest probabilities (fractals) which are no different than your own thinking. You think certain thoughts, visualize images, ideas, and landscapes and you affirm over and over. If all of this goes along with what you have been consistently working with you have created a pattern of highest probability. This is the pattern you will experience as your three-dimensional world. The choices you make doing this creates the different universes or dimensions that are available. What you experience corresponds to the choices you made.

We all have five basic selfs: the physical self, the social self, the self-concept, the ideal self and the real or true self. Each self has a complete reality all its own. Together they combine and form the dimensions of your total personality.

We all exist in both conscious and unconscious realities. We also exist in the realities of other object-events. For an object to be perceived two consciousnesses have to combine to create that perception. That means there is a feedback loop created between perceiving objects.

There are times when we are on the surface of the fourth dimension. Night dreams and daydreams are possible examples. Interestingly, in the space-time dimension there is no space and time.

In order to accomplish your goals they must be realistic. This means that the goals must be: attainable; not egocentric; making full use of your talents, abilities, skills, and strengths; kept privately to yourself; and planned and carried through.

By controlling your daydreams through the use of visualization, having the appropriate emotional content, changing your personal identifications, and affirming your desires appropriately you can begin to deconstruct and reconstruct your reality.

There are exercises you can use to aid your ability to visualize a complete sensory experience. It takes time to do these exercises properly but you will gain much by working on them. They will help you to accept your visualization as a reality. When your visualizations are stronger and more vibrant they are much easier to accept as a reality.

The brain produces images through top-down and bottom-up

processing. There are ways you can use this processing to aid in your visualization. There are different therapeutic systems that use visualization to aid in physical or psychological healing.

We live in a world that seems to have lost its imagination. With the advent of television our ability to visualize has decreased. No longer is our creativity piqued. No longer do we take the time to read. No longer is our imagination aroused. It's something else that is in control of the pictures in our mind. Now you can control what is going in and out of your mind.

Endnotes

i James Gleik (1987) **Chaos, Making a New Science**, Penguin Books, New York, NY

ii Alexander S. Holub, Ph.D. (2007) **From Victim to Victor! Defeating a Victim's Consciousness**, Bridger House Publications, Inc., Carson City, NV

iii Anna Abraham and D. Yves von Camaron (Mar. 2009) *Reality=Relevance? Insights from Spontaneous Modulations of the Brain's Default Network when Telling Apart Reality from Fiction*, **PLoS ONE**, Vol. 4, No. 3, e4741

iv M. Samuels and N. Samuels (1975) **Seeing With the Mind's Eye**, Random House, Bookworks Books, Toronto, Canada

v *IBID*

vi Alexander S. Holub, Ph.D. (2007) **From Victim to Victor! Defeating a Victim's Consciousness**, Bridger House Publications, Inc., Carson City, NV

vii A. Girogi (Fall 1970) *Toward Phenomenologically Based Research in Psychology*, **Journal of Phenomenological Psychology**, Vol. 1, No. 1, P. 75-98

viii Susan R. Walen, Raymond DiGiuseppe and Richard L. Wessler (1980) **A Practitioner's Guide to Rational Emotive Therapy**, Oxford University Press, New York, NY

ix Francine Shapiro, Ph.D. & Margot Silk Forrest (1997) **EMDR: The Breakthrough Therapy for Overcoming Anxiety, Stress, and Trauma**, Basic Books, New York, NY

Words have a longer life than deeds.

Pindar (c. 518- c. 438 BCE)

Chapter 8

Effective Change Statements

There are a lot of rather humorous stories about people who talk to themselves.[1] As much as you would hate to admit it, you spend a lot of your waking time doing just that. Unfortunately, you also spend a lot of time shrugging off that internal conversation as meaningless idle chatter and not paying a bit of attention to what is being said. You can learn a lot about yourself and your universe if you would take stock of what you say in the confines of your mind.

To begin, let us start with an exercise.[2] Take out a sheet of paper and for the next fifteen to twenty minutes simply write down *all* of your thoughts or you may take a tape recorder and just speak into it. This may seem like an easy task but you will find that it is not so. You may have a tendency to write or say what you *want* to think, not what you are actually thinking. The difference is this; what you want to think ends up being something like this:

> "I really feel good now. I'm focused and clear in what I'm thinking and what I want. I know what I want and like what's happening to me and in my life. …"

1 It used to be that if someone was walking down the street alone and talking or yelling everyone gave that person a wide berth for he was probably schizophrenic. Now it's difficult to tell if the person is schizophrenic or on a cell phone.

2 This exercise can also be seen in more detail in **From Victim to Victor! Defeating a Victim's Consciousness** by Alexander S. Holub, Ph.D.

What you are actually doing is repeating an affirmation. This is not what you are really thinking. It is a contrivance. What you are actually thinking tends to go something like this:

> "Well, it's Saturday. I'm sure glad this week is over with. What do I have to do today? The weekend is too short. It'll be Monday before I know it and I get so tired thinking of work. Today I have to go to the bank and do some shopping. I'm going to have to clean my apartment one of these days. I'm really tired of cleaning my apartment. Maybe I'll hire a maid. Later I'll get together with Babs and Chuck and go to a movie. I have so much to do and the weekend just isn't long enough. Boy, work sure makes me tired. I wish I could win the lottery then my life would be set for sure. Whenever I think of all I have to do, oh man! …"

You will notice a difference between the two. The first is controlled and based on an *idealized* internal monologue. The second is often connected and rather jumbled but there is a theme that tends to come through. This is what actually goes on in most thought processes. Go on and complete this exercise before reading further. It is important that you write this down. When you use the tape recorder instead of simply listening to what you said when you have completed the fifteen minutes transcribe it. It is important to see what you're saying and the only way to do that is to write it down.

What is Your Self-talk Doing?

Take a look at what you have written. There will be one concept, idea or statement repeated several times. You may see something like, "I'm tired" stated three or four times. Others may see, "I can't …" Maybe you will see, "What's wrong with me?" or "I don't understand …" These statements come from years of training and learning as well as proving of the self-fulfilling prophecy. This means that as you were growing up you were told many things. Anything that you were told often enough you came to naturally assume was part of your identity and responded appropriately. More knowledge of yourself came through other statements and other things that you learned. If you were told that you were stupid enough times, you would finally come to the point that you would accept that statement as being factual. You were also taught to accept certain actions that you would do as correct. These would all be placed in your unconscious mind and you would act in accordance with them. You would then view reality filtered through all that you were taught you were supposed to be. The fact is the more you repeat a particular statement the more you will act on it. Repetition imbeds the concept into consciousness: The deeper the imbedding in the system the greater the chance of realization.

This does not mean that you force yourself to repeat only positive statements. The problem with this is that you do not believe or accept the positive statements. Because of this no amount of repetition is going to do any good until other things are changed in your unconscious. What you need to do is to find a way to accept and trust in other statements so you can make the appropriate changes.

Recall that the greatest influence you have on your life is your early training in your family. Due to the fact that, as some researchers say, something like 90-percent of your personality was formed by the age of five, then much of what you think yourself to be comes from your very first learning experiences. Besides being told who and what you were you would also employ imitation, identification and role modeling to cloak yourself in personality. All of these processes will ether get rewarded, ignored or punished and there would be a resulting behavior.[i]

All children will hold some adult in high esteem and because of this he or she will imitate and emulate that person's behavior, values and attitudes. This may be rewarded and become part of the personality structure. Your habits, attitudes, behavioral responses and learning patterns were formed by early conditioning. Your inner feelings of self-esteem, self-confidence, degree of self-love or –hate, tendency toward being a winner or loser, your general life's goals and your basic self-image were all learned early in life. These are the patterns that you tend to continue throughout life without thinking. Consequently, you can easily say that you live in the past and are constantly trying to get the approval of your parents. Only later do your parents become concepts and not physical people. You are locked into constantly making choices based solely on your past experiences as you continue to try to get their approval.[ii] But you do not have to, nor do you need to live in the past.

No matter what your state of life you are there due to the choices that you have made. In essence, *you put yourself where you are*. It is so much easier to place the blame on something or someone else. You will say that you have no control over your conditions; that someone or something "greater than you" has some kind of power over you; or that you are at the mercy of an unkind Universe that tosses you around wherever and whenever it so desires. Then there's today's favorite new-age cop-out: "It's my karma from a past life." All this does is give you another excuse to have destructive relationships, make unrealistic choices and to set yourself up for failure. The fact remains that you've made the choices which put you where you are and those choices are *present tense* choices, *not* past tense.[3] They are, though, based on past experiences in *this* life; not some dubious existence in some unverifiable past.

Whenever you experience anything you do not see it clearly. It is filtered through your past experiences, your attitudes, your expectations, your values and your belief system. All of these directly affect your choices. If you are in a situation where you are very unhappy, have low self-esteem and level of aspiration and are constantly seeing no way out it is because that is what you feel you deserve. What you feel you deserve is based on what you were

3 That is, choos*ing* not chose.

taught to be and to expect from yourself and your life. You are the person that you are because that is who you believe you are and with what you have identified. Whatever you believe yourself to be and to deserve has much to do with your early training in life. Realizing this, you can set about changing your belief system and as it changes so also does your Universe. But you have to commit yourself to it and work at it constantly for changes to result.

You are the creator of your personal universe, not simply an observer being swept along by the winds of chance. Not only are you the creator of your personal universe but your universe, as we've noted, partially creates you.[iii] In other words, you begin the creative thought process and your thoughts begin manifesting. These manifesting thoughts are the people with their own ideas, your behavior and habit patterns, your attitudes and the objects to which you are attracted and which are attracted to you. Further manifestations are the conditions associated with the people and objects which you brought into your universe. These conditions will in turn affect you and recreate some of your thoughts which will attract to you other objects, people and conditions and so forth and so on.

To review the basic processes which occur and attract to you that which you believe you are and what you believe you deserve recall that you are an electro-chemical system. All of your sensory systems operate electro-chemically. Since your brain is the main unit for processing of all of your sensory information, it operates on the same principle as the senses.[4]

Here is a simplified description of how a sensory message gets to the brain and back out: At the sense organ (e.g. the eyes) a sensation is received. (Figure 8-1) The sensory receptors have the first group of neurons that pick up the sensation and react to it. Initially, this is through a stimulus at the receiving point of the neuron. This is then transferred into a change in the body of the nerve cell. At a point in the body of the neuron the chemical stimulus is turned into an electrical impulse which travels down

4 Some theorists see the sense organs as extensions of the brain.

Figure 8-1

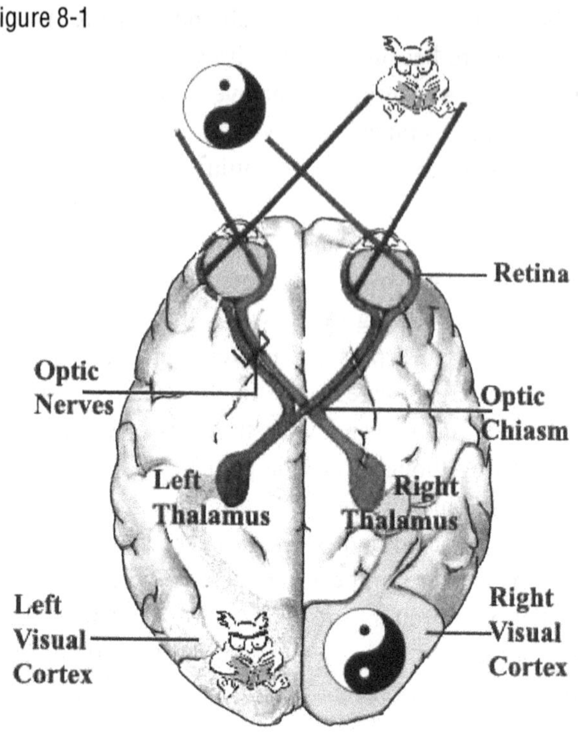

a "wire" called an axon. At the end of the axon are terminal bulbs which contain biochemicals. These biochemicals are released when the electrical impulse reaches them. When the biochemicals are released they stimulate the next neuron and this same process goes on in the next neuron, and the next neuron until it reaches the area in the brain where it becomes interpreted. A group of neurons that fires in order is called a neural pathway. A neural pathway is made by your learning, your habit patterns and your consistent thoughts. The action for the neural stimulation is taken in the cortex of the brain. The cortex is the outer portion of the brain, the gray matter, that you usually see pictured in books.

This process of electrical to chemical change through each neuron not only goes for the physical activities that you learned but for your thought processes as well. It must be remembered that every thought that you think is a sensation containing a multitude of sensory messages, images, internal conversations, emotions, desires and needs. These are all treated by the brain as a totally physical event. Your brain cannot tell the difference between a physical or imagined event. Consequently, any thought that you spend any amount of time pondering over could become an objective reality since it has created a neural pathway in the brain.

Since the human body is an electro-chemical system and since it also contains trace minerals (e.g. copper, iron, and zinc), as long as the certain electro-chemical action (e.g. the thought) takes place there may be a tendency toward you becoming like an "electro-magnet" drawing to you those objects and persons which harmonize with that thought.[5] This is why only certain conditions, experiences, persons and objects are available to you at a certain period of time in your life. The electro-magnet that you are is based on the thoughts that you think and you will recall that your thoughts are the after-effects of your consciousness. So, what you experience is the result of your consciousness and your consciousness is the outcome of your experience.[6]

It then becomes quite apparent that if you change your thoughts you can change your life. This seems like a major task for in order to change your thoughts it is necessary to go deeply into yourself and change your very consciousness. When this happens your reality changes as do your perceptions of reality, your attitudes, habits and beliefs about yourself and your created universe. With

---

5 You must also consider that your constant thoughts set up expectations and you will unconsciously select out of your environment those objects, people and events that correspond to those expectations.

6 In essence, you are creating a mental set through which you are viewing the world. Once that mental set is engaged you will pay close attention to what harmonizes with that mental set. An example is a racist. He can see nothing outside of his mental set and will behave in accordance with it. This will attract the people and conditions to him that will verify that his mental set is correct. Anything outside of that mental set will be disregarded and discarded.

this change you will come to view yourself and your conditions differently.

The main concern here is that the mind and body act in harmony and this harmony will affect your conditions. For as long as a certain thought is thought, a state of consciousness continues, the mind affects the body from another reality level which draws to you the proper conditions which harmonize with that thought and accompanying state of consciousness. Since the body has become "magnetized" it will attract these certain conditions, persons and objects. All of these will become part of your environment and the environment affects what, when and how you think as well as what, when and how you think affects your environment in an ever-flowing feedback loop.[7]

How often do you really pay attention to what you say to yourself? You may spend tens of thousands of dollars and go through years of therapy to have someone trained in listening guide and direct you into paying closer attention to what you are telling yourself.[8]

It is unfortunate that a lot of what you say to yourself tends to be negative and irrational. What you are constantly doing is interpreting, and often incorrectly, your environment. Of course you will say, "I know what I saw!" You must remember that you are seeing things filtered through your consciousness, your experiences, your beliefs, your values and your expectations about yourself; much of which was from a child's point of view.

You received many labels early in life that you hold on to throughout your adulthood. Maybe you were told that you were unattractive. This would carry over and due to the created neural pathway in the brain and the "magnetizing" of yourself you

---

7 This feedback loop can be positive or negative such as synchronicity being positive or negative.

8 Many will do the same with "pseudo-therapies" and think they've been helped. It was noted more than 2000 years ago by the Greek philosophers how people think that if they pay a lot for something they have the idea that they've gotten more from it than they actually have.

would be reacted to *as if* you were unattractive and the self-fulfilling prophecy would prove that your knowledge of yourself is correct. You will recall that the self-fulfilling prophecy states you will assume something about yourself to be true and will go out of your way to prove it.[iv] Much of the self-fulfilling prophecy involves the deletion and distortion of information that is contrary to the prophecy. So, you will see and hear what you want to hear — even in your own self-talk. In essence, negative self-talk leads to perceptions and behaviors which can only be classified as self-defeating. Your external behaviors will reinforce your negative internal conversation and this goes on and on.

Your internal conversation can give you a clue to your self-concept. What you really think of yourself you say to yourself. This was the purpose of the exercise at the beginning of the chapter. On the surface is one statement or behavior, but inside is another. You will attempt to compensate for this imbalance, in most cases, not internally with introspection and self-analysis but externally with actions and attitudes which are incongruent and ego defensive. Still in all, you will continually talk to yourself.

Changing Self-talk

If you change your self-talk you can make other changes in your views of yourself and your life. If you speak more positively to yourself about yourself you will begin to gain more confidence in yourself. You will gain a greater sense of self-worth and feel better about who you are and what you want and need. You will be able to see the difference between egocentered desires and your true needs.

The basic steps to changing self-talk or internal conversation are:

1. ***Listen to what you are saying to yourself***. Like most people, you probably have the idea that it is necessary to constantly talk to yourself. All of the chatter that you tend to have going on in your head keeps you from getting in

touch with what really matters. If you only say what is necessary to yourself you will not have the problem of over-emotionalizing. Remember, your thoughts are your choice. You can choose what you want to say to yourself.

2. ***Question your statements to yourself.*** Like a child wanting to understand something, ask yourself questions like: "What is the reason for this?" "What does this really mean?" "What am I really saying to myself?" Whenever you come down on yourself, question in order to find out the truth in what you're saying:"Who said that I'm stupid?" "Where is there a law that I *have* to be competent *all* of the time?" "What If I don't succeed at this? Does it mean that I *never* will succeed at anything?" "Where is the absolute proof that I'm a failure?" A very easy and effective way of getting into the habit of doing this is by stopping yourself whenever you start coming down on yourself with your self-talk. You can tell this is going to happen because you will hear words like would, should, have to, need to, must, ought to, I can't ___, I can't stand ___ or a demanding internal tone of voice. Pay attention even to the slightest demand. For example, you have had the experience of going shopping and forgetting to purchase something that you wanted. When you got home you would say something like: "Damn! I *should have* picked that up when I was down there. Now I *have to* go down again to get it." As innocuous as this sounds, deeply hidden in this statement is an underlying deeper meaning like, "How could I be so stupid for forgetting to get that?" If you keep repeating this statement after a while you are going to be making so many mistakes that you will not be able to keep track of them. As soon as you hear yourself make these personal demand statements stop it immediately and begin questioning logically: "Who says that I *have to* go down again and pick it up?

Was the one that I forgot to get the *only* one or the *last one* in existence? Who says that I *should have* picked that up *now*? Does it make any sense to come down on myself for forgetting something?" After you have done this reframe the statement to something like: "It would have been nice if I would have picked it up when I was out at this time. I'll just pick it up the next time I go shopping. This time I'll write myself a note and I won't forget."[v]

3. ***Act positively on your self-talk***. This will help you out of your negative self-fulfilling prophecy and on to more confidence.[vi] Do things that are fulfilling and success oriented. Even little successes can be built up to become big successes. The more success you have the more you will look for. Little successes can be as simple as finishing reading a book in a certain time or cleaning your apartment or signing up and taking a seminar or workshop or stopping procrastinating on something or even completing a project for work or school early instead of waiting for the last minute. The more of these you do, the more action that you take the better the chance you have that you will become more success oriented.

4. ***Pay attention to your emotional reactions***. You may think that you have no choice when it comes to your emotions. That is not completely true. As you have seen, many of your reactions were installed by the age of 5 or 6 so what you are emoting over is something to which you were trained to react. In order to deal with your emotions, *verbalize* your feelings. Do not just feel something and hide what it really is with rationalizations, intellectualizations and excuses or other defenses. State specifically *what* you are feeling *when* you are feeling it. The fact is that there are only six basic emotions. They are: joy, sadness,

> fear, anger, surprise and disgust.[9] The point is, if you take your emotions down to the six basic emotions and state what you are feeling when you are feeling it you will find yourself being able to deal more effectively with your emotions. Bringing your emotions to the surface like this helps you to see them for what they are and to control and understand what it is you are feeling. The most basic emotion is fear. As a modern human being you do not have to worry about lions, leopards or packs of wild dogs, wolves or hyenas attacking. Being a member of a group you have to concern yourself with the effect that you are having on others and what you are doing to yourself. Most of the fears that you will encounter daily are fears based on *possibilities*. In other words, you are *anxious* about the future: "What *might* happen if I do that?" "*What if* this doesn't work?" and so on: These are your greatest concerns. The fact is that you have a tendency to be *overconcerned* about those things and this overconcern leaves you little time for things you need to do to live a better life. These anxieties are felt quite often as a "cringe" inside. As soon as you have this feeling question it: "What am I afraid of?" If your response is "What if …?" then question with: "What if it does happen? Will it be the end of the world?" You could also go to the other end with, "What if it doesn't happen? What will happen then?"

With processes like these you can change your self-talk. Changing your self-talk can help you to see yourself more clearly. In fact, you will be able to work through many problems encountered from your past experience when your self-talk is changed. Your past experiences and all of your beliefs, attitudes toward yourself and others, your habits, your emotional and psychological

---

9 These emotions are on a continuum from the mildest form to the most intense form. All of the other emotions we experience are variations of these six emotions which vary due to their placement on intersecting continua.

stability, some of your values and so on are probably the greatest weapons you have in your arsenal against yourself. They limit your consciousness, your expression and the experience of your potential reality. Consequently, you are not responding clearly to a situation because, to all intents and purposes, you were taught to see it, to hear it and to react to it in a certain way. You do not have to accept that. You can change. Changing what you say to yourself is one way. One technique of making change is generally called an affirmation. Affirmations will be referred to here as *Effective Change Statements*.

You spend a lot of time talking to yourself. The effective change statement is a way of doing that talking in a positive and constructive way. Presented will be several ways that effective change statements can be constructed for specific objectives.

The effective change statement is *a positively asserted statement of fact for the future made in the present*. There are several ways of constructing effective change statements. One of the earliest types was the *incantation* which was used in magical practices. The incantation usually consisted of four or five lines of a poetic nature designed for a specific purpose. This is useful because the meter is easy to remember like a poem that you learned in your early years in school. Another type of effective change statement is the one or two line *written* statement. This is usually an assertion of an objective written twenty or more times a day for about a month. With the written statement you will be involving your senses of sight, sound because you will be stating it out loud, and feeling because you will be writing it. Similar to the written statement is the *shouted* statement. This is a line or two which is shouted several times a day. Lastly is the *complete effective change statement*. This is a complete statement concerning a specifically desired result. This is what will be discussed at length and the other effective change statements can be better understood both in context and effect.

An effective change statement is tailored to suit the desired objective. There are six basic rules to follow when creating an effective change statement:

1. ***State it only in the positive.*** It is unwise to use any negative words or words that have a negative prefix. Negative words such as; no longer, can't, won't, am not, don't have, will not, unable, inconceivable and so on tend to cause problems. What seems to happen is that the unconscious takes whatever is placed into it literally and only responds to it from the perspective of a positive statement. Consequently, any negative statements introduced will be responded to as if they are positive. So, using a statement such as "I am not limited …" the unconscious will respond to only the positive placing limitations in your path. Some positive statements that work well are: *I now have ..., I am now ..., I am doing ..., I am manifesting ...* and so on. Remember that the unconscious works to keep you in harmony at all times. It does what it can do to eliminate negatives and strengthen positives. So making sure that you use only positive wording helps it do its work.

2. ***Statements need to be made only in the present.*** Using a phrase such as "no longer" is a statement of admission of a past problem which the unconscious will continue to see. Remember that there is no time or space in the unconscious. Phrases of the future such as "will be" or "will have" do not work well either because it puts everything just slightly out of reach in time. Always use the present tense such as, "*I am now ...*" "*I now have ...*" "*I am doing ...*" and so forth. Whenever you can, use an "*-ing*" suffix on a word. A statement such as, "*I am living ...*" can have a powerful effect on your thinking. Even though it may sound silly adding an –ing suffix to some words this can change it from a static concept into a process (e.g. success*ing*). What you want from using present tense words is to make the goal something you *are* achieving — now!

3. ***Make your effective change statement in the first person singular***. This usually gives the best effect. This seems to work more universally than any other method. This is stating, "*I am now* ..." or "*I now* ..." Using the second person singular ("*You are now* ...") may be effective to some persons and for some goals and seems to work well in hypnosis but it is not as universally useful. Actually, there may be times when the second person singular may be more appropriate. One of these times is when you make a self-hypnosis tape with your effective change statement repeated in it. To find out if the second person singular is useful, simply do your effective change statement in the first person singular and note the effect. If it does not seem to work well, change to the second person singular. If you make a tape repeat it each way to take care of all possible states.

4. ***For the greatest effect, personalize it***. In other words, use your name. Here also, notice the effect with and without the personalization. You will find by adding your name it generally becomes more effective. One thing more, the name that would tend to work best is the name you were called when you were about three years of age. This is done because the unconscious mind is still at that level of experience and still is experiencing things as a child. So, if you were called some sort of nick-name such as "Punkin'" or "Poopsie" use it even if you now hate it. It will most likely be much more effective. In fact, since the unconscious is at the child's level it would be best to use the language you understood at that age as well. So, if English is a second language, use your first language.

5. ***Be thankful — especially to your unconscious***. This must never be forgotten when constructing your effective change statement. The reason for this is simple: You are accepting the situation *as if* it is already happening. This

aids in the realization of the objective by opening yourself up for the total acceptance of it. Also, thanking your unconscious seems to bring along with it a very positive emotional response so when you have completed each session you will come away feeling good about it.

6. ***Always remember that it is an experiment***. You are trying to find out what is going to work best for you. Once you know what is going to work you can continue using it to accomplish more and more.

Now, let us consider examples of effective change statements. It must be understood that these are examples. They cover only specific areas of life and the effective change statement should be made up *by you* and directed toward *your specific goal*.

There are several main areas of life where most people have problems and desire change. These areas include: 1) ***Health***; 2) ***Career Success*** and ***Money***; 3) ***Love and Attraction***; 4) ***Self-awareness*** or ***Spiritual Expression***; 5) ***Guidance***; and 6) ***Emotional Release***.

You will notice that there will be overlap in many of the effective change statements. The reason for this is that there is overlap between many areas of change. One area of change can affect other areas. It is a fact that if you lack awareness or control in one part of you life there can be problems in some related, but not all, areas of life. So, it is necessary to be precise in the desire for this begins to straighten things out step-by-step. Be specific except when ***Guidance*** is wanted. Also, you will notice that the bottom line of all objectives is ***Self-awareness*** or ***Spiritual Expression***. It is the uplifted spirit, the more fully-functioning self which contains all things and objectives.

The first area to be considered is ***Health***. Two things are necessary to understand immediately: 1) This is to be used in accompaniment *with* your doctor and his advice and *never* instead of; and 2) You should know what you would like to accomplish. If you want general good health, then an appropriate effective change statement such as the one following could be used. Remember, there is no such thing as *perfect health.* You can have *excellent health* or an *excellent healing*. Perfection of any sort is impossible and unrealistic. In fact, a general good health statement could be used even in specific situations to take care of other problems which may be there. Remember, one organ always affects another. With a specific case rearrange the statement to suit your problem. If after one problem disappears another occurs or if the illness does not subside then something else may be occurring: 1) Where you're focusing your effort is at the wrong organ; 2) There may be some other deep-seated psychological problem you need to deal with before the healing can progress; and 3) You may not even truly want the healing. In the last two instances it would be wise to consult a *good* psychotherapist and rearrange your statements toward ***Self-awareness*** and personal understanding.[10]

A typical ***Good Health*** change statement could be:

> I _______ am complete in all ways — NOW! My whole body, mind and spirit vibrate in a healing harmony vitalizing and energizing my whole being. My whole being: every muscle, every bone, every fiber, every nerve, every cell, every atom is permeated with new life and energy making me whole, complete and pure. I reflect the completeness, beauty and love of the whole Universe in all my ways. I give thanks to my unconscious for helping to bring about this wonderful healing.

In the poetic form the statement may be:

> I ________ now manifest,
> A Universe within at its best,
> As my mind, spirit and body somehow,
> Take on a complete new healing right — NOW!
> I thank my unconscious for the healing I attest.

10 A good book that can help you to understand and work through some personal problems is: **From Victim to Victor! Defeating a Victim's Consciousness**. Another approach that can be very useful is **Psychokinesiology: Doorway to the Unconscious Mind** both by the author.

The written statement could read like this:

> I _______ am now in total harmony and at one with the Universal principle of complete expression and healing throughout my whole being and thank my unconscious for this wonderful change.

The second area is ***Career Success*** and ***Money***. There are several questions that are necessary to answer in order to affect this part of your life. They are: 1) What is success to you? Many people have no idea or a very limited concept of success. To many it is nothing more than making a lot of money. It does not matter how emotionally distraught they may feel with a lot of money. The money is what is important. If this is your definition of success you need to ask yourself what you would do if you came into the money that you desire. Money is best looked at as a *means to an end* and not an end in itself. So, begin by defining your terms and you will be able to make more satisfying gains; 2) What are your real needs? Here is another aspect of defining your terms for success. Many people confuse their real needs with what their ego wants. What do you honestly need to exist and live comfortably? Compare this with what it is you want. Is it to prove something to yourself or to anyone else or is what you want something that will cause you to be envied[11] or give you power; 3) What does your ego want? Knowing the difference between an egocentric want (something not really necessary but used to impress others or to satisfy some self-centered want) and your real needs helps to define success more appropriately for you. Straighten these terms out and you will be able to accomplish more. You will no longer pursue egoistic goals and see your real needs. That will certainly make achieving your goals much easier; and 4) Is this career choice permanent or a means to an end? It is necessary to understand this because you will be gaining a greater understanding of your life's choices. You will also know better if the career is an ego

11 You may define envy as admiration. Be clear with what your definition is because envy and admiration are quite different.

choice, something you were told would be a good paying career or something you really want to do.[12] If you cannot make a choice, then go for ***Guidance***. After that, then you can begin to focus on your direction.

A typical (kind of long) ***Success*** change statement may read like this:

> I _______ have complete success in all areas of my life. I am now in harmony with the Universe and flow with the energy of the Universe. All of my choices are appropriate for achieving my success. I always have whatever I need whenever I need it because the Universe is abundant and freely flows through me — NOW! I am filled with peace, harmony and joy and radiate this to all whomever I meet. I identify myself with success and am attracting to me all of the people and conditions necessary for my total success — NOW! I am prospering in mind, body and affairs and give thanks to my unconscious for helping me to achieve my success.

The poetic version may sound something like:

> I ________ with success now do identify,
> The Universe to me now does reply,
> What I know success to be,
> I now give thanks to my unconscious for living successfully.

The written statement can read like this:

> I _______ am in harmonious connection with the Universal energies which yield to me great success, personal income and fortune — NOW! And I give thanks to my Unconscious for bringing this about.

The third area is that of ***Love and Attraction***. There are a few things necessary to understand before dealing with this area: 1) What are your motives for the love relationship? Are you out to get back at the person because you were rejected? Are you

12 "Follow your bliss" as Joseph Campbell so aptly stated.

trying to manipulate the other person? Do you have some other egocentric or selfish reason for this affair or is real love the only reason? Do you know how to really love another? Are you being realistic in this instance? 2) What type of love is desired? Is it physical, emotional, spiritual or a combination? Remember, any relationship that starts out with sex is a sexual relationship. That is all that it is; That is all it will ever be. To try to make something different out of it by rationalizing and intellectualizing your feelings and fantasizing about it is immature, irresponsible and unrealistic; 3) Are you willing to openly share your deep inner feelings with this person or with any other? In other words, do you trust this person *implicitly* with your innermost secrets and trust that these secrets will not be used against you at some later time? If you have even the *slightest* doubts, forget about the relationship. You will always be anxious; 4) Have you decided how long this affair will go on? You usually have an idea at the very beginning, and sometimes even before, just how long a relationship will last. Look deep inside for your feelings toward this; 5) How much do you really know of yourself? Before you can enter into a truly deeply committed relationship you have to know yourself at least well enough that you can trust yourself and your feelings. Do you honestly trust yourself enough to get out of a destructive relationship? In essence, how much do you love yourself? You need to be able to love and trust yourself before you can express those same feelings to another; 6) Do you really *know* the other person? Is there any kind of attraction from the other person? Often you will get involved with another and think you are in love and to not really know the other person. What happens many times is that you will fall in love with an ideal or something about the other person or with the idea of being in love rather than with a human being. The fact is that most people not only do not know the other person, they do not even like that person (see #7) but being in love is what's important. This does not bode too well for the relationship. Unfortunately, by the time that the person comes to some realization of this his/her ego is involved and they will refuse to give up going after the relationship continuing to say it's "love"; and 7) Do you *like* the other person? This may sound strange but many people "fall in love" and don't really like the person that they claim to love. You cannot really love another unless you like that person first. Love takes time to develop. Love best develops from liking, not the other way around. It is best to take your time. In this way you can get to know the other person and love *may* develop naturally.[vii]

In most instances you will have someone in mind. It is necessary that you be very realistic in your choice. Otherwise, lacking in realism, the affair will either never be or will be very emotionally trying. Remember, love is not blind; insecurity is.

To more fully understand your reasons for the current choice ask yourself these questions: 1) Am I seeing this person as completely as possible or am I hiding some important facts from myself? Am I seeing the other person as *I would like to see him or her*? You tend to see only what you want to see in a lover and you place unrealistic expectations on that person without telling him or her. You will become disappointed when that person does not live up to your expectations and due to your "love" of him or her you will hide important information from yourself even though that information continually surfaces; 2) Am I idealizing this person as a "Prince Charming" or "Snow White?" When you put someone on a higher level than yourself, you tend to refuse to see that person as he or she is expecting more from him or her than is humanly possible.[13] In this type of situation you are showing your immaturity and an unrealistic view of life and relationships; 3) Am I rescuing the other person from him or herself or a situation which *I* see as being not good for that person? Many relationships are rescue attempts and sympathetic, not empathetic, associations. There are those who mistake sympathy for love and become involved so deeply in another's problems or emotions that they are dedicated to "making that person happy." The assumption is made that the other person

13 This is called the "halo effect" in Social Psychology.

is unhappy and "needs" your help. Rescuing also includes going after the social "underdog" and rescuing him or her from a life that they are living or have chosen to live or even feeling sorry for that person because of some unfortunate situation(s) that person had experienced. It is important to remember that the rescuee actually does not want to be rescued; 4) Is my attraction purely sexual or does it go beyond the purely physical level? Here again, problems develop. Many people mistakenly assume that sex and love are the same. Sex can exist without love and love without sex. When both are together then the relationship can become much more enjoyable. Remember do not expect real love to develop from a purely sexual relationship. The question to ask is just how long will the relationship last without sex? To many, physical attraction is more important than anything else. These people will seek out certain types of persons to be their partners and omit others. As a matter of fact, physical attractiveness is the first thing that attracts people to people. What researchers have found is that 80-percent of married people have married someone who resembles their opposite sex parent, a sibling or themselves in values, attitudes, behaviors and even appearance;[viii] and 5) Am I willing to commit myself to this relationship? Today many want the oxymoron of a "non-committed relationship." This is impossible for in order to have a relationship in the first place there has to be commitment. Without commitment there is nothing.[14]

The best thing to state for ***Love and Attraction*** is a statement of general attraction. It is kind of a call to all who fill the bill to come over and then you can have your choice. If the person that you have in mind is the most appropriate one for your present and future needs that will be quickly seen. Your statement for love could read as:

---

14 For a detailed discussion of relationships, love and sex see chapters 7 and 8 in **From Victim to Victor! Defeating a Victim's Consciousness** by the author.

I _______ am now filled with the joy and love of the Universe. I am feeling secure in knowing that true love is mine —NOW! I am radiating love, peace and happiness to all I see and they radiate the same back to me. I am attracting to me the person who harmonizes precisely with me in all ways and with whom I harmonize and am able to grow physically, emotionally, mentally and spiritually. We communicate true love and trust in all our ways and live together in harmonious loving response. I give thanks to my unconscious for my loving mate.

A love poem for this purpose might state:

I ________ am now attracting to me,
One with whom I harmonize exactly,
In every way that there may be,
In mind, in heart, in life agree,
Thank you unconscious for the mate I see.

A written love statement may say:

I ________ give thanks to my unconscious for attracting to me someone with whom I am in precise harmony and who harmonizes exactly with me.

The fourth area is ***Self-awareness*** or ***Spiritual Expression***. Needless to say, this is the basis for all of the other areas of life. For you can neither have nor comprehend a thing until you have the proper consciousness for it. Further, once you have achieved a higher state of consciousness more self-awareness develops. With more self-awareness comes a greater knowledge of the difference between your real needs and your ego desires as well as a greater responsibility for your choices.

To restate, the effective change statement, along with all of the other techniques, is intended to bring you to the state of consciousness needed for the perception of and acceptance of a desired objective.

A typical self-awareness statement may say:

I ________ am now at peace and in total harmony with myself

and the Universe. I have a new strong knowledge of my inner being and the Universal Presence within. This Presence uplifts my body, my mind and my spirit to greater heights daily. My Spirit guides, protects and permeates all of my life, conditions and affairs. I dwell in love and all I do is with love. I give thanks to my unconscious for my new awareness and my new life.

A poetic statement could sound like this:

I ______ now do feel,
My Spirit being lifted high,
My life glows with light so real,
My conditions now glorify,
My thanks to my unconscious I now testify.

The written style may say:

I ________ now give thanks to my unconscious and feel the Universal Presence within me permeating and raising me up high in all areas of my life.

The fifth area is ***Guidance***. This would probably be the best thing with which to start. It could open up all sorts of possibilities and probably give several choices that were not seen initially. In any case, if you have some trouble deciding which direction to go or if you have no idea of a direction, then guidance is what is needed. Even after direction is seen it is best to look over all of the possibilities carefully before deciding exactly what to do. Then, proceed by focusing in on one direction.

To gain ***Guidance*** state something like this:

I _______ now accept the guidance and urgings of my deeper self. I am guided now in thought, word and deed and I am a direct channel for the guiding energies of the Universe. I am now in my True Place doing what I love to do using my talents and abilities to their fullest, freely giving of them in many ways and receiving great compensation in all my ways. I reflect the power, glory and love of the Universe. My True

Will is completely and fully expressed in all I do. I give thanks to my unconscious for the wonderful guidance I am now receiving in all I do.

A short ***Guidance*** poem can go like this:

I ______ now accept,
Direct guidance from deep inside,
My whole life is now being kept,
In wondrous harmonious stride,
Thanks to my unconscious I give from deep inside.

The written statement of this type can read:

I _______ give thanks to my unconscious that I am now in precise union with Infinite Guidance and am being exactly directed in all my ways.

The last major area of change is that of ***Emotional Release***. There are many persons who choose to hold on to someone after they have gone. It does not matter if it is a broken romance, a runaway child or a death, emotional release is necessary. Being concerned and to care is fine. Tenaciously holding on is psychologically unsound. In the case of a broken romance, if the romance was good and positive and one that can grow, the release may bring the person back. In the case of the runaway child, the release could help you to find ways to contact the child or the child will return. But the child ran away for a reason and it is necessary that all persons involved begin to look within themselves and decide to change their relationship with each other — and the child. In this latter case, many things within the home must be looked at and changed. Finding a *good* family dynamics counselor or therapist can be one of the best things that can be done for the child and parents.[15] In the case of a death, the greatest gift that you can give to another who has made the transition is to allow him or her to go on through your emotional release. By continually

15 Again, **From Victim to Victor! Defeating a Victim's Consciousness** is an excellent source for personal development.

holding on to that person you are not only being selfish but you are not allowing him or her to go on to fully experience what may be beyond. The emotional release allows this to happen. It is good for you emotionally, psychologically, mentally and spiritually and it is good for the other because it allows him or her the freedom to choose their own path. The sign of true love is to allow the other the freedom to choose whatever she or he may feel is appropriate and you accepting that choice.

Written and spoken, the ***Emotional Release*** statement may say:

> I _______ totally release _______ to the Universe knowing that whatever you do is what you desire to do. I know you are guided, protected and prospered in all of your ways and wish you all of the love, peace and happiness possible. Thank you for the experience of your being and I thank my unconscious for the freedom to release you.

The poetic form may read:

> You _______ I _______ totally release,
> You are being loved in all of your ways,
> I now accept complete peace
> And happiness throughout my days,
> I give thanks for the experience of you
> And to my unconscious for the release, too.

Intonation

One thing that is always omitted in the books that speak of and use affirmation is proper intonation. As previously mentioned, just speaking your change statement with a normal tone of voice works fine with some persons and with some objectives but not with all. Also, thinking the change statement without speaking it works fine with others but not with all.[16] What you are looking

16 In ceremonial magick internally intoning in a loud "voice" is called "the great voice."

for is the most effective and dynamic method of getting your statement into the deeper mind where it can do its work.

There are three dynamic ways of impressing something into the unconscious. First is *shouting* it. The idea behind this method is that with the shout the ambient resonance from the volume will vibrate the shouter and cause the impregnation of the idea. You will better understand how this works if you will stick your head in a large bucket or barrel and shout. This method can be effective when you want to remove a bad habit or some sort of problem. One major drawback with this method comes when you live in close proximity to other people.

The second method of impressing the unconscious is by *lowering your voice about an octave lower than your ordinary speaking level.* Then speak your change statement. The theory behind this method is that the resonance of the lowered voice will cause a vibration throughout the body thus relating the vibratory level to the degree necessary to begin the change. If you vibrate mantras during meditation you will notice that certain parts of your body will vibrate during the mantra. With an appropriate effective change statement vibrated in this manner you can get your whole body charged up.

The third and final method, and probably the most universally effective method, is the *whisper*. The whisper should be loud enough to hear the change statement well. The reason that this method is so effective is because as a child the most loving statements were often given to you in a whisper. You long remember the rewarding feeling you got after grandma whispered how wonderful a child you were. Consequently, you would do all that you could to prove to her that she was right. The whisper technique has been described: "It's like loving yourself."

The method of shouts and whispers stems from childhood. Whenever you were told not to do something it was usually shouted at you. Conversely, the whispers were invariably loving kinds of statements. You must remember that your unconscious is still at about four years of age and so in order to get the most effect from your change statement you must give it to your unconscious as if you were giving it to a child.

There is a system in the use of whispered effective change statements. Stay with one statement until you begin to feel somewhat frustrated and uncomfortable then switch to another. ***Self-awareness*** and ***Healing*** statements can go on for years. Others would be best done in this manner: Use one change statement for one or two months then go to another for the same amount of time. The other may be totally different or it may be another aspect of the one with which you are currently working. Keep repeating this process continually and synchronous changes may begin to come about throughout and in many aspects of your life.

Another aspect of the effective change statement that is rarely discussed is when to do the statement for the most effect. As far as timing, there are two best times during the day that can be most effective. The first is in the morning as soon as you wake up. This is an excellent time because the mind is fresh from sleep and your first thoughts of the day set the mood for the whole day. Also, you are still emitting a great deal of alpha brain waves so the change statement has a better chance of getting into the unconscious completely intact during this time.

The second time is right before you retire for the night. The brain waves begin to slow down in the late evening and the unconscious is slowly opening. The change statement can get into the unconscious at this time as well. In both the morning and evening about twenty minutes or so of stating at each sitting will usually be sufficient. Properly done, you should notice an inner response within a few days. If not, experiment with different methods of intonation, stating and wording. Remember, it is an experiment.

It is also wise to have a written change statement that you can sit down with during the day. By doing all of this you can inundate yourself with the one idea that you have in mind.

For Those Who Need a Boost

A concept which is usually not discussed in reference to affirmation or effective change statements is the use of external aids. Outside aids can help to impregnate an idea into the unconscious. Also, when the conscious mind sees that you are doing something on the outside it begins to focus and move over to allow the unconscious to open up.

The thing that sets human beings above many of the lower animals is the ability to make and use complex tools.[17] In this instance the tools that are being discussed are simple aids to help activate the unconscious mind to do its job. What is being referred to here is the use of color and fragrances. It has been known for centuries that colors and fragrances can be used to assist in changing one's consciousness. For some strange reason, many people who use affirmations are averse to using an outside implement to help them trigger their deeper mind into action. The tools are there only as an aid.[18] Once the technique has been mastered, then the tools can be discarded.

Candle burning is a very ancient practice. The candle works on two basic levels. The first, and most obvious, is that of the burning candle or flame helping you to get into a meditative state. This will open your deeper mind. People are always fascinated by fire because it tends to relax the conscious mind and open the unconscious. With this happening, an idea can be shifted from the conscious into the unconscious more easily.

The second level is the effect brought about by using a candle of a specific color. No one can deny the effect that color has.[ix] By

17 Although this separation in tool use is getting smaller and smaller it is the use of complex tools that sets humans apart from the lower primates and other animals.

18 Often you can see televangelists use tools. Some will say, "Touch the television while I pray for you." Others will say, "Get out your 'healing towel.'" Then there is the use of pieces of bone or wood or engraved medals, etc. They are all tools to activate the unconscious mind and all extensions of magickal practice.

working with (a) specific candle(s) a subtle effect can be promoted in your consciousness.

The traditional colors and their effects and influences are:

White -	Self-awareness and consciousness raising; healing
Black -	Removal of unwanted behaviors, attitudes, etc. and energies
Red -	Physical energy; healing; physical attraction
Pink -	Good health; emotional attraction
Orange -	Mind clearing and focus; courage
Gold -	Courage; success
Yellow -	General success; mental clarity
Green -	Material growth; physical healing
Blue -	Peace; meditation; concentration; deeper understanding; communications
Purple -	Power over situations; material or business gains; dealings with the law; overcoming of obstacles
Brown -	Special requests and intentions

The sense of smell is probably the most neglected sense that humans have. Both eastern and western medicine has long known that certain diseases emit specific fragrances. Science has just gotten into the basic understanding of the pheromone, the natural attracting scent in animals and insects. There are suggestions now that specifically formulated fragrances could prove instrumental in healing, working, psychological intervention and a number of other processes.[x]

Some of the basic fragrances which can be used to promote an idea are:

Frankincense -	Meditation; raising awareness; healing; purification

Cinnamon -	Meditation; increase focus
Carnation -	Speeds healing
Cloves -	Overcome depression
Eucalyptus -	Healing
Geranium -	Spiritual strength; overcome depression
Jasmine -	Overcome depression; love
Lavender -	Love; encourages peace, relaxation and sleep; restful dreams
Lily of the Valley -	Calms the nerves
Lotus -	Calms the nerves; raising awareness
Magnolia -	Psychic development
Musk -	Physical attraction; self-confidence
Narcissus -	Calmness; harmony; peace of mind
Patchouli -	Separates energies; love
Peppermint -	Physical energy
Rose -	Peace in the home; attraction of affection
Sandalwood -	Purification; healing; success and good fortune
Wisteria -	Good feelings
Vanilla -	Good fortune
Violet -	Marital peace and happiness
White Rose -	Peace and serenity; spiritual strength

The use of candles and fragrances is centuries old. The reason that it still is in use is that it works well as *an effective aid*. But it is important to understand that these are only tools to help you to get into the proper state of mind where suggestions in your effective change statements and your visual imagery can reach the unconscious more strongly. Using the *tools* and the change statements and visual images inundates your whole system for a period of time with the one idea upon which you are working. This has a better chance of affecting your whole system and your life. The idea is not to get dependent on the use of the tool. It must never be an absolute necessity. It is an *adjunct* to what you are doing and may be a nice thing to use. The point is to find the visual imagery and effective change statement process which works best for you. Then changes come with your thinking.

A final method of controlling self-talk and developing your will-power is this: For a period of time, start with a few days, do not use the words "I" or "me" or any other self-reference in internal or external conversation. It is not as simple as it seems. You may also choose to not think a certain thought that gets in your way. This is almost like telling you not to think about a purple elephant. This will make you more keenly aware of the thought. Then, finally, do not perform a certain act for a period of time.

Since you spend a lot of time talking to yourself you may as well say nice things to yourself — the right way. The change statements are an effective method of doing just that. You may feel that you do not have any choice as to what you will say, why you will say it and when you will say it. That is not true. All of your thinking, your self-talk, is all your own choice. Your whole life is a product of the choices that you can do something about.

All of these exercises are designed to make you see how much unnecessary time is spent on useless and self-defeating talk, thoughts and actions. This time can be put to a lot better use. In order to insure that you will work your way through these exercises and learn to control your mind you can take away something which you find rewarding whenever you fall back into your old patterns. After you have completed these exercises for several weeks or months, depending on what you want to change in your life, then you will find more time to use your visual images and effective change statements. The change statement and visual imagery of an objective will more productively fill up that time and you can finally take total responsibility for your whole life and take total control of your existence.

Summary

Much of your internal conversation is shrugged off as idle chatter. By paying closer attention to what you're saying to yourself you can learn a lot about yourself and your universe.

Self-talk affects you depending on how often you repeat it. After years of saying things to yourself you end up proving a self-fulfilling prophecy about yourself. The more you repeat a statement the more you will act upon it. Repetition imbeds the concept into consciousness and the deeper the imbedding the greater the chance of realization. Repeating only positive statements won't necessarily work because of the lack of belief in them or intent behind them. Without the appropriate change mentally and emotionally the statements will have little or no effect.

Your feelings of self-esteem, self-confidence, degree of self-love or –hate, tendency toward being a winner or loser, your general life's goals and self-image were learned early in life. These patterns continue throughout your life without your thinking. Because much of this was learned at home and after a while your parents became concepts and not physical people. That doesn't mean you're still not trying to please your absent parents. But you do not have to live in the past.

You are where you are due to your choices, and you are totally responsible for your choices. There are many excuses that you can have for your present conditions but it is your choices that are to blame. You are where you are because that is where you want to be and that is what you believe you deserve.

To make the changes you desire you have to commit yourself to get busy at making the changes you want.

You are the creator of your personal universe. You begin the creative thought process and these thoughts begin manifesting. These manifestations will affect you and recreate your thoughts. All of these thoughts cause biochemical changes in the brain. Thus the thought becomes imbedded in the brain. If this process continues properly your consciousness for change may draw specific conditions to you. So, if you change your thoughts (your mind) you can change your life.

Much of what you say to yourself is negative and irrational. This will affect how you are interpreting your environment. Your total experience is filtered through your consciousness, past experiences, beliefs, values and expectations.

By changing your self-talk you can make other changes about yourself and your life. There are steps to changing your self-talk. After a concerted effort to change your negative self-talk you'll need to replace the self-talk with something more positive: Effective Change Statements. There is a pattern for creating Effective Change Statements that can make them practical and useful. There are also practical methods for the repetition of the Effective Change Statements. If you need a meditation tool to help you can use things like candles and fragrances. The point is to commit yourself to changing your thinking and thus changing your personal universe.

Endnotes

i Alexander S. Holub, Ph.D. (2007) **From Victim to Victor! Defeating a Victim's Consciousness**, Bridger House Publications, Inc.

ii *IBID*

iii Bob Toben (1975) **Space-Time and Beyond**, E.P. Dutton, New York, NY

iv *Op cit*

v Alexander S. Holub, Ph.D. and Evelyn Budd-Michaels, Ph.D. (1999) **Psychokinesiology: Doorway to the Unconscious Mind**, Bridger House Publications, Inc.

vi B. Berglund, U. Berglund and T. Undvall (Nov. 1976) *Psychological Processing of Odor Mixtures*, **Psychological Review**, Vol. 83, No.6, P. 432-441

vii Alexander S. Holub, Ph.D. (2007) **From Victim to Victor! Defeating a Victim's Consciousness**, Bridger House Publications, Inc.

viii *IBID*

ix F. Birren (Apr. 1973) *Color Preference as a Clue to Personality*, **Art Psychotherapy**, Vol. 1, No. 1, P. 13-16
M. Sahlins (Oct-Dec 1975) *Colors and Culture*, **Rassegna Italiana di Sociologia**, Vol. 16, No. 4, P. 591-610 (English Translation)

x B. Bergland, U. Bergland, and T Undvall (Nov. 1976) *Psychological Processing of Odor Mixtures*, **Psychological Review**, Vol. 83, No. 6, P. 432-441
W.S. Cain (Feb. 1977) *Differential Sensitivity for Smell: 'Noise' at the Nose*, **Science**, Vol. 195, No. 4280, P. 796-798
S. Schiffman and C. Dockis (Nov. 1976) *Multidimensional Scaling of Musks*, **Physiology and Behavior**, Vol. 17, No. 5, P. 823-829
W.B. Weitzel, J.J. Horan and J.W. Addis (Jan 1977) *A New Olfactory Aversion Apparatus*, **Behavior Therapy**, Vol. 8, No. 1, P. 83-88
The Subtle Persuasion of Scent (1981) **Science Digest**, Vol. 89, No. 10, P. 97

Endnotes

Nothing endures but change.

Heraclitis (c. 540 - c. 480 BCE)

Chapter 9
Conclusion

How do you know when **you have changed**? This may seem like a rather strange question but most people have no idea when change has occurred in their lives. If you have no idea when change has occurred how will you know if **it has happened**? Often change is assumed to be due to a major or drastic event. Actually, immense changes occur only after a myriad of small changes. Around ninety-nine percent of the changes that occur to you are ones you are unaware of because they are so small. Major change comes from small steps leading up to it. It is sort of a pyramid effect as many small changes build up to a peak that finally gets noticed.

The main idea presented in this book is that you can build the small steps upon which change can develop. You have seen that scientific principles from the new physics may effectively be used in order to explain the functioning and programming of your mind. But all of these techniques, principles and exercises are of absolutely no use. They are a waste of time and of literally no good —— if they are not used. Reading about them and agreeing with them is simply worthless. In order to get anything to happen in the direction that you want to go you have to make changes. You must begin those changes on the inside with your thinking about yourself, your experiences and your created universe. If you're waiting for the Universe to do the changing for you while you sit idly by *expecting* something to happen, you are in for a rude awakening. There is an ancient proverb: "The gods help those who help themselves."[1] If you are not going to do what needs to be done *with yourself* first, how do you expect anything to happen *for* you?

All too often after reading a book, after a seminar or workshop or even in therapy[2] you will come away being excited and motivated to do something.[3] The problem comes when you attempt to apply what you have learned after returning home and to work. You run into the same old problems that you had before. So what you do is end up responding with the same behaviors, attitudes, thoughts and emotions as before. What happened to the changes that were supposed to have occurred from the techniques in the books, seminar and workshop or therapy session? Psychology defines learning as a "*relatively permanent change* in behavior brought about through *practice*." With this definition it becomes obvious what has happened. For something to be learned and installed in behavior so that there is change it has to be *practiced*. Without the practice there has really been no deep and worthwhile learning that is going to do anything in your life. If you want to really make changes in your life you need to continually practice. When you were a child and you first learned to walk one of the first things that you did was fall down. If you sat on the floor and said, "I'll never be able to do this. I'm a failure at walking," you would still be sitting on the floor. The fact is that you did not sit there. You got up and went at it again — you continually practiced walking. Then, before too long you were walking all over the house with adults chasing you and you certainly did think that was funny.

1 From Aesop's fable, *The Old Man and Death.*

2 The reference here is to actual therapy sessions. There are organizations who have pseudo-therapy sessions based on emotional trance state manipulation.

3 There is even one well-known seminar leader who says that all you have to do is buy his book and keep it with you. You don't even have to read it. The "energy" from the book will surround you and affect your life. What a great way to sell books! I guess it's too late to say the same thing about this book. You've already read this far.

So you come away from the book, the seminar, the workshop or the therapy session all excited and the minute that anyone hits one of your triggers the first thing you do is respond as you normally do. Believe it or not, that's absolutely normal. What you need to do is to go into your deeper mind to find out what you could do to make a change in your response-ability. You expected the change to be automatic. It wasn't. When it was not you became disappointed and disillusioned thinking that all of the information you were so excited about was of little value. Without practicing the things that you want to change, there will be no change. But the trick is to know what actually needs to be changed.

It is the same with the techniques that you read about in this book. How many of them did you look at and either not consider using or say, "I *tried* that and it didn't work." The statement will give you an indication as to exactly what happened. It is not true that "it" did not work. *You* may not have worked with it long enough or with the proper intent, emotions and desire. Most often the problem is that you have no idea what you need to change in order to get what you want or you have your ego involved in your choice or you have no idea what you want to have in the end. Maybe you do know what you want in the end. The problem is how will you know when you have gotten what you want? Just by thinking about what it will be like *if* you got it is not going to help you at all. You have to have a *completely detailed picture* of what you will *experience* as soon as you have it. Often people are expecting others to change and *as soon as* the others change then things will be different. Nothing could be further from the truth. Those people are not living your life. You are. If you do not take responsibility to do something about you it will be business as usual. There is an old maxim: "If you keep doing what you've always done, you're going to keep getting what you've always got."

The techniques presented here are a means of having you assume total responsibility for your past and future. They are a means of having you assume the total responsibility for the change that you want as well. As you well know, the change begins inside you with a change of consciousness, for as your consciousness changes so does your manifested universe. A change in consciousness rarely, if ever, occurs instantly. It takes time.[4]

There is an old proverb that states: "The journey of one-thousand miles must begin with a single step."[5] The decision to do something is not the first step. That is because decisions are constantly being made and nothing comes of them. What then is the first step?

The actual first step to making changes or accomplishing any purpose is the ***intent*** to do it. Intent is a *deliberate* act of will *and* the decision to do a specific thing or to achieve a certain outcome. Once the intent has been made there is the definite commitment to follow through. It is easy to say, "I'll be going to Europe."[6] But you can put that off for years and eventually forget about it or rationalize the reasons for not going. But once you have deliberately intended to go, your definite ***commitment*** will arrange getting all of your affairs in order so that you may go at the time that you have decided to go. So, as you can see by rewording the statement to, "I'm going to Europe the first two weeks of May of this year where I will visit London, Paris and Rome" creates a definite plan. With your intention and commitment you will see yourself going. You will see yourself there and you will talk to yourself about all of the things you will do and see. You may even get pictures from magazines of many of the sights in Europe and see yourself at them or you may make a collage of these places and intersperse them with your picture.[7] But the point is, you have engaged your intentionality and made a definite commitment. Once this is done there is very little that will hold you back from your goal.

---

4 Unless you're taking some mind-altering substance.

5 Lao-Tzu (c. 604-531 BCE) **The Way of Lao-Tzu**

6 One female comedian put going to Europe this way; "It's a pain in the ass, but you got to do it just once."

7 This is called a *treasure map.*

After commitment comes the ***conceptualization***. This is done through any or all of the methods that have been discussed: visual imagery, effective change statements, using candles and scents, and/or even creating a collage. This brings the desire to the part of the deeper mind where the work is done.

To involve yourself more in your conceptualization follow this simple process:

1. ***Relax***. This is very important. Relaxation brings you to a more accepting state where learning is quicker and more effective and where tensions cannot block your thinking. It also gets your ego out of the way keeping you from talking yourself out of what you want to do. For just dealing with visual imagery and effective change statements you might try some simple method such as what has been called *progressive desensitization*. This is done by beginning at one point of the body (usually the feet but sometimes the head) and tensing and relaxing each part of your body while stating the relaxation as you go along. This is an example of what you may do: Beginning at your toes you will tense and relax your toes a couple of times. As you do this you will state, "My toes are relaxing. Feel them relax. More and more relaxed ..." Then tense and relax the ankles and feet and state, "My ankles and feet are relaxing. Feel them relax. More and more relaxed ... as I can feel the relaxing warmth move throughout my whole body," and continue on until you have the feeling of relaxation throughout your whole body.

2. ***Combine the mind and body***. Both the mind and the body are interconnected. Through many of the techniques available you can gain control over what goes into your deeper mind and consequently what goes out to your body. By combining mind and body you are getting yourself totally involved in the idea of what you are moving toward. What this actually means is that you are

effectively manipulating your visual imagery with the proper emotional response in order to make them more believable to both your conscious and unconscious. By bringing in the appropriate emotional responding you will be able to apply a deeper intention to your outcome. In order to get an appropriate emotional response what you can do is to go back to a time when you were successful at doing something that you had set your mind to do. Re-experience it *through your own eyes* and get the emotions as clearly as possible. Hold on to those emotions and bring them up to what it is that you want to do now. Then, do your visualization and apply those emotions to it. This will help you to get the proper emotions into the present goal. If you have a difficult time getting the appropriate emotional responses then you will have to build the emotions. Think of something that you feel confident about: a sport, an art, fixing your car, music or whatever. Bring up that confidence and hold on to it as strongly as possible. You can use a key word such as, "Oh, yeah!" or clenching your fist to trigger this response. Then go to another response such as "being focused." Bring that up and do the same thing using the same trigger. Bring in another response such as "happy" and do the same thing. The point is to figure out what emotions and responses you want to have and build them. After you have built three or four of them use your trigger to see how well they are working. If they have not been built strongly enough intensify each one by adding stronger responses to them. Then, do your visual imagery and use your trigger. Once you have gotten the feelings that you need for your visual image then you can do your visualization *and* trigger your emotions at the same time on your own.

3. ***Be patient***. Expecting wonders in a day or so is unrealistic. Impatience breeds tension and tension blocks any programming on which you are working. Impatience is

actually nothing more than the ego getting in your way. It is a demand on the Universe to accede to your will. Patience allows you to see things much more clearly. Hurrying to get things done or to see things happen prevents them from happening. Patience actually can speed up the accomplishing of many things. This is so because you are no longer trying to consciously "force" something to happen. You are allowing it to unfold.

4. ***Keep going forward.*** By going forward you will be able to see what needs to be done as you go along. You can also see what *not* to do as well. When you decide to go backward you lose all of the potential you had. Remember, potential energy is the energy a body has by virtue of its position. By going back your potential for experience and expression lessens and you will tend to attach emotions to incorrect responses. That is, you can become angry (both direct and indirect aggression), fearful, frustrated and unhappy. Your responses to your environment will be unrealistic and irrational causing you to create immense generalizations of lack, inability and failure. The past is something to learn from; not something to become stuck in.

5. ***Master the ego of the senses.*** All that you perceive on the physical level is a transitory reality. Your interpretations of them as actual permanent realities are the illusions. You must not think or believe that what your senses view is the only reality or what is. The fact that you perceive only one-one millionth of a meter of the whole electromagnetic spectrum gives you proof. Hence, your senses are extremely limited and function on a low level.

   Humans are actually interdimensional beings. Even if you only consider humans as existing on the fourth dimension of space-time along with the other three-dimensions this makes humans interdimensional. What you perceive as life is to be experienced and learned from; not something upon which you must become dependent. Once an experience has been completed, it is completed. Holding on to it means that you have not learned from it. Until you are able to make a positive statement of what you have learned from a seemingly negative situation, you will continually repeat it.

6. ***Apply your energy to what is positive and constructive***. Once you begin to direct your energy into positive outcomes you will be adding to the positive direction of the Universe. There is an ancient Celtic maxim: "An' that ye harm none, do what ye will." Do no harm. Prevent no one from achieving their full potential nor prevent yourself from achieving your full potential. Remember, if you take the time and energy to block another you are wasting the energy that you need for yourself. See to it that you are directing and focusing your energies into the direction that affords you the most complete self-expression and greatest experience of the Universe possible — not at the expense of others. Instead, realize that what you want to accomplish is for the good of all.

7. ***Strengthen your will-power***. As a young child you could will things into existence. You were not bound by, "You can't do that," or "That's not for real." Instead, you just went ahead and *wished* it to happen — and often it did happen. As you grew older you lost that ability because rational explanations such as coincidence seemed to make more sense. So, what you did was to forget about and no longer accept that you could do anything about making changes in your life. From this point you came to accept whatever came along as your "lot in life." You no longer had the confidence in your own deeper self and your abilities to do the change work.

   You strengthen your will-power by understanding that you have created your whole existence and that you can recreate it. You further strengthen your will-power by beginning working on those things which are realistic and have a good chance of being accomplished. By doing this you will find the techniques that work best for you. You can then apply those techniques to more difficult tasks.

8. ***Have no ulterior motives***. This means to get the ego out of what you are doing and be honest with yourself and with others. Whenever you want to accomplish something and you have any sort of ulterior motives you limit the possible outcomes. Your only motive should be to express and fulfill yourself to the fullest in such a way that it will be the greatest benefit to the largest number of people. Never should you want to do something because it is what you want for yourself, nor because you want to show-off ("I'll show them!"). That is your ego talking. Most often, by maintaining this attitude, you will not succeed when you go into your change work. If you do succeed the gains tend to be rather empty because whoever you were trying to impress just does not care and is not impressed. It is best to want to express yourself to the fullest because you are in your rightful place and doing what you love to do.

9. ***Encourage others***. Throughout this book the self and the spirit have been referred to as pretty much the same thing. Self-awareness increases your spiritual growth. Begin to become more fully aware of all that is around you. Become more fully aware of your reasons for doing what you're doing and wanting what you want. Learn to experience life more fully by expressing yourself more openly and more fully. Become more in harmony with the Universe by applying Universal Principles; principles that are directed at what are right and good for all, into all that you are doing. Do not be fooled by the objectives of your ego for the truly great person has power over his lower nature. Learn to consider yourself as part of the Universe

> and not just a name and/or a member of a group with a title. Accept no pat answers for the Universe does not work that way. Remember, pat answers are lies because they are human devices that keep people in bondage.
>
> Nature, you will find out, is illogical. From sub-atomic particles which simply appear and disappear for no reason, all of nature is chaotic. Some aspects of nature are easy to understand. The vast majority of what nature is all about makes no sense at all. The main reason for this is that the Universe is constantly changing and nothing remains the same. Accept that you are constantly changing as well and that you are part of the Universe and are able to come into harmony with that constant change.

Mental imagery is not the only important thing you need to get things moving; you also need organization. Organization means that you are putting things together mentally, psychologically and physically in order to make your mental image more effective. Know exactly what it is that you want or need or where you want to go. You cannot visualize until you have decided what to visualize. You cannot use change statements until you have decided where the change is going and what actually needs changed. It is an interesting fact that through visual imagery and change statements your previous organization will reorganize your conditions in order to bring about your purpose.

Most people would not recognize being given direction if it came at them with a brass band. You must open yourself up to be more aware of the possibilities available. When you are locked into one idea by fear, ignorance of fact, ego, vanity and so on you are not open to other experiences. You need to learn to recognize the positive and negative synchronous events and flow with or away from the direction that they are leading. You need to also be aware and recognize possibilities as they occur.

Through recognition of your direction you can actualize your desires. By flowing with your proper direction you can place the proper energies into the proper space at the proper time and get things accomplished when they are either set into motion or just waiting for the energy to move them. Manifesting of desires comes from doing what needs to be done appropriately and effectively. If manifestation does not occur or there is no inner response quickly check your reasons for wanting the goal. You may feel that you really *do not* deserve the objective. It is rather difficult to know if you are on the right path unless you are looking at the synchronous events that are occurring. The easiest method for finding out what the problem may be is to look honestly at yourself and your reasons for doing what you want to do.

If life's changes are truly desired then commitment to a program that will place the mind into the proper space for accepting the desire is necessary. One possible program that you may follow could be: 1) Buy a blank book to use as a journal where only certain things will be placed. These things are, first, positive events. Second, you will list those events that you ordinarily would have handled badly but have handled differently and their outcomes. Third, you will list the ways that you came down on yourself and confrontational questioning procedures that you used to prove to yourself that what you came down on yourself for was factual. Finally, you will list those things you handled badly and ways that you can handle them better if they ever occur again; 2) Buy a tablet where you will write your effective change statements at least twenty times every day; 3) Decide exactly the *realistic*, not egocentric, changes you are needing to make; 4) Design a visual image that will accompany your effective change statement; 5) Wake up a half-hour to forty-five minutes earlier in the morning to do the visualization and whisper your change statements; 6) Prior to going to sleep take the time to write in your journal; 7) Do more change statements and visual imagery before going to sleep; and 8) Go to sleep feeling and visualizing accomplishing your working.[8]

---

8 The word "sacrifice" actually means to exchange one energy for another. Remember, energy just is and can neither be created nor destroyed but can be transformed.

The effective change statements can be written at any time you so desire. This usually takes only about ten minutes. One thing that can be done during the day is to have a simple one or two line statement and short visualization which can be invoked at any time. The statement that you will have needs to be one that forces you to think about what it is you are saying and what your goal is. Vain repetition does nothing for your accomplishing anything. You need to keep your mind directed toward your objective constantly. It is also important to remain faithful toward your desires and *do not tell anyone else what your desires are or what you are doing*. It is none of their business and they would just love to talk you out of what you are doing so they can say, "See! I told you so!"

If visual imagery seems to be a problem then whisper the change statements and work to strengthen your ability to visualize. Constantly keep in mind that the visualization *is* a reality and accept it as such. Without this acceptance it becomes nothing more than another fantasy. The more you accept it as a reality the more real it becomes.

Many persons are dissatisfied with their present conditions for several reasons: 1) They think that someone else has something that they *should* have; 2) They cannot accept the fact that *they* are responsible for where they are; and 3) They cannot accept that what they have and are now is *their* reality. If you look deeply into these statements you will see that they are all intertwined. If you blame another for your conditions, whether that person is real or imagined you are claiming that whoever or whatever it is has the power to single you out from the billions of people on this planet and those existing on other planets for an unhappy existence. This may come in the form of acting out, envy, jealousy, negative religious, economic or social philosophies or whatever is so desired. What you're thinking is that someone or something has given what you think you *should* have to someone else or is withholding something from you. Consequently, you cannot accept the reality which exists for you and which you created. You will then become frustrated and do one of three things: strike out at others in overt and/or covert ways; actually do something about your conditions; or give up.

It is necessary to begin to accept what you now experience as being the precise response to your present state of consciousness. This means seeing and accepting what you have as your creation and your present reality is caused by your thoughts. Accept all that you are experiencing, all that you are doing, all that you are and all of the people and conditions as your own concepts and you can begin to grow from there. Once you start to accept all of this then what is not right can be made right by the Universe.

Accepting does not mean that you become complacent, sit back and do nothing and feel that what you have is all that you deserve. Accepting means that you understand first, that you are responsible for who you are and what you now have and that all you perceive is temporary and since it is temporary you can affect it. This does not mean that you make statements such as, "Of course it's a reality, but it's not mine. I'm not supposed to have it." How asinine of a statement could anyone make? The point is that you are supposed to have it or you would not have it. What you are experiencing *is* yours. You created it with or without your conscious knowledge, so take responsibility for it and accept it as yours.

This is the beginning point. From here the understanding of your effect on your existence starts to emerge. As you grow from here, you can begin to set about changing your perceptions, and you will probably do it. Once you really become determined to do something, as long as it is realistic and does you or another no harm, you most likely will accomplish it.

To do this you need to be self-disciplined. By the term self-disciplined is meant *voluntarily* disciplined. Many mistake punishment for discipline. Discipline means to teach and doesn't involve physical or psychological harm. Punishment does not necessarily and often does not teach anything. In order to discipline another, a learning experience must be presented. With the learning of a lesson the discipline accomplishes its purpose.

Discipline helps you to more fully express yourself. It gives you an inner strength that is totally unmatched by the undisciplined. It gets you more in touch with the spark of the Higher Self within. Punishment and discipline are not the same things; especially when it comes to self-discipline. Self-discipline means that as you make your choices you are learning from the outcomes of your choices. Without the learning process there is no true discipline.

Any imposed means of discipline, such as coercion or fear, is not true discipline. When you, through your own desired (not manipulated) choice begin to regulate your own behavior for any positive and constructive learning purpose you are disciplining yourself. True self-discipline is totally voluntary. In this discipline you will realize that you will be gaining mentally, emotionally, psychologically, physically and spiritually.

Through voluntary self-discipline not only do you learn from experience but new experiences will be sought from which to learn. Coercion or fear-oriented “discipline” locks you into certain behaviors, learning experiences and a constant state of anxiety. It confounds and confuses and sets up pat answers. It invents “mysteries” in order to keep your mind bound up onto one track. It promotes personality problems and paranoia in order to manipulate your emotions. It does not give. It takes and convinces you that you are getting so much from it. It takes your inner being and gives you membership in a group. It takes your mind and the freedom to think and tells you what you are to think, when you are to think and how you are supposed to think. It creates a uniformity of people making you like everyone else. It takes your empathetic emotions toward all life and tells you that their philosophy is right and good and everyone else’s is wrong or evil. You become judgmental toward others who are not involved. The others who will not buy into the philosophy become a means of displaying how right the group is. The coercion or fear-orientation of these groups is a means of not wanting you to think as an individual for without their members they would not exist, nor do they have the answers that they claim. Fear is their only means of control not of discipline and especially not love, although they do a good job of convincing you that you are loved — by them.

Real learning is from being and experiencing. As you learn you become proud of yourself and your accomplishments. You become action and goal-oriented and your behaviors become life-ward.

The American society is, unfortunately, a society of pandemic undiscipline. A good conservative estimate of those who are voluntarily disciplined for positive gains would be less than 5-percent of the society. That would be less than five-hundred thousand people in a society of over 300-million people who have any real sense of discipline.[9]

When Benjamin Franklin wrote, "Early to bed; early to rise makes a man healthy, wealthy and wise," he probably was implying that a disciplined individual is the one who makes the greatest strides. The founding fathers of the United States, almost all of whom were highly disciplined and learned and experienced Freemasons, knew the value of discipline.

Today, everyone seems to be looking for the easy way: fast foods (which are ruining our diet and our health); fast money (which is causing people to sell themselves out, to sell themselves short and an increased victim and victimless crime rate); fast love (which is causing a lack of deep intimacy and honest caring, a high divorce rate and an epidemic of sexually transmitted diseases); and fast enlightenment (which is causing people to pay exorbitant amounts of money and attach themselves to anything which affords them a sheltered environment where they can be spoon-fed someone's contrived version of a philosophy). Very few are willing to take the time out of their day to be with themselves or work on accomplishing their desires. That is basically where voluntary self-discipline comes in. Being self-disciplined you

9 I recall reading this statement somewhere: "Only about 5-percent of the people in the world think; ten-percent think they think; the other 85-percent don't know what they're thinking." This is a variation of a statement of Thomas Edison.

will sacrifice the time in the present to insure a better future for yourself and everyone with whom you are in contact. Essentially, being self-disciplined means that you are taking the time to be good to yourself.

Many will say that they do not have the time to do a complete change program; that they have to make a living. They are partially correct: They do have to make a living. That part is correct. The only reason that they do not have the time is because *they do not want to take the time*. Other things are more important: Who has the highest averages in a favorite sport?; Who is doing what to who in the latest episode of the soap opera or in the neighborhood or in Hollywood?; What is happening on Oprah or Ellen or some other talk show?; What is the latest hit record?; Who is the latest member of what group?; Who is in love with who this week?; Will I get seduced this weekend?; Why did so-and-so get that job (raise, promotion, etc.) and I did not?; Who is getting paid the most in sports, movies, business and so on and why?; Who can I manipulate to get what I want?; How much more money can I make if I hold out, cut corners, use cheaper materials, lay-off this many employees, raise the rents this much and so on?; This car, this house, these clothes, this attitude, and on is what I need to impress the businessmen, lawyers, doctors, boys, girls, church group, whoever; I need a young woman/man because it makes me look better in public; Can I break my last/best score on the video game or golf or tennis?; and on and on.

By now you have the idea. Most people waste so much time cultivating crass, inane and absolutely useless objectives that they fail to take the time to discipline themselves in any constructive ways. They assume that just because they get up at a certain time for work five days a week and that they do some work around the house on the weekend that they are disciplined.

Discipline means that you take the time to do something *useful and constructive* in *your own life*. It means that you have got objectives in mind that *you* want to accomplish and *you are* setting yourself up in order to accomplish them.

Along with discipline, another totally misunderstood term is *sacrifice*. You have been taught that sacrifice means that you give up something for some rather dubious reason: a martyr sacrifices his or her life for a philosophical or political idea;[10] a "religious" person sacrifices something they like during a period of religious observance. It is ideas like these which have been brought down to us and keep us misinformed as to the true meaning of sacrifice.

Sacrifice simply means that one energy is *exchanged* for another. This also is the point being made concerning voluntary discipline. Once a program of visual imagery, effective change statements, journal-keeping and so on has begun the energy that is expended building the physical manifestation will be exchanged for the manifestation itself. So, it comes to reason that the greater the energy expended the more joy there will be when the manifestation working is objectified. Once begun, there is also the distinct possibility that the manifestation can come around more quickly or at least you will have a better idea of the direction you need to go.

To discipline yourself is to sacrifice your time and expend energy at present to make future gains. You are not doing it because of some religious, philosophical, egocentric, political ideology, social tenet or economic reason. You are doing so because you *want to do it* and you realize the total manifestation of the objective will be of benefit to everyone.

It is easy to rationalize and say that you want to discipline yourself but once you begin to inquire and you find yourself making statements such as: "Because so-and-so says to do it" then it is not voluntary and it is not a sacrifice nor is it discipline.

10 The only time this type of sacrifice works is if the specific religion or political philosophy wins-out. Otherwise, it goes unnoticed. Quite often the sacrificed is unnamed no matter who wins.

Discipline is a necessary adjunct to life. Without any discipline you will wander aimlessly from place to place, job to job, idea to idea, person to person, relationship to relationship and never have anything settled. When you find a group that affords you the discipline that you refuse to give yourself then you will attach yourself to it and defend it to the death. Being undisciplined you tend to go in one of two directions and sometimes swing back and forth between a complete lack of discipline such as the beatnicks, yippies, hippies and flower-child cults of old and the punk and new-wave of this present time, to a total discipline such as fundamentalist Christianity or Islam and its tens of thousands of splinter groups; those groups classified as cults such as the Unification Church, the Hari Krishnas, Jehovah's Witnesses, Scientology, Alcoholics Anonymous and other quasi-religious groups as well as pseudo-political philosophies such as the neo-Nazis and the Ku Klux Klan. You will be looking for someone else to give you the discipline that you lack because you either received too little, none or totally extreme doses of "discipline" (punishment) as you were growing up. There tended to be no real training in your life: a training which helped you to become more responsible. Consequently, you turned to other persons to do the work for you.

We all have limitations. That does not mean that you cannot accomplish *anything*. You can overcome many limitations and become a really active participant in the Universe. You have the ability and power within you to create your personal heaven on Earth if you so desire. That is your choice. No one is holding you back but yourself. You cannot blame your parents for what is happening to you now. You cannot place the blame for your present situation on any deity; benevolent or malevolent. You cannot blame the nebulous "they" for anything you are going through. You also cannot blame the government and their policies for the government of a nation is the consciousness of the majority of the people of a country who helped to place those people in power. You are the only one who has control of your world and your Universe.[11] You are where you are due to your own choices and nothing else. So, now it is up to you to do something about it. You have to choose to do it and you have to do it yourself. You cannot depend on someone or something else to accomplish your purpose. What is most important is that you have to stick to your decision. You need to sacrifice as well. You need to sacrifice some of your present time and energy for future rewards. For you will reap great benefits with dedication, determination and *discipline*. You are going after the change for yourself, but not in an egocentric manner because you want everyone to benefit. When you are happy and satisfied in yourself and your life others with whom you interact cannot help but to be the same.

In essence, then, it can be said that your sacrifice is out of *love*. First it is the love that you have for yourself. Second, it is the love you have for everyone and everything in your created universe and beyond. This love is a feeling of one-ness or unity with your surroundings. This brings you feelings of exhilaration and life transformation. Scientifically this feeling deals with spontaneous altered states of consciousness and specific brain functions attached to the right hemisphere.[i] This is termed *quantum solipsism* and it is the feeling of unity which is the aligning factor to who you really are and your place in this unity. It is also the same experience that has been described down through the centuries as *insight*, or *enlightenment*, or *the experience of God*.

All that is done in love reaps the rewards of love. Once you get into the habit of love you see it in everything and everyone — including yourself. Love is a deep concern and respect; a feeling of unity with yourself and the Universe. Although there are persons

11 This is true to a large degree in those countries where people have the right to vote. What must be considered is the fact that often poorer countries have their governments manipulated by the more powerful countries' governments with promises of protection and material aid. The material aid *never* reaches the people who need it most and the poorest people are *never* protected from the ravages of their own government. The greatest asset a country has is not under ground but the creative drive of its people. Give them a chance and the country will prosper.

who will by their actions perform a rather cruel and unjust activity which none will consider positive this does not exclude them from this feeling. You cannot love their choice and their action but they still deserve your respect simply because they are another human being. The action is separate from the actor even though it is a choice that the individual made which interferes with the lives of others. Since they are the same as you when you give them respect, you give yourself respect for all things are interconnected.

This unity is the bottom line to all existence. If the Universe were egocentric it could have chosen to remain as Chaos or Nothing. But the Universe understood that in order to express itself to the fullest it had to love itself and it could not love itself without allowing the evolving of objects that could experience and express love. All that exists on all planes is the result of love. All that is created is created out of love.

Love is unity and unity is love. The more in union you feel with your deeper self the more you respect the individual that you are. The greater this respect for yourself the more this respect generates outward to all other object-events. In response, all other object-events return your feelings of respect and with this response comes a greater feeling of unity with all existence.

What you most love or unify with you express. In this expression are the created conditions for the experience. You love yourself to the degree that you experience your created universe. The happier and more prosperous your conditions the greater are your feelings of self-love. Whatever you have is what you feel you deserve.

How can you begin to create the universe that you want to experience? A possible formula for the mechanics of creation could be:

$$\left(\left[T\left(\frac{sD\left(\frac{PI}{RM}\right)\frac{1S}{O}(i)}{\sum e} \right) - f \right] C \right) L^{n+1} = U$$

T = Thought
L = Quantum Solipsism
U = Created Universe

S = Sacrifice
1 = Self-love
M = Mental Clarity

D = Discipline
O = Other Awareness
C = State of Consciousness

R = Degree of Relaxation
P = Perceptual Ability
I = Ability to Interpret Subtle Energies

I = Ability to Interpret the Physical Reality
f = Fear Orientation
$\sum$e = The Sum of the Experience

Unfortunately, with this formula is the fact that we are dealing with immeasurable items. Consequently, just about any formula could work as long as the legend accompanying it was explanatory enough.

The point to this is not to attempt to provide a mathematical model, as feeble as it is. The point is to bring out the fact that L (Quantum Solipsism or Universal Love) is the multiplying agent. The greater this aspect of life, the greater is the experience of U (the Created Universe).

Learn to love all things for who or what they are for they are part of you and you are part of them. You are a creation of the Universe as you also create your own specific universe. Understand that you are always in the process of becoming or in potential and that what you perceive now is already past. Take control and become all that you were meant to be. For what you are seeking is seeking you.

To paraphrase Gary Zukav;[ii] *If we are to learn anything from our past we should learn the folly of holding on too fast to any particular idea or concept.* Ideas and concepts are devices of man and man alone. There are no concepts apart from those produced by the mind of man. If man was not here to conceive of an idea there would be no ideas or concepts conceived. Everything would be in potential and would not be stopped even for a moment in time and space to be perceived. It would become what it was intended to be without any distraction or disturbance. But there are object-events here that do perceive. They do slow time down in order to perceive. They do create intents which recreate what they perceive distracting and disturbing the Universe and they are also in potential. The object-events occupying the Universe are here to give the Universe its eyes, ears and other senses experiencing and expressing themselves following the changing structure of the Universe. This structure is constantly changing, becoming and is not the same from moment to moment. Those object-events perceiving the Universe are also changing. To "go with the flow" allows those object-events to make the changes necessary to experience and express the Universe to the fullest. By their innate property of distracting and disturbing the Universe the perceiving object-events can change their own experience of the Universe and become that which expresses the Universe to the fullest. The Universe will more completely flow through those object-events which exercise their potentiality more fully. This means that the object-events which take change into account will become what they were meant to be and will do what they were meant to do.

Begin to drop pebbles into the still water of your mind and your experienced Universe. Each pebble sends out waves of creativity which will return in kind. These pebbles are the thoughts which can change your perception of your reality. From a new perspective you can see yourself and your life differently and gain in peace of mind, respect and love of yourself and all that exists in the Universe and assume responsibility for the choices you make. From this perspective you will be accepting yourself as a Child of the Universe having the right to be here or you would not be here. Remember, whatever you accomplish, whatever pebbles you drop into the still waters you are helping the Universe unfold and know itself.

Endnotes

i M. Black (Aug. 1982) *Brain Flash, The Physiology of Inspiration*, **Science Digest**, Vol. 90, No. 8, P. 85-87, 104

ii Gary Zukav (1979) **The Dancing Wu Li Masters**, Bantam Books, New York, NY

Glossary of Terms

Bell's Theorum – Particles once in contact will continue to influence one another no matter how far apart they are; there is no such thing as "separate parts," everything is part of a unified whole which is interconnected.

Biogravitational Field – A field similar to the gravitational field governing the structure of matter and this in turn structures reality; consciousness.

Causality Violation – Observations occurring simultaneously; superposition.

Coincidence – The principle of non-causal events; an acausal principle in nature; synchronicity.

Complementarity – Light has both wave-like and particle-like characteristics but cannot be both at the same time.

Condition, Necessary – A condition that must be fulfilled in order for a second condition to be met; contingency.

Condition, Sufficient – A minimal condition; a weaker, demanding condition.

Correspondence, Principle of – Quantum and classical "rules" correspond; wherever the world appears to be continuous.

Consciousness – "That element outside of the physical universe that collapses the quantum wave function, producing the observed result from its range of possible situations" (F.A. Wolf, *Taking the Quantum Leap,* p. 215); the awareness of any particular branch of parallel universes of which you happen to be aware; the process wherein potential reality becomes physical reality; a wave function collapse.

Contingent – Predictable only within statistical limits; necessary condition.

Entanglement – Nonlocality; once one particle is in contact with another particle it continues to influence that particle (see Bell's Theorum).

Formative Causation, Hypothesis of – Characteristic organization of systems depends on the influences that lead to a repetition of forms and patterns of precious systems; morphogenesis.

Fractal – Natural, uncontrolled regularly irregular patterns and formations in real objects.

Ground State – The lowest energy state of an atom.

Implicate Order, Hypothesis of – Space and time are derived from a deeper level of objective reality called "the implicate order." (F.A. Wolf)

Indeterminism, Principle of (Uncertainty Principle) – The impossibility to predict the outcome of an experiment no matter how much we know about matter. (Hiesenberg)

Information Transfer, Superluminal – An "instantaneous" change in the quality (coherent structure) of energy in two fields causing a faster-than-light communication between two events which cannot be connected by a signal; synchronicity; quantum potential.

Intentionality – Directed consciousness; the central and essential characteristic of thought, the will.

Interaction – When something influences something else.

Learning – The ability to turn initially conscious acts into unconscious habits; a relatively permanent change in behavior brought about through practice or experience.

Matter – A series of patterns out of focus; matter, like light, has a dual nature and manifests both as a wave and as a particle; gravitationally trapped light.

Metaphysics – The branch of philosophy that includes ontology (evolution), cosmology. causation and the nature of being, life and the Universe.

Morphogenesis (Hypothesis of Formative Causation) – The structure or forms of characteristic fields (e.g. molecules, crystals, cells, tissues, organs, and organisms) are influenced, shaped, and maintained by fields derived from previous similar systems.

Observables – Features in nature that are considered fixed or determined.

Organic – Responds to processed information.

Particle – A thing which is confined to a region in space; a tiny object distinguished from a wave due to its localization.

Particle, Virtual – A particle that doesn't exist except in essence or as a mathematical calculation; an elementary particle.

Potential, Quantum – Interaction between quantum mechanical events that exist outside of space and time; signal given by particles to inform other particles that their probability has been fulfilled; interconnection between particles without any interaction apparently through a signal of some sort; information exchange; superluminal information transfer.

Reality – An order.

Solipsism, Quantum – The view that one is the whole universe.

Superposition – One or more things imposed on another.

Superposition, Coherent – Thing-in-itself which is distinct from its components as its components are from each other and which *reflect* the nature of experience.

Symmetry – Space being the same in all directions (isotropic) and in all places (homogenus).

Tachyon – A particle conceptualized by Einstein that travels faster than light.

Twistor – Roger Penrose's conceptualized object containing eight dimensions and which is neither a particle nor a point but lies somewhere between; the most fundamental object in the universe.

Uncertainty Principle (Principle of Indeterminism) – No matter how accurately one tries to measure the position and momentum of a particle, there will always be uncertainty in the measurement; one can never be sure of both the position *and* momentum of a particle at the same time, we can know one or the other.

Wave Function Collapse – Occurs whenever someone looks at an observed system, or "I" look at the system, or when the system is measured; consciousness.

Bibliography

Albert, David Z. and Galchen, Rivka (March 2009) **A Quantum Threat to Special Relativity**, *Scientific American*, Vol. 300, No. 3, 32-39

Arcaya, J. (Fall 1973) **Two Languages of Man**, *Journal of Phenomenological Psychology*, Vol. 4, No. 1, 315-331

Barnes, Deborah M. (11 July 1986) **Brain Architecture: Beyond Genes**, Research News, *Science*, 233, 4768, 155-156

Bear, M.F., Cooper, L.N., and Ebner, F.F. (3 July 1987) **A Physiological Basis for a Theory of Synapse Modification**, *Science*, 237, 4810, 42-47

Berglund, B., Berglund, U., & Undvall, T. (6 Nov. 1976) **Psychological Processing of Odor Mixtures**, *Psychological Review*, Vol. 83, No. 6, 432-441

Birren, F. (Apr. 1973) **Color Preference as a Clue to Personality**, *Art Psychotherapy*, Vol. 1, No. 1, 13-16

Black, M. (Aug. 1982) **Brain Flash, The Physiology of Inspiration**, *Science Digest*, Vol. 90, No. 8, 85-87, 104

Cain, W.S. (Feb. 1977) **Differential Sensitivity for Smell: "Noise" at the Nose**, *Science*, Vol. 195, No. 4280, 796-798

Calhoun, J.F. & Acocella, J.R. (1978) **The Self-Concept: How to Change it**, *Psychology of Adjustment and Human Relationships*, Random House, New York, NY, 104

Campbell, J. (Ed.) and Hull, R.F.C. (1971) *The Portable Jung*, Penguin Books, New York, NY

Capra, F. (1975) *The Tao of Physics*, Shambala Books, Boulder, CO

Cowen, M.W., et al (21 Sept. 1984) **Regressive Events in Neurogenesis**, *Science*, 225, 4668, 1258-1264

Crick, Francis H.C. (1979) **Thinking About The Brain**, *Scientific American*, Vol. 241, No. 3, P. 221

Dumont, J.P.C. and Robertson, M. (22 Aug. 1986) **Neuronal Circuits: An Evolutionary Perspective**, *Science*, 233, 4766, 849-852

Eccles, John C. (1984) **Facing Reality**, *Institute of Noetic Sciences Newsletter,* Summer 84, 12, 2, 8-9

Feher, L. (Winter 1977) **Natal Therapy and Theory**, *Journal of Psychohistory*, Vol. 4, No. 3, 309-317

Gazzaniga, M.S. (1 Sept. 1989) **Organization of the Human Brain**, Articles, *Science*, 245, 4921, 947-952

Gill, Victoria (14 July 2010) *Plants 'can think and remember,'* **BBC News Science & Environment**, http://www.bbc.co.uk/news/10598926... extracted 14 July 2010

Girogi, A. (Fall 1970) **Toward Phenomenologically Based Research in Psychology**, *Journal of Phenomenological Psychology*, Vol. 1, No., 75-98

Gleik, James (1987) *Chaos, Making a New Science*, Penguin Books, New York, NY

Gliedman, J. (March 1983) **Mind and Matter**, *Science Digest*, Vol. 91, No., 68-72, 115

Greenfield, Susan A. (1995) *Journey to the Centers of the Mind*, W.H. Freeman & Co., New York, NY

Hall, C.S. & Nordby, V.J. (1973) *A Primer of Jungian Psychology*, New American Library, New York, NY

Hoffman, Paul (Sept. 1987) **Your Mindless Brain**, Reflections, *Discover*, 8, 9, 84-87

Holub, Alexander S., Ph.D. and Budd-Michaels, Evelyn (1999) *Psychokinesiology: Doorway to the Unconscious Mind*, Bridger House Publications, Carson City, NV

____________________ (2007) *From Victim to Victor! Defeating a Victim's Consciousness*, Bridger House Publications, Carson City, NV

Hugston, L.P. *Twistors and Particles* (1979) Springer-Verlag, New York, NY

Hurley, Thomas J. III (Spring 1987) **Beyond the Modern Worldview**, *Noetic Sciences Review*, 2, 19-24

Jones, Edward E. (3 Oct. 1986) **Interpreting Interpersonal Behavior: The Effects of Expectancies** ***Science,*** 234, 4772, 41-46

Kihlstrom, John F. (18 Sept. 1987) **The Cognitive Unconscious**, Articles, *Science*, 237, 4821, 1445-1452

Korzybski, Alfred (1958) *Science and Sanity* (Sixth Publishing) The International Non-Aristotelian Library Publishing Co.

Kracklaner, C. (Spr. 1972) **Exploring the Life-World**, *Journal of Phenomenological Psychology*, Vol. 2, No. 2, 217-236

Kroepel, Robert H. (2006) **Operational Psychology: Introduction**, *Operational Psychology: The Complete Theory*, www.bobwebsite.com, Extracted February 27, 2011

Lanza, Robert & Berman, Bob (May 2009) **The Biocentric Universe**, *Discover*, 53-55

Leggenhager, B. et al (24 August 1997) *Video Ergo Sum: Manipulating Bodily Self-consciousness*, **Science**, Vol 317, 1096-1099

Lenard, Lane (Dec. 1983) **The Dynamic Brain**, *Science Digest*, 65-66, 118-119

LeShan, L. & Marganan, H. (Mar. 1983) **Discovering Alternative Realities**, *Science Digest*, Vol. 91, No. 3, 71

LeShan, L. (1966) *The Medium, The Mystic and The Physicist*, Ballantine Books, New York, NY

Lewin, Roger (8 May 1987) **The Human Psyche Was Forged by Competition, The Origin of the Modern Human Mind**, *Science*, 236, 4802, 668-669

Lewis, Peter J. (2003) **Life in Configuration Space** at **http://philsci-archive.pitt.edu/archive/oooo/272/ol/Configuration-Space-2.doc/** extracted 4-2009

Long, M. (Nov. 1981) **Visions of a New Faith**, *Science Digest*, Vol. 89, No. 10, 36-42

Love, J. (1976) *The Quantum Gods*, Samuel Weiser, New York, NY

Merton, R.K. (1948) *Antioch Review*, 8, 193

Musser, George (June 2010) **A Simple Twist of Fate**, *Scientific American*, Vol. 302, No. 6, 14-16

Netherton, M. & Shiffrin, N. (1978) *Past Lives Therapy*, Wm. Morrow & Co., Inc., New York, NY, 123-132

Parsons, A.S. (Fall 1973) **Constitutive Phenomenology: Schtuz's Theory of the We-Relation**, *Journal of Phenomenological Psychology*, Vol. 1, No. 1, 331-361

Penrose, Roger (1994) *Shadows of the Mind*, Oxford University Press, New York, NY

Phillips, Tony (12.23.2009) **Voyager Makes an Interstellar Discovery**, *science@nasa*, science.nasa.gov/…/23dec_voyager.htm, extracted December 29, 2009

Pietsh, Paul (Feb. 1982) **Brain Swapping**, *Science Digest*, 76-81, 112

Restak, Richard (1994) *The Modular Brain*, Lisa Drew Books, New York, NY

Sahlins, M. (Oct.-Dec. 1975) **Colors and Culture**, *Rasegna Italiana di Sociologia*, Vol. 16, No. 4, 591-610 (English Translation)

Samuels, M., & Samuels, N. (1975) *Seeing with the Mind's Eye*, Random House-Bookworks Books, Toronto, Canada

Schiffman, S. & Dockis, C. (Nov. 1976) **Multidimensional Scaling of Musks**, *Physiology and Behavior*, Vol. 17, No. 5, 823-829

Shapiro, Francine, Ph.D. and Forrest, Margot Silk (1997) *EMDR: The Breakthrough Therapy for Overcoming Anxiety, Stress, and Trauma*, Basic Books, New York, NY

Sheldrake, R. (Oct. 1981) **Rupert Sheldrake's Hidden Force**, *Science Digest*, Vol. 89, No. 9, 54-57

Talbot, M. (1981) *Mysticism and the New Physics*, Bantam Books, New York, NY

Thines, G. (1977) *Phenomenology and the Science of Behavior*, George Allen & Unwine, Boston, MA

Toben, B. (1975) *Space-Time and Beyond*, E.P. Dutton, New York, NY

Underwood, Benton J. (1966) *Experimental Psychology*, Second Edition, Meredith Publishing Co., New York, NY, 5-8

Verney, Thomas, M.D. and Kelly, John (1991) *The Secret Life of the Unborn Child*, Dell Publishing, New York, NY

Waldrop, M. Mitchell (Mar. 1985) **Machinations of Thought**, *Science 85*, 38-44

Weitzel, W.B., Horan, J.J. & Addis, J.W. (Jan. 1977) **A New Olfactory Aversion Apparatus**, *Behavior Therapy*, Vol. 8, No. 1, 83-88

Whitson, Jennifer A. & Galinsky, Adam D. (3 Oct. 2008) **Lacking Control Increases Illusory Pattern Perception**, *Science*, Vol. 322, Pp. 115-117

Wilshire, B. (1968) *William James and Phenomenology: A Study of "The Principles of Psychology"*, Indiana University Press, Bloomington, IN

Wilson, R.A. (Jan. 1982) **Mere Coincidence?** *Science Digest*, Vol. 90, No. 1, 82-85, 95

Wolf, F.A. (Dec. 1981) **Taking the Quantum Leap**, *Science Digest,* Vol. 89, No. 11, 88-92

Wolf, F.A. (1981) *Taking the Quantum Leap*, Harper and Row, Publishers, San Francisco, CA

Wolman, Benjamin B. (Ed.) (1973) *Dictionary of Behavioral Science,* Van Nostrand Reinhold Co., New York, NY

Zukav, G. (1979) *The Dancing Wu Li Masters*, Bantam Books, New York, NY

The Subtle Persuasion of Scent (1981) *Science Digest*, Vol. 89, No. 10, 97

Personal References

Dryer, I., **Science, Mysticism and the Future**, *U.S. Psychotronics Conference*, Taped Talk, Nov. 1979

Huddle, N., *Interview with Robert Beck, D.Sc.,* Taped Jan. 1983

About the Author
Alexander S. Holub, Ph.D.

Alexander S. Holub has been teaching Psychology in the Los Angeles Community College District for more than 35 years. He holds a Bachelors Degree in Psychology, a Masters Degree in Educational Psychology, and a Doctoral Degree in Psychology. He is a member of the American Association for the Advancement of Science. Dr. Holub has certification in Rational-Emotive Behavioral Therapy being taught by its founder, Dr. Albert Ellis. He has further certifications in Neuro-Linguistic Programming where he possesses Practitioner, Master Practitioner and Trainer Certifications.

For five years he had been a facilitator for a S.M.A.R.T. (Self-Management and Recovery Training) Recovery group. S.M.A.R.T. Recovery is an alternative to the 12-step approach based on the work of Dr. Albert Ellis and cognitive therapy. Dr. Holub has been a practicing hypnotherapist for more than 40 years.

He has Applied Kinesiology certifications in Total Body Modification (TBM), Emotional Complex Clearing (ECC), and Neurolink 2000. For more than twenty years he has been pioneering in the use of Applied Kinesiology in counseling and therapy doing presentations at many conferences in the western United States. Among the conferences were: *The Western States NLP Conference* in Park City, Utah; the *American Board of Hypnotherapy Annual Convention* in Irvine, California; the *1995 NLP Comprehensive International Conference* in Denver, Colorado; and *The Whole Life Expo* in Los Angeles, California. In 1999 he had published,

Psychokinesiology: Doorway to the Unconscious Mind detailing the basic techniques used in the therapeutic adjunct. He has written articles for: *The Journal of Borderland Sciences, The Psychic Reporter, Anchor Point* (an NLP journal) and *The Journal of Educational and Psychological Measurements.*

Currently, he has three books published: ***Psychokinesiology: Doorway to the Unconscious Mind, The Gospel Truth: The Heresy of History,*** and ***From Victim to Victor!: Defeating A Victim's Consciousness.***

He had studied Southern Shao-Lin kung-fu from the renowned late Grandmaster Wong, Ark-Yuey (the "father of kung-fu in America") and has written articles on kung-fu for *Martial Arts Masters, Black Belt, Karate/Kung Fu Illustrated,* and *Inside Kung Fu* magazines.

Dr. Holub's interests are wide and varied ranging from Theoretical Physics, Cosmology, Mystical Traditions and Mysticism, Mythology, and Art, to Ancient History, Archeology, Anthropology, Paleontology, and Human Behavior.